T.J. ROHLEDER'S...

FOOLPROOF SECRETS of Successful Marketers!

POWERFUL Direct-Response Marketing Methods That Make YOU Rich!

Also by T.J. Rohleder:

The Blue Jeans Millionaire
How to Turn Your Kitchen or Spare Bedroom into a Cash Machine
The Black Book of Marketing Secrets (Series)
The Ruthless Marketing Attack
How to Get Super Rich in the Opportunity Market
Five Secrets That Will Triple Your Profits
Ruthless Copywriting Strategies
Ruthless Marketing
50 in 50
Secrets of the Blue Jeans Millionaire
How to Make Millions Sitting on Your Ass!

Printed in the United States of America.
For information address:
Club-20 International • 305 East Main Street • Goessel, Kansas 67053-0198.

Cover and book interior designed by Mary K. Jones

FIRST EDITION

ISBN 1-933356-45-6

TABLE OF CONTENTS

INTRODUCTION:

These Foolproof Marketing Secrets Can Take You From Where You Are To Wherever You Want To Be!

This unique book was written to help you dream up all kinds of newer and better ways to make more money in your business. It will help you work **'on'** your business and not **'in'** it.

This requires more thought than action. It requires you to THINK BIGGER. It also means you have to change your thinking and see your business in an entirely different way... For example, it means thinking about your business through the eyes of all of the people who are most important to its ultimate success: Your customers, staff members, business partners, suppliers, and your prospective customers and buyers who have never done business with you. Your goal is to sit around and try to figure out as many ways as you can to give all of these people the things they want the most so they will give you the things that you want the most. It also requires you to think like a marketer and get really good at doing all of the things to attract and retain the largest percentage of the best customers in your target market.

Seems so simple, doesn't it?

Well it is simple. But it's never easy.

In fact in today's overcrowded marketplace, doing all of the things I just mentioned is getting harder all the time. <u>Don't let that fact discourage you</u>. All you have to do is think bigger... think differently... and think even more! Sometimes you're thinking on your feet and other times you're doing it on your butt... But however you do it — the key to achieving your greatest success in business is TO DO MORE OF IT. Do this, and...

The more time you spend working 'on' it and not 'in' it — the more money you'll make!

Does that excite you?

If so — good! Building your business is exciting! **So many books on business and marketing are boring as mud!** The authors are trying hard to show off and prove they know so much more than you do. They make everything way too complicated and confusing — they throw around big words to prove they're smarter than you are... they talk down to you... and what's more, many of the ideas they give you suck! You must dig through the entire book to get a few good ideas that you can use to make more money in your business.

This book is different.

You won't find too many big words and fancy language in this book. There are no confusing theories or overly complicated concepts... I'm definitely not trying to show off and pretend that I know so much more than you do. Instead, what you will get are simple business and marketing ideas that I use to bring in millions of dollars a year in my own businesses. These ideas work! They have brought in many millions for the companies that I have started or been part of and they can do the same for you. I don't care how much money you want to bring in, you can do it with the simple strategies and methods in this book. As you'll see, everything I have to teach you is simple to understand and easy to put into action.

Just spend a little time going through this book every day and...

You Will Gain A Genuine Unfair Advantage Over All Of Your Biggest Competitors!

Does that sound too good to be true? Maybe. But it's not. *Here's why:* Most small business people are working way too hard for too little money. They are trying to wear all the hats... They're too busy working in their business instead of working on it. And finally, they are terrible marketers because they spend VERY LITTLE TIME AND ENERGY thinking through all of the ways to attract and retain the very best customers. They simply do not understand the basic principles of marketing and, because of that, they have never developed a well thought out marketing strategy.

But You Won't Make This Mistake.

The ability to become a great marketer and do the activities that are necessary to attract and sell to the largest percentage of the best people who are perfectly suited for whatever you sell is within your reach! This book shows you how. The tips, tricks, and little known marketing techniques you're about to see as you flip through these pages have been proven to generate many tens of millions of dollars for my small businesses and for many others. In fact, these rare and unusual methods are making a fortune for many other people right now — and they can make a fortune for you, too. Use these methods and gain a genuine unfair advantage over all of your competitors!

And finally…

Working on your business is a lot like getting in top physical shape... It takes constant activity and great discipline to work yourself into shape and stay fit. You can't just go to the gym when you feel like it. So do spend at least one hour a day in concentrated thought of all the ways to build your business. That's 365 focused hours of <u>nothing</u> but thinking and dreaming creatively! One hour a day of doing <u>nothing</u> but focusing on how to build your business will help you dominate your market and destroy your competition! That's over two extremely productive weeks a year of <u>nothing</u> but planning — plotting — and scheming!

So with all that said, let's start dreaming and scheming together…

SECTION ONE:

The Blue Jeans Millionaire!

The 16 Secrets That Took Me From $300.00 to Over $10 Million Dollars in Less Than Five Years... And How <u>You</u> Can Do It Even Faster

SECRET ONE:

Develop a Deep Understanding of Your Target Market

Secret Number One is our greatest secret, the one I believe served us best when we first got started. **You see, although we were new to the business itself, we were already very familiar with the market.** I was 28 years old; my wife Eileen was 30. This was back in 1988, when we were just a couple of kids who had never made more than $26,000 a year combined. I had a little carpet-cleaning business at the time, and that's how I met Eileen: I stopped in at the filling station where she was working for minimum wage and asked for directions. I was looking for a street that was just two blocks long, and I thought it was in the area where her filling station was. As it turned out, it was on the other side of town, but I still got lucky: I met the woman who would become my wife of 22 years. We started dating, and she was the only girlfriend I'd ever had who actually wanted to come with me on my carpet-cleaning jobs. Even though she had multiple sclerosis, and still does, she would come along and do all the physically demanding work it took to do those jobs. I actually fell in love with her on one of those jobs!

By then, I'd had the carpet-cleaning business for about two years. All that time (and for years before) I'd also been sending away for all kinds of moneymaking plans and programs, and I had all these moneymaking ideas in my head. Luckily, Eileen was very ambitious; she was looking for an opportunity, too. **When I told her about my plans for getting rich, her eyes just lit up.** Even though I could barely afford a roof over my head at the time, she knew that it *was* possible to get rich — and so did I.

We had nothing going for us at all. I wasn't even a high school graduate. I went and got my G.E.D. because my dad insisted that I do so, but I didn't even have a real diploma. Eileen had graduated from high school, but she never went to college. We were dirt poor. And yet Eileen saw me sending away for all of these plans and opportunities, and she got excited about some of them. That was in 1987. **We were trying different moneymaking plans, we were joining multilevel marketing companies,**

---

and I saw that she was the kind of woman that I could work side-by-side with. She wasn't one of those women who was always critical, cutting down all my ideas — and that was part of the key to our success. **I think having a spouse who's supportive is vitally important.**

Before we met, Eileen didn't know anything about the opportunity market. But when she started seeing all these crazy sales letters I was getting, and the fact that I was spending all my money on these programs, she got it in a big way. **I remember her telling me, "T.J., the way to get rich is to be in this business. We need to come up with a plan of our own to sell."** That was incredibly insightful of her. She saw all these plans and programs, and she saw that most of them were total crap; that was obvious because I lost money on most of them. Her telling me, "I think the way to get rich is to actually *sell* these plans and programs," was what changed our lives for the better.

About nine months after we got married, we took two programs we really liked, programs that we thought were a cut above the others, and combined them in a unique way to make a little booklet — more of a brochure, really. It was a terrible little thing, filled with typographical errors, that embarrasses me to look at to this day. It was called *Dialing for Dollars*. Then we took $300 that we'd earned from selling a beat-up old carpet-cleaning van and ran a one-sixth page ad in a moneymaking magazine to advertise our program. That was September 1988. **Within less than five years, *Dialing for Dollars* had brought in over $10 million.**

We had a lot of help along the way, and

it took a lot of hard work, but one of the most important factors in our success was Secret Number One. We were familiar with the market, even if we didn't know it. Like I said, I'd been sending away for all these plans, programs, and opportunities for years. I was what we lovingly call an "opportunity junkie" — I couldn't get enough. Little did I know that there were millions of people out there just like me. This is a very lucrative market — and before we got started in the market, we already knew a lot about it.

That first little ad was the spark that started our mighty fire — and it took me a whole weekend to write it. I knew that we only had $300, and that we could only run a one-sixth page ad, which today will probably cost you $500 to 600. **I knew we had a limited amount of space, and the ad had to be just right — because if we didn't get off to a good start, there went** *that* **idea.** So, it took me a whole weekend to write this little, tiny ad. I laid it out like all the other little ads that I'd seen running forever, and I ran it. We used the profits from that ad to buy two more, and the profits from those two ads to buy four; then we built to eight and sixteen, and *then* we started running full-page ads. Eventually we started doing direct-mail and card-pack advertising, and we just kept expanding.

We got a lot of help from a lot of good people along the way. **The first person who helped us in a big way was Russ von Hoelscher,** a man I now consider one of our mentors. Now, Russ didn't help us out of the goodness of his heart! He started out as a consultant, and we had to pay him thousands of dollars for his help. This is a business, and time is the one element that is precious to us all. It's a limited resource we can never get back once it's spent.

The opportunity market is the best-kept secret out there, and we didn't even realize it at the time. It's such a lucrative market. There are millions of rabid buyers, people who are just like I was for years, people who are sending away for every single plan and program they can. I call it the second largest niche marketplace in the world. Now, let me explain that to you. First of all, **a market is simply a group of people who have something in common.** This commonality causes them to feel and act a certain way, which causes them to buy certain kinds of products and services — and to rebuy them. There are people in the opportunity market who are multi-millionaires. They're just looking for the next million-dollar deal, or they're bored, or they want to get into something new. Some of them are doctors and lawyers who are sick and tired of their professions, or now they're retired and they want to try something else. And on the other end of the scale, there are people who are illiterate. I'm not being judgmental; it's just a fact. They can't read or write and they're on welfare. I was somewhere in the middle of the field. I was dead broke, sending away for all these moneymaking plans and programs, and yet I had a small business and **I was fully committed to being an entrepreneur.** I was doing the best I knew how, even though I wasn't making very much money.

There are reasons why we were able to turn $300 into $10 million in our first four years. First of all, we were very familiar with the market — that's our Secret Number One. We also had a lot of help from a lot of people (as I'll explain in more detail in later sections of this book), and we were willing to do whatever it took to succeed. I like to call us the "Forrest Gumps." Remember the movie with Tom Hanks? Whatever you told Forrest Gump to do he did, and he ended up becoming a multi-millionaire and having a great life. He just did what he was told: He didn't question it. That's how it was for Eileen and me. **When Russ von Hoelscher first came along and started working with us, whatever Russ told us to do, we just did it.** At the time he already had 20 years of experience. He'd already made millions of dollars and lost a few too, and we were just getting started. His experience became our experience, and he helped us take something that was already working for us and expand it. We already had a good solid foundation.

It also helped that we had some business experience under our belts. When you're in business, you realize that there's no such thing as a perfect world. You have good days, you have bad days. Just like a good marriage, it goes through droughts, hills, and valleys, but you know you're committed. **People with business experience tend to do very, very well in this market** — and not just because this market is so lucrative. You see, they're already used to the learning curve, and they realize that it's not a perfect world — that there's a price to pay for success. A lot of people who lack previous business experience just want everything handed to them, and they give up when the going gets tough. **But a seasoned businessperson knows that there's no such thing as something for nothing, and they realize that if money is spent right, it's an investment towards future profits, not an expense.**

There are two basic things here that can make you rich, and you **need both. One is product knowledge: You've got to know everything about the product or service you're selling.** This is so you can communicate it in the clearest way to all of your prospective customers and buyers, answer all their objections, and be 100% sold on it yourself. **The second thing is market knowledge: a real understanding of the people to whom you're trying to sell and resell.** Of those two things, **the most important is market knowledge.** The opportunity market can make you rich, because this market is so absolutely huge and so needy. Millions of people desperately want to find a way to make more money but they don't know how. They're scared, confused, and frustrated. There are rabid buyers out there spending all kinds of money looking for ways to make more money. They're more than happy to spend huge sums of money. We've had customers spend thousands and thousands of dollars with us on our various products and services — the kinds of things I'm going to tell you more about in this book, and show you how to create on your own. But that said, it's also a very skeptical marketplace, because there are so many scam artists out there in the opportunity market. Ironically, that's a great thing for you — because if you handle your business with complete honesty and integrity, you can win people over. They'll be more than happy to continue to do business with you once you earn their trust.

Another reason I love this marketplace is that there's an endless array of products and services that you can create. It never ends, and it's such a creative way to make money. Another great thing about this market is that **most of the competitors in it are very easy to beat.** Again, I don't mean to be disrespectful; that's just how it is. Now, I'm hoping that you, the reader, are going to get fired up about this market, get started in it, and make millions of dollars in it just like we have. I'm not worried about the competition; I *need* competitors. **We need more good people in this marketplace.** Since our company mails millions of pieces of direct-mail, if nothing else we need more companies that will put their lists up for rent — and I'm hoping to rent your list someday. I'll explain more about that when we get to our direct-mail secrets. Direct-mail is the exciting medium that's made us so many millions of dollars in this market — and I don't mean to brag. When I talk about all the millions we've made, it's to inspire you. **I'm bragging on this marketplace; I'm bragging on the secrets that I'm trying to share with you in this book.**

The more familiar you are with this market, the better; and when I started, I was very familiar with it. I knew that the competitors who were really kicking ass and taking names were few and far between; and they still are. When you get right down to it, **the competitors in this marketplace are very easy to beat, because there are so many fly-by-nighters out there.** These fly-by-night companies don't understand what real business is all about — and I'll explain more about that. I'll make that crystal-clear for you by the time you finish this book.

Another reason I love this marketplace is the fact that **the best years are still to come, and it won't be long now. The Baby Boomer generation is just starting to retire.** Now, what happens when people retire, after they play golf for six months and gain twenty or thirty pounds and watch too much TV, they start looking for something else to do. They find out that retirement isn't all that it's cracked up to be; in fact, it's terrible for most people. They have too much time on their hands; for years they've lived a structured life, where they've had a job to go to and they had people they worked with and things to do and places to go and people to see. Now they're retired, and the phone stops ringing. The friends they worked with are busy doing the deal every day. This is one of the driving forces that causes people to start looking for business opportunities.

A lot of those bored retirees are going to be taking a closer look at the opportunity market. Millions of new people are going to be getting into this marketplace, year after year. **Another thing about this marketplace** — and I'll make this clearer to you as we go along — **is**

that it's very easy to get started in. There are all kinds of ways to reach those millions of people who are desperately seeking a way to make more money, all kinds of magazines you can advertise in, plus direct-mail, card-packs, and the Internet. **It's constantly evolving.** The millions of people in this marketplace share something in common, even though they're from different demographic groups. **They all have that same insatiable desire to get rich.**

I'm the perfect example. Back when I first met my wife, when I was sending for all these plans and programs, I couldn't pay my bills. My electricity kept getting shut off. Why was that happening? Because I was using every last penny I had to buy all these get-rich-quick plans and programs. I was delusional — all my friends and family told me so. It's true; I was obsessed. **A large percentage of the people who perpetually buy these plans and programs on a regular basis are overtaken with the same sense of delusion I had in the beginning.** I don't mean to be judgmental about it; I was an opportunity junkie for years. **That's part of what makes this market so lucrative.** These people are rabid buyers.

Now, the way for you to get started is pretty simple, really. **In fact, everything I have to share with you here is simple, and a lot of the ideas you're going to hear throughout this book are repetitive in nature.** When you see the same things over and over again, though, you should feel good. Highlight those things. Write them down in a notebook. Each one is a common denominator in the business, and each is very important for you to know and remember. That's why I'll repeat them over and over.

Here is one example: **Start building a swipe file. Send away for all the different plans and programs that you can find — they're everywhere.** If you're not already on an opportunity mailing list, go to the nearest bookstore and find some opportunity magazines. Or go look in the back of *Popular Mechanics* or *Popular Science* — they've got great business opportunity sections. *USA Today* has a great biz-op section. Some of the most popular tabloids are good for business opportunity sellers, too. **Do this, and send away for fifty or a hundred programs. Pretty soon your name will be traded;** it'll go out to all the different mailing lists, and it won't be long before your mailbox will be jam-packed, stuffed with different opportunity offers. That's how you start building your swipe file — and then you have to start studying it.

When you start buying up these different moneymaking plans and programs, you'll see there's a lot of garbage in this market. **That should make you feel very confident.** Remember, the competitors in this market are very easy to beat.

This is the last point I'm going to make before we go on to our next secret: **I want you to think carefully about all the unhappiness in this marketplace. You see, that's what causes people to buy.** There are a lot of people who are frustrated when it comes to money. They want to get rich, they want to make more money, they're desperately seeking a way to do it; but they're so frustrated, and they're so confused. They're even desperate. A lot of them are fearful; they know that the window is closing. They know that they only have a couple of good decades left in them, and they're desperately searching for a way to make more money. Plus, they want some excitement. **There are all these emotional factors,** and I've already talked about one of the biggest ones, which nobody else will tell you about — the sense of delusion in this market.

There are millions of people like me who have never made any money. That's the way I was in the 1980s, just barely getting by, but spending every last dollar. In some cases, I was even saving it up. If I found a good plan or program I wanted, I'd save all my money for six or eight weeks, until I had a couple of thousand dollars, and I would spend it all at once. So don't think that just because a lot of people in this marketplace are broke right now that they can't get their hands on hundreds or even thousands of dollars. **Because they can save it up, and they're willing to spend it once they do. It's a rabid marketplace.** The marketplace is driven by emotional factors; the obsessions that people have, the insatiability. These folks are driven by a strong, overwhelming desire to make more money. They dream of getting rich. It's what they think of from the minute they get up to the minute they go to bed at night. As a result, there's a small group of people — I'm one of them — who are making millions and millions of dollars in this marketplace. You can be one of them too, and Secret Number One is so vitally important for you. **It's just to become familiar with the marketplace.**

So consider carefully about what I've said here; break it down and think about it. **The opportunity market really can make you rich, and I'd like for you to start thinking carefully about this marketplace and start buying some of the available opportunities, and start building** and studying your swipe file.

Become Self-Employed Today… *and* _Never_ *Give Up!*

I've already mentioned the fact that Eileen and I had a little bit of business experience before we started M.O.R.E., Inc. At the time, I couldn't have told you just how important that previous experience was; it's only through reflection that I'm able grasp this principle. **If you don't have any previous business experience, that's fine — just pay attention to what I'm going to tell you.** If you *do* have some previous business experience, whether positive or negative, it can be a great asset for you. But it's only an asset if you recognize it, and I'm going to help you do that.

I started my first business in December 1985. It wasn't much, just a little carpet cleaning business, and I started it with a friend at the worst possible time of the year. Plus, it was a bad time for me personally. I didn't have a roof over my head; I was staying with friends and basically living in a sleeping bag on a floor. This is the real story; I was dead broke, and it was in the wintertime, right around Christmas. Nobody wanted their carpets cleaned; everybody wants to wait until after the snow melts in the springtime. But we had an idea… and it was my friend's idea, really. If it weren't for him, I never would have done it. I was cleaning carpets for another individual, and I was doing most of the work. I had a truck and equipment that he supplied, and I'd to go out and find all my own jobs. Then I'd to give this guy 40%. In a good week in the peak season, I was bringing in $1,000 a week. Then my friend came along, and

> Giving people <u>multiple</u> <u>options</u> to choose from is very important because people do not buy in a vacuum. They must have one thing to compare to another. It is this contrast that influences them to buy.

SECTION ONE — The Blue Jeans Millionaire
19

▼▼▼▼▼▼▼▼▼
MARKETING SECRET

Overview of c successful marketing campaign...

a. Take the best sales points and "schemes" that have worked before...

b. Find new ways to hook them together... new themes, new angles

c. Then smooth it out... So it sounds new and different.

I told him the kind of money I was bringing in. Of course, it was during the fall that I told him this.

Knowing what I know about business and marketing right now, I could have easily doubled or tripled what I was making with the other guy. But $1,000 a week was a lot of money back in the mid-1980s, so my friend talked me into going out and doing it ourselves. **It wasn't much of a business, but it helped me get started, and it helped me learn some things I needed to learn.** When I met my wife, she helped fill in all the gaps that were missing in my life; she's the Queen of Common Sense. I was a pretty good salesman, and I was confident I could do a good job cleaning carpets; if I knocked on your door, which is how I got a lot of my work, there was a one-in-three chance you'd let me come in and clean some carpets. That was how good I was. I just knocked on doors and I wasn't afraid, because I was confident and really focused on helping people. I learned a few things, and little did I know just how important all that was; but I realize how important it is now. I started figuring this out years later, when we were selling our *Dialing for Dollars* program and we had people who were making ten, twenty, thirty, fifty thousand dollars a month.

We even had one guy in Provo City, Utah, an ex-lawyer named Jay Peterson, who was doing *$5 million* a year with our program. I know that because we were selling him our products at wholesale. They were just little booklets, but I know from the volume of business he was doing that that **he was grossing about two-and-a-half times more than we were!** Of course, he put a lot of his own ideas into it. When we were

---

bringing in about $4,000 a week, he was bringing in about ten grand every week, using our secret, the principles that we'd laid out.

We tried to get a handle on our success, because at the same time we had so many people who were criticizing us. They were saying things like, "You guys are cheating us; we're not making any money off this program," and we'd get all these letters from people who wanted a refund on *Dialing for Dollars*. That used to really upset me. I would take it personally before I understood that **refunds are a normal part of doing business.** People would want their money back, and they would accuse us of selling them a program that was fraudulent or misleading, or that wouldn't work. Or they would tell us how terrible it was. And then we had other customers who bought that same, exact program who were jumping in their cars and driving in from four or five states away, or hopping on airplanes just so they could come and thank us, because it was the only program that had ever worked for them. It was so frustrating because I cared deeply, and I really wanted to help people. **Even back then that was my goal; of course I wanted to get rich, but I also wanted to help people.** I wanted to make a difference in their lives, so I took it personally when people accused me of cheating them, of selling them worthless programs that didn't stand a snowball chance in hell of working.

But they *did* work. In some cases, people were getting rich with these programs. I also knew that just like Jay Peterson, the guy in Provo who was doing five million a year, they were using a lot of their own ideas. Jay was very secretive; he was one of those business people who kept his cards close to his vest. I have friends and business partners like that; they try to be secretive about everything. I'm the exact opposite. You want to see my cards, I'll show you my cards; I don't care. You'd probably love to play poker with me, but I would *never* want to play poker, because I would give it all up! I love to be free with my ideas; **I share my best secrets with people all the time.** I hope they benefit from them. I believe in an abundant universe; I believe that you can make millions and I can make millions, too. That's especially true in a marketplace as big as the opportunity market, or the diet market, or the self-improvement market, or many other markets out there. They're so enormous that it doesn't matter; we can all make millions. Just because you make millions doesn't mean that you're making money that would otherwise be going to me. Now, it's true that there are competitors out there. **Somebody's going to make these millions**

of dollars, so it might as well be you. But the market is so huge that you can reach people that I won't be reaching, and I can reach people that you won't be reaching, and together we can all make a fortune.

But back to my story. The unbalanced responses we kept getting in the mail really bothered me, month after month. We'd get letters in the mail where people would say, "Eileen and T.J., I love you guys! You're changing my whole life with this program of yours. I'm making $10,000 a month; thank you, God bless you, and God bless your family," and we would start feeling good about ourselves; we'd start patting ourselves on the back. We'd say to each other, "God, we're so good, we're helping people, we're achieving our dreams. We're not only making millions of dollars ourselves, we're helping other people achieve *their* dreams" — and it felt so damn good. But then we'd get another letter in the mail and it would say, "Dear Eileen and T.J. Rohleder: You scumbags! You cheated me! I spent thousands of dollars on your program, and it didn't work!" Imagine the frustration of *knowing* that you had a program that was tested, was proven, that other people were using to make thousands of dollars — and yet you had people who claimed that the program did *not* work, and that you had lied to or misled them. **That bothered me so much so that I became determined to find out, what were the common denominators?** What were the successful people doing that the rest of them weren't?

Take Jay Peterson; he's the perfect example. He was making more money than any of our other distributors — millions of dollars — before he cut us out and started doing it all on his own. **Incidentally, this is something all of our most successful distributors always do, and that we *encourage* them to do.** In fact, I encourage you, the reader, to try that, if you like: To break out on your own, use our products and services as a way of getting started, learn what you have to learn, develop your knowledge and confidence and experience, and *then* start developing your own products and services. Eventually, cut us out. If you want to make the most money, you should be developing your own products and services; that should be your ultimate goal. We can still do business together.

Jay was our most successful distributor, and oddly enough he was doing everything exactly the *opposite* way we told all our distributors to do it in our book. He had his own theories, and he tested everything out himself. He was like most entrepreneurs: He was stubborn and independent, and wanted to do everything his own way. One of those things was the way he handled his scripts. You see, *Dialing for Dollars* used answering machines to replace a live salesperson to sell the products and services for you; it was a little ahead of its time that way. Incidentally, all the principles of *Dialing for Dollars* still work to this day; we use them on a daily basis, except that voicemail has replaced the answering machine.

Whereas we told people that their scripts should move quickly and shouldn't be too long, Jay's scripts were all very long, and they were boring. I once told him, "Jay, I can't even listen to one of your scripts," and he replied, "Look, T.J., the reason why you won't listen to one of my messages from start to finish is, you're not the prospect. You're not the person calling from these ads. A lot of those people hang up too, but I know that when they do hang up, they were just tire kickers anyway; they weren't that serious." He had his own theory — and he was making millions of dollars, so you can't argue with it. Other people were making money doing other things too. **The neat thing about this business is you can do it your way, and I can do it my way, and we can still make millions of dollars.**

The only real common denominator I found with all these successful customers was that they had some previous business experience. That's it. Case closed; look no further. That was the *only* thing. Now, that led us to some very interesting theories that I want to share with you. Keep in mind that these are generalizations. I want you to think about this: These people had some previous business experience, and so they tended to try things a little harder. Plus, they weren't expecting things to be perfect. They had more realistic expectations. **They didn't just give up when things went wrong, because they'd been in business before.** It's kind of like a guy and a gal living together. If you live together and there's no marriage contract there, what's to stop you from just saying "Adios," and packing up as soon as something goes wrong?

The people who had previous business experience were more committed; they were more persistent, had a greater level of confidence in themselves, and had broken through a lot of the fears that were holding the inexperienced businesspeople back. They had already suffered through some major setbacks; I know I have, and each time I've continued to move forward, I've always come back stronger. That's the way you develop your entrepreneurial skills and ability. **These experienced people had the confidence that came from experience, and they also had a strong**

MARKETING SECRET

The E-Factors that influence every sale:

- Pride — Desire to be better than others...

- POWER

- Love

- Fear

- Greed

- Guilt

That's it!

These are the 5 reasons people buy anything and everything! Every reason to buy can be linked back to these 5 powerful emotional factors.

work ethic, because successful entrepreneurs are used to doing things on their own. They don't need somebody to tell them what to do, and they don't need somebody to constantly stay on their butt, keeping them busy all the time. Look, I love employees; I thank God for them. But I have to admit, a lot of employees — well, without supervision they're never going to work to their fullest capacity. **Becoming successfully self-employed does require a new set of skills that must be developed.**

Nobody told me that 20 years ago when I first got started, so I'm telling you now. **Your awareness of that one principle is a skill.** There's a new set of skills that you've got to develop, and your willingness to develop those qualities is all it takes. There will be some temporary pain and a learning curve; there will be struggle, adversity, and some challenges. The more money you want to make, the more pain you have to go through. But you see, you shouldn't even look at it as pain or problems; these are just part of the price you pay to get where you want to go. It's just like with a bodybuilder or a champion athlete. They know they've got to go through some pain. **But the pain of discipline is far greater than the pain of regret — far, far less.** Remember that. You've got to feel good about paying the price.

Again, the more money you want to make, the bigger the price you pay. If anybody tells you all that money's going to come out of nowhere, that you're going to make millions of dollars without learning a lot and developing new skills and facing challenges and adversity — well, then, you shouldn't do business with that person, because they're lying to you. They

---

may be trying to tell you what they think you want to hear, but they're not telling you the truth, and why would you want to do business with somebody who's not going to tell you the truth? I'm trying to be honest with you here. If this is one of your weak areas, we can help you. You may be further along than you realize; if you've got some previous business experience, then this is an area you won't need any help with. You're already on the path. You've already experienced the challenges, and you're stronger than you think. That's what I want to share with you. It's a true advantage.

If you don't have the previous business experience, don't despair! **You can develop these skills.** When I ask myself the question, "What does it take to be a great entrepreneur?" I see that you must be disciplined, because you have to get yourself out of bed in the morning to do the work. Nobody's telling you what to do anymore, so **you have to be self-motivated, you have to be focused, and you have to have a strong work ethic.** You have to see things conceptually from the top down instead of the bottom up. **You need the ability to work *on* your business, not *in* it, to pull back a little, to delegate your weaknesses.** Before you delegate those weaknesses, you've got to face up to them. The more money you want to make, the more you're going to have to build a team of people to help. You can't do it by yourself, and you can't get bogged down in the details, although the details are important.

Now, part of what made us millions of dollars has to do with the fact that my wife and I had complementary skills and abilities. By her own admission, she's not a good sales person; she's not a good marketer either. She focuses on the details. She has a lot of common sense, and she's very conservative. I tend to be reckless and wild, and thank God I've picked up enough of her qualities over the years that some of her behavior, ideas, thoughts, and philosophies have rubbed off on me — so I now have the capacity to be a little more conservative. Getting older helps there too. With age, you do tend to mellow somewhat. I've faced up to my weaknesses, and many times the only way I've been able to do that is by suffering through the pain, going through the problems necessary to get to the place where I've said, "No more!" I did that several years ago with being a manager, when Eileen stepped down from the company because of health reasons, and I took over as President and CEO. Before that I'd just been doing the marketing. The first fourteen years, she had the company; I just focused on the marketing, selling, and product development, and I let her do everything else. Well, I don't want to say, "I let her" — that would be wrong. She *took on* everything else. Then she stepped down eight years ago, and I tried to be a general manager. I tried to fill her shoes, and I beat myself up, and I really gave it my best. I wasn't making excuses. **I found out that I'm a terrible manager. I found out that I just don't have the right skills and abilities.**

So when I'm telling you to delegate all your weaknesses, it's because I've learned that I had to do that. **I finally came to grips with the few things that I'm really good at, and I put all my focus there — and you've got to do that too.** You're going to get a really good understanding of this by the end of this book. I'll give you a hint right now: Your focus needs to be marketing. That's the one area that will to make you millions and millions of dollars; and if you can't be a good marketer, then you have to find somebody who can help you. The more money you want to make, the more help you're going to need in this area; and if you're a natural marketer like I am, then you'll need to find people who can handle the day-to-day workings of the company.

You see, business is pretty simple. You've got to see it simpler and believe it bigger. There are a lot of details out there, a lot of different things you can think about when it comes to business. It's like a game of chess. The number of moves is endless, but the basics are pretty simple. **You've got what I call the three M's: 1)** You've got **marketing,** which is what makes you all the money; **2)** You've got **management,** which keeps it all organized, keeps it all controlled; and **3)** You've got **margins.** You've got to watch your profits. **A business has to do just two things: Serve its customers and make money, and that's it.** No matter what business you're in, every business in the world has those two objectives. We've got to serve our customers (which means different things to different businesses), and we have to make a profit.

Marketing is all about attracting and retaining customers. Part of the secret of business is to study the successes of other companies. See yourself as an entrepreneur, subscribe to *Forbes* magazine, read some great biographies. There are some wonderful books on business that aren't "how to" books necessarily; they were never designed to be such. No, **these are biographies of successful business people.** Two of my favorites, both of which I would strongly encourage you to read, are *Behind the Golden*

Arches: The Story of McDonald's and *Gates*, by Stephen Manes and Paul Andrews, respectively. That latter is a wonderful book about Bill Gates and the story of Microsoft. And then there's another great book that really influenced me earlier on: It's a book on Steve Jobs, the co-founder of Apple Computer, and it's called *The Journey is the Reward*.

▼▼▼▼▼▼▼▼▼▼▼▼▼▼▼▼▼▼▼▼▼

Price resistance usually only lives in the business owner's mind.

The biggest obstacle to raising price is in the business owner's mind.

I would just encourage you to think carefully about what I've said here. It sounds like common sense, in a way. If you do have some previous business experience, you should pat yourself on the back. If you don't, that's fine too, but you'll have to realize that it's a limitation you have. **So just develop the awareness that you need to constantly develop some skills, and that you're never going to get there 100%** — you're always growing. There's new knowledge to learn and experiences that you have to go through, but you can learn these things. You really, truly can do it. I know you can do it.

I've struggled so much to be an entrepreneur; it's been such a painful thing with me. Why? Because I wanted to make millions of dollars. If I'd only wanted to make a couple of hundred thousand a year, it would be no struggle at all. I can do that in my sleep right now. I don't mean to sound arrogant or cocky; it's simple fact. I can go out there and make $100,000 without even thinking about it, without even working. Why? Well, it's like that bodybuilder who goes to the gym every day. Year after year he pumps these massive weights; he's always adding to the bar, and he develops this very strong body, and eventually he can handle a massive workout. That's the way it is in business, too. **These abilities and skills you develop as you go out there to make millions of dollars, to move forward in the direction of your dreams, to take on newer and better challenges, to learn more and more things will make you a very strong, very capable entrepreneur.**

I'm here to tell you this: **If I can do it, you can do it.** But it's not going to come without a lot of challenge and pain and struggle. You have to be willing to go through it, to accept it. I hope that you do. With that said, let's move to the next secret.

Get Help from the Right Wealth-Making Experts

MARKETING SECRET

▼▼▼▼▼▼▼▼▼

Money buys you one thing and one thing only: MORE CHOICES.

- This is not power. But it is potential power.

- Power is the ability to act. More choices give you more ability. This is the one th ng money can buy you: more ability to act — for the good or bad!

Our Secret Number Three is that we had the right moneymaking help along the way. **That's a recurring theme throughout this book: Nobody ever gets rich by themselves.** If it weren't for all the people who helped us, I wouldn't be a millionaire today. I've already mentioned that terrible myth that I call the "Entrepreneurial Hero Myth," where successful entrepreneurs want you to believe that somehow they made it all on their own. Nothing could be further from the truth. I needed a lot of help to get where I am today, and all the people who make the most money share that secret with me.

For me, it started with the people I met in multilevel marketing meetings. When I first got the idea that I wanted to make millions of dollars, I started getting hooked on all these multilevel marketing companies. With most of them I never stood any chance of making any money, and neither did any of the people I met at those meeting — **but at least they were positive people.** They weren't like all the other people I was running around with. **These were people who really believed it was possible to get rich.** They wanted to do something with their lives. They weren't happy; they had what I call "inspirational dissatisfaction." They wanted more out of life; and so they, like me, joined all these stupid multilevel marketing companies —

and a lot of them *are* stupid, by the way; many are absolutely worthless. The only people who ever make any money with those are the heavy hitters and the companies themselves.

But you know what? **That's okay, because they can be great places for you to get some support — and I would encourage you to join those companies for that, if for nothing else.** Do the minimum it takes to become a distributor, just so you can go to their motivational rallies. Surround yourself with people who are moving forward, doing big things. Of course, there are also other groups that allow you to do that. Once you go into business for yourself, you can join the **Chamber of Commerce.** You may not feel like you fit in, but some of the people who belong to those organizations... well, don't let them fool you. Even though they have traditional businesses, most of them, they're still people who are doing something positive with their lives. **There's also Toastmasters, and other independent, local groups you can join for inspiration.** For me, that was so vital, having help from people who were positive. They were motivated, they were dreamers like I was, they wanted more out of life, and that's really what got me started. The more I hung around with those people, the less I hung around with people who seemed to be happy where they were, and didn't want anything more out of life.

My first two business partners also helped me a great deal, and by the time I met my wife Eileen in 1987, I'd already had 18 months of business experience. Of course, I burned through those first two partnerships very quickly. Those partners were exactly like I was, and when I met Eileen, little did I know that I'd stumbled on to that secret of synergy that I've already shared with you. She was very different than I was, and together we combined our talents and created something that was truly powerful. **By the time I met her I was ready to succeed, and her help was vital. She had all the right skills to compliment mine.**

Then, in 1989, we met Russ von Hoelscher — and from that point forward, our lives were changed forever. Now, we paid Russ many thousands of dollars over the years, but he helped us make millions of dollars in return. **It's not what something costs but what it will make you that counts, and that's the *only* thing that counts.** I want to do the same thing for you. It's my sincerest goal to help you, just like Russ von Hoelscher helped us.

Our multimillion-dollar help didn't stop with Russ von Hoelscher. In 1992, we met the great copywriter Luther Brock, and we mailed millions of sales letters that Luther wrote for us. He's a great and experienced copywriter, and no matter how hard I tried back then to write advertising copy that did a great job of profitably attracting new customers, I just couldn't do it. I wasn't talented enough — and that used to bother me so much. I've always thought of my customers as friends, so when I wrote to my existing customers, I was writing to friends; **but when it came time to write copy to new people who had never done business with us, I was dependent on these outside copywriters like Luther — and what they did was inspire me.** Admittedly, it was mostly the kind of inspiration that comes from anger. I was so upset because these copywriters were able to bring in millions of dollars of business from new customers. They were able to write direct response marketing and advertising copy that was so compelling that it drew in people who had never had a relationship with us. Now, once those people were attracted to us, I could write from there and do all the promotion myself.

Of course, I've gotten better over the years: what used to take me three months now takes me three days, and what used to take me three days now takes me three hours. I'm better at drawing in new customers on my own today. **But getting the right help from other people when we needed it has been very important in our success.** I've had people like Russ von Hoelscher, Luther Brock, and Dan Kennedy, who came along in 1993 and wrote a lot of copy for us, helping me every step of the way. Watching them do what I couldn't do inspired me to do a better job. **It inspired me to learn how to write copy.** Of course, with Eileen running the company, I could focus all of my time and attention on marketing — coming up with great ideas for products and services to sell to our customers, developing promotions, learning the skills of writing copy. **It's another reason why you need help, so that you can focus in on that one thing.**

In 1996, we joined Dan Kennedy's Platinum Group, and again, that was crucial to helping me become a better marketer and to helping Eileen understand some of the principles of marketing. We met four times a year, and at that time I think we paid $6,000 annually. By the time we quit it was up to close to $10,000 a year, and I wouldn't be surprised now if it's up $15,000 or even $20,000 a year. Whatever it costs, it's worth it.

In 1993, we came across **Alan R. Bechtold. He's a living legend in electronic marketing.** He was one of the very first people to started selling stuff online, a true expert who helped us make millions and millions of dollars. When the Internet came along and started taking over everything, it changed our entire business. **But we had Alan, helping us profit from the changes.**

That's the point of this particular secret. Russ, Dan, and Alan all helped us make millions of dollars — not just by profiting from their help, but also through various partnerships that we formed with them. **The millions of dollars we made with them, and all our other joint-venture partners, was in the most part money that we would never have made without their help.** That's an important principle that most people just don't get, because they're unwilling to make an investment. They see a coaching group that sells for $5,000 a year, $10,000 a year, $30,000 a year and they say, "No way am I going to pay out that kind of money!" They hear about a seminar that sells for $5,000 or $10,000 — or even $25,000, for some of Jay Abraham's seminars — and they say, "There's no way I'm going to pay out thousands of dollars to go to a seminar, or even to buy the tapes!" **They don't realize that just a few ideas could turn everything around for them.** That's all it takes: just a few well-implemented ideas, with the right help — and what costs you thousands of dollars can make you millions of dollars. Because they're unwilling to spend that money (they could get it, if they really wanted to) they always stay broke.

In 1995, we started our One Hundred Million Dollar Roundtable Group, where we get together with other marketers for product development and develop products as special partnerships, and it was the start of something that continues to this day. **We have members coming and going constantly, but we're doing a lot of things as a group that we never would have done on our own — ever.** It's been very profitable for us, these things that we've learned just by freely helping each other. You can never really reach out to try to help somebody without helping yourself, too. That's an important principle to remember; it's a spiritual principle, but it also applies to business and making money.

In 1992, we met Chris Lakey, who is now a vital part of our organization. Chris was just 15 years old when I met him, and he's 32 years old now. So he's been in and around our business for more than half of his

Work on your business — not in it. Be the architect of your business — not the worker or foreman.

Definition: The architect designs the building — and sees to it that his plans are followed by the builders.

The same is true in business. We must design successful marketing systems — and then monitor them closely.

Work ON it — not IN it.

life. He's very smart. He started out as an employee, but somewhere along the line a switch inside of him just flicked. He got interested in the business and I told him, when he decided to create his own company in 1996 or 1997, "Look, if you'll just do what I tell you to do, you can make $100,000 a year within your first three years, and you'll just work part time." He wanted one day a week where he could just focus on his business and come in four days a week, but I needed him to stay at M.O.R.E., Inc.! Well, he was open and he was receptive, just like we were when Russ von Hoelscher started working with us, and in his first year he made more than $100,000. Again, it's all about the power of getting the right help, and learning the right shortcut secrets.

So let's talk about those secrets. Other people who have gone where you want to go have already figured out the problems that you need to figure out. **They have experience, they know shortcuts, and they've done what you want to do, so they can shorten your learning curve by revealing their secrets to you.** If you're open and receptive to those secrets, it can make all the difference in the world to your success.

We met Jeff Gardener in 1996. When he first got started, he was just 15 or 16 years old, still living at home in Dodge City, Kansas. He would come home every day and say, "Mom, how many orders did I get for today?" and his mom would say "Well, son, here's your mail," and he'd open it up, and there would be cash in the mail. That was his dream, even from the time he was very young. Of course, his parents told him to forget all this garbage about making money and direct response marketing, and they encouraged him to go to college and get a degree, which he did. But he never used his degree, and he's a millionaire now — probably a multi-millionaire. He learned it from the ground up, and he's been a vital part of our group. The same thing with **Don Bice: we met him in 1999,** and he's helped us make millions of dollars.

We've also had a great staff over the years, and I'm going to talk more about them in other parts of this book. In 1990 and 1991, Eileen hired Jeff McMannis and Randy Hamilton. Those two gentlemen are still with our company. Randy is a numbers genius; Jeff is an implementation guy. If you need anything done, there's Jeff. In 1997, I met Jeremy and Shelley Webster, and now Shelley's my general manager and Jeremy's a vital part of our organization. There are many others I could mention. **These folks are the foundation of our group, and yes, they've helped us make millions of dollars. And I've got to mention our suppliers, like our mailing house printers.**

I just cannot stress enough how finding the right people and sticking with them is a real secret here. It sounds like common sense: get all the help you can, and find the right people. But when it comes time to pay these people, a lot of entrepreneurs balk, because the right people don't come cheap. Russ von Hoelscher, as everybody knows, has been one of the key factors to our success — but over the years we've probably paid him about half a million dollars. So although he's helped us a great deal, that help has cost us. Even though he's a dear friend of ours, he has a business that has to make a profit. His time is money. That's a limited resource. So we pay him thousands of dollars an hour, in some cases, but it's worth it because it makes us so much more money than we pay him.

The people you surround yourself with, especially when it comes to finding people who are talented in the areas that you're weak in — those people will help you stay focused, and that's important in business. Too many business people spend their time doing what I call 'putting out the brushfires' every day. That's all they do. They come into the office, they've no real strategy, no real plan, they're not focused at all, they're trying to wear all the hats, they're trying to control every aspect of their business, and they refuse to delegate. I did this for several years when Eileen stepped down, so I can tell you what a waste of time and resources it really is. It's the worst thing you can do, and yet most businesspeople do it constantly. They have no agenda; they just walk in the door and solve problems, every day, that other people could be solving. They feel important; it strokes their ego, and they feel like they're getting something done. But the truth is, they're undisciplined and unfocused. They never get rich, and it's no wonder so many businesses go broke. **They refuse to spend the kind of money you have to spend on the infrastructure.** They refuse to spend the kind of money you have to spend to get the best experts, the best consultants. In some cases, these are people you're going to pay $10,000 a day to, but it's going to be worth that if you'll implement their ideas. **No amount of consulting work, going to seminars, reading good books, or studying great programs is ever going to make you any money unless you implement the ideas.** With the right implementation, you can make millions by learning shortcut strategies, by acquiring the important contacts that these people offer you, by learning the things they had to learn by going through a lot of pain and struggle themselves.

Eileen and I tell people that we were like little Forrest Gumps — you know, like in the Tom Hanks movie. Forrest just does whatever you tell him to, and he ends up becoming rich and having a very happy life even though he's mentally challenged. Well, see, I think in some ways *I'm* mentally challenged. I'm not the smartest guy out there, and I never really fooled myself about that much. **Some part of me always knew that I needed help.** I see people who are so much smarter than I am, people who are multi-talented; they can do lots of things, whereas I'm good at just a few things. I'm a great conceptual thinker, I can develop product ideas that make millions of dollars, and I'm a great copywriter to the market I serve; that's about it. But I have friends who are skilled in all areas and more — and it's a weakness. **It's a curse, not a blessing, because they try to do everything themselves and they never stay focused on what's most important.** Some of these guys are geniuses. They could be worth a whole lot more money than my wife and I are worth — and yet because they don't practice Secret Number Three, they're putting in 12 and 14 hours a day and are always broke.

So find people and lean on them. Find the very best people you can, and then grab ahold of them and don't let go. Pay them whatever money they ask for and let them become a vital part of your success; that's been our secret. **The experts can give you the shortcuts that you need; they can help you do more with less, and they'll make you money, not cost**

you money, if they're the right people.

That's why paying consultants $1,000 an hour or more is usually worth the investment. I hope you can see that just a few of the ideas that they can provide you can make all the difference, turn everything around for you, and help you make the millions of dollars you want. **Similarly, the more money you want to make, the more important your staff is, because you need that infrastructure.** I'm going to talk a lot about that in this book, because it's extremely important. A great staff can free up your time and energies to allow you to focus on what you need to focus on. The good people you surround yourself with will help you do and be and have more of everything that you want.

> The delay of a sale is usually the death of a sale.
>
> Do as many things as possible to create a great deal of urgency to make them want to take action now!

And then there's the emotional element. Now, this is something that nobody talks about — and I don't know why, because it's such an important thing. It's something that will never show up on a profit/loss statement, but here it is: Good people will keep you in the game. They'll not only keep you playing at a higher level, but they'll keep you playing, period. You're going to go through some good times, but you'll go through some bad ones, too. The more you want to make, the more struggle and adversity you'll have to face. **You're going to hit the peaks and you're going to hit the valleys, and to survive both you need good people that you really trust, who are capable and competent, who have the skills that you lack, who have the knowledge that you need, who can stay with you through thick and thin, through the ups and the downs.** They'll take the lows and help smooth those out, so the pain will be less than if you were all alone; and in those times when everything is great, when the money's pouring in, the joy you'll feel will be intensified. They'll make the good times better and they'll make the bad times less painful. **I'm so fortunate that I'm surrounded with people that I love and care about, who are also with me in the business.**

Even though my wife Eileen officially stepped down as General Manager in 2001, she's still my business partner. We still talk about

The universal common denominator of why people buy:

People buy things to feel better about themselves!

- Everyone wants to feel better about themselves.

- The products/ services they buy let them do it somehow/ someway. (emotional)

business all the time, and she helps me manage some of my joint-venture partnerships. Plus, she's my confidante. She understands the business and has helped me a great deal on a daily basis. But I also have Chris Lakey, who's worked his way up to the top of the company — he's also my son-in-law. And then I have my son Chris, who's only been with the company now for a few years, but he's coming around, and he's learning more and more all the time; and then I have staff members who are really more like honest-to-God family. The company could fall apart tomorrow, and I'd still be in touch with these people on a regular basis, and I'd always have a warm, loving, caring feeling about these people till the day I died, if I lived to be 100. This is something that doesn't show up on a profit/loss statement, but I know that it's been a vital part of my success, and the successful people I know who have opened up to me off the record (because nobody likes to talk about this) have said the same. **It's the people you surround yourself with who make it all worthwhile, and they'll keep you in the game — even when you want to give up.** But you won't quit; you don't want to let them down, and they'll inspire you. As they get excited about the business and as the business becomes more important to their lives, it'll help you.

Even your joint-venture partners help you, as you help them. Helping people like Eric Bechtold has been a wonderful experience for me, because I knew him for a few years before he broke away from his uncle Alan and started his own business. I've been part of helping him from Day One. He's 15 to 16 years younger than me, but he's exactly like I was back then — only he's so much smarter, and he's going to make so much more money by the time he's my age. He'll be worth ten or a hundred times more money than I'm worth, and that's okay — he's inspired me. Helping other people will help you at the same time; that's how you need to look at it. **These aren't just people who are going to give you things;** these are people who are going to play a role in your success. But you're also going to do everything you can to be there for them and to give them what they need, and that includes suppliers, staff members, joint-venture partners; that includes your customers too, your customers and your clients. **You're going to do everything possible to reach out to help them, and you're going to benefit greatly in the process.**

SECRET FOUR:

Master the Art and Science of Direct-Mail

Secret Number Four: **We leveraged the power of direct-mail to make our fortune.** People who are familiar with our story know that when Russ von Hoelscher first started working with us, we were bringing in $16,000 a month. That was more money than we'd ever made in our entire lives. You see, Eileen and I had never made more than $26,000 a year, ever, and that was combined. Yet here we were, brand new in the mail-order business, getting rich. I'd already had a couple of years under my belt as a business owner, so there was some experience there, and we'd done a lot of different things. But once we got into mail **order, that's when preparation met opportunity. We had the right opportunity at the right time with our** *Dialing for Dollars* **program.** We were doing pretty well — but Russ von Hoelscher helped us take that income and turn it into almost $100,000 a *week*.

Everybody who knows us knows that story, and they all ask us the same question: "What exactly did Russ do to help you go from $16,000 a month to almost a $100,000 a week in just nine months?" The main thing that he did was to give us all his greatest tips, tricks, and strategies, and really help us to see what we had. We didn't realize just how many advantages we had, and what a great thing it was. You see, Russ von Hoelscher, back in 1988, was in some ways where I am right now. He was able to recognize a great thing when he saw it. That's the one advantage I have now, with more than twenty years of experience under my belt. **I can spot a great opportunity when I see one, and I can spot a winner when I meet one. I'm just smart enough now to quickly see when somebody's got a multimillion-dollar idea.** When they're going in the wrong direction, I know that too. It just comes from years and years of experience.

Direct-mail is the most powerful sales medium on Earth. It helps you instantly reach and sell to millions of people. **It's fast, it's direct, and you're in total control.** Direct-mail lets you do a complete job of selling from start to finish, and when you do it correctly, a thousand great direct-mail packages is the same thing as having a thousand of the best salespeople. **I call it "direct salespeople in an envelope."** But you don't have to put up with all the crap you normally have to put up with salespeople. I'm a salesman myself, and I can tell you that salespeople can be real pain in the butt. The best ones tend to be very egotistical. They're not team players, they want to do everything on their own, but hey, they're making you money, so you've got to put up with their crap.

But when you use direct-mail, you could have the best of the very best salespeople, the ones that go out there and bring back the money. They'll never call in sick, and you'll never have to pay them the big bucks. Direct-mail does a complete job of selling. **This is a powerful medium, and it's a great way for you to build strong bonds of loyalty with your customers because you can stay in touch with them on a regular basis.** You can separate out your best customers from the rest, and you can make special deals for them. You can do things for your best customers that you can't do for any other group of customers. I can't think of a better way to sell and resell customers. Remember, that's all marketing is: all the things you do to first attract new customers, and then to resell to them. There's no better way to do that than direct-mail. This is a vehicle that allows you to be in total control, unlike space advertising. We got started in space advertising, where you wait 6-8 weeks for your ad to run. If you run it in all the national magazines, you're at the mercy of the media ad departments. They can tell you if they don't want to run your ad. They can dictate the layout to you. But when you're using direct-mail, you're in total control. It's pretty simple, too, and it gets simpler the more you do it.

So what do you need to create a top-notch direct-mail product? **First of all, you need a great offer.** This consists of a great product or service, something that's designed for the exact people you're trying to reach. There are good profit margins in it, and some kind of a special deal for them. People always want some kind of a special deal. **So when we talk about a great offer, we're talking about prices; we're talking about the value that you build up and establish in the minds of the prospect, and if it's the right product or service for the right market, then it'll have a high pursuit value.** It also includes all the special things that make people want to give you their money right now — powerful, compelling offers, things that make people *excited* about giving you their money.

That's part and parcel of great advertising copy, which is also absolutely necessary. Writing great copy consistently is something that takes years to develop — **but I want you to know that you can start learning how to write great copy immediately, by focusing in on your customers, attracting groups of them, and then writing to them like they're your friends.** That's the one thing that every letter that you get in the mail has in common; it says, "Dear friend." So write to your customers as if they're your friends — and they *should* be your friends, because they support you. So you'd better think of them as friends, and you'd better treat them as friends. **You learn how to write great copy over a period of time, and you do it by doing everything you can to serve your customers in the highest way possible.**

You need a great graphic artist, somebody who's going to get your stuff ready to go to press. We have two graphic artists at M.O.R.E., Inc., and one of them, Mary Jones, has been with us since the very beginning. She used to design all the little fliers for the first business I started in 1985, and she's been with me right along the way, the whole time. Every great copywriter needs a great graphic artist to work with, to help them turn their copy ideas into powerful direct-mail packages and products. **You also need a good list broker,** and that was one of the things that Russ von Hoelscher helped us do. He introduced us to Stewart Kogan, who has been our list broker since 1989. A list broker's job is just like a bloodhound's, or like a detective's. They go out there and track down the very best mailing lists. They're constantly looking for mailing lists that are just right for whatever it is you're offering, so that you'll use those mailing lists and then keep

Strong motivators...

- Some products/ services can be sold because people want to avoid a negative situation

- People will do more to avoid pain — than to gain pleasure

- Use the P.A.S. (Problem — Agitate — Solution) Formula

using them. Every time a new quarterly hotline comes up, you re-rent that list through your list broker, and they get 15 or 17% — a nice little percentage. Now, with the best mailing lists you're always going to have to take 5,000 names, and the list is vitally important. **In fact, the list you mail to is probably the most important thing when it comes to direct-mail.** There are a lot of lists on the market; and there are a lot of sharks in the business who are going to take advantage of you by giving you bad mailing lists. So you've got to find a good list broker who'll give you the very best names.

Next, you need a great printer you can trust, somebody you can work with. Ideally you need someone who can give you the very best prices, the very best turnaround time, the very best quality. Sometimes you can't have all three; maybe you can only have two. If you want the best quality, it's going to cost you more money; if you want the best turnaround time, you're going to have to give up on some of your quality. So you've got to find the best printer possible who's going to give you all three of those things, and realize that sometimes you'll pay him a little bit more. **We have a great relationship with our printer; his name is Steve Harshbarger, from CityPrint.** We've been using him since the mid-1990s. Here's why: when I met him, I was so impressed. You see, earlier on, Eileen and I had started our own printing division — and it was the wrong idea. That department grew and grew, until we had all these huge presses and hundreds of thousands of dollars worth of printing equipment. It seems funny now, but that's the way it was, in the first five years of our business. In the beginning, no printer would take us seriously; we were small potatoes. But we were kingdom builders, so we built this huge printing department. The whole thing worked for a little while, and then it all caved in on us. I met my printer when it came time to sell all of that equipment, and he's been with us since that time. **The first thing he said to me made a really deep impression, and told me that I was dealing with somebody who was very honest.**

I was asking him about his prices, and he said, "I have a certain amount of equipment in my shop; it allows me to do some jobs and be very productive, as far as price and speed and quality go. There are other jobs you may have for me that I can make work on my equipment, but I can't make work for the best price. So you're better off using different printers to do those jobs for you — the ones whose equipment allows them to do it at the best price possible, the best turnaround time possible, and the best quality possible." Now, that really let me know I was dealing with someone who was telling me the truth. Because somebody who's lying to you says, "Oh, you bet, we can handle any job that you have! We'll always give you the best price at the best possible quality!" But that's not what Steve said; he told me the truth. What I've had him do since then is this: When they can use their equipment at the best price and give us the best turnaround quality, they do it right there in-house at CityPrint Printing in Wichita, Kansas. Whenever we have certain jobs that other printers can do faster and cheaper and at better quality than Steve can, **then he's our broker: He goes out and negotiates for the very best prices, then adds a small percentage on for himself and makes a little extra money that way.**

And then you have to find a good mailing house, a company that mails all your products out for you. We started with a company in Hutchinson, Kansas, and they cheated us every step of the way. They didn't mail the stuff they were supposed to, and so our responses all varied — that's how we found out they just were not honest. **We switched over to another company in 1990 called CCI, and we've been with them ever since.** Conservatively, they've mailed 200 to 300 million pieces for us, and they've done a fantastic job. That's one of the nice things about direct-mail. If you're mailing 50,000 pieces a week and you've got an offer that's just making you tons of money, all you have to do is pick up the phone, call your printer, and say, "Hey, instead of printing up 50,000, I want you to print up 100,000." Then you call your mailing house and say, "Look, I want you to mail 100,000 pieces a week instead of 50,000." Then you call up your list manager and say, "Get me 50,000 more good names." Pretty soon, you can double your business. If you've got an offer that's really working like gangbusters, that's causing people to drop everything to send you their checks, cash, money orders and credit card authorizations, all you've got to do to make it better is make a few phone calls. Suddenly you've got millions more dollars more coming in, and it's the most beautiful feeling on Earth.

I want you to experience that feeling. You *need* to experience that feeling. **First of all, to get paid for other things than your time — to get paid for the products and services that are sold, rather than the hours that you have in a day — is just phenomenal.** Most people make their money by selling their time. Even the highest paid people — models, brain surgeons, lawyers, doctors — they're getting paid for their time. Even though they may be making an enormous sum per hour, they're not getting the kind of money you could get when you're selling products and services that have nothing to do with the amount of time you're spending on those items. Personally, I can make more than $1,000 an hour by writing sales copy that sells thousands, tens of thousands or even hundreds of thousands of products and services. I don't mean to be egotistical; quite honestly you'll find, if you use these principles here, that *you* can make more than $1,000 an hour too. There have been times when we've had promotions that worked so well that when I take the time that I personally spent writing the sales letters and putting the whole thing together, and then you take the millions of dollars that we've made on the promotions, divided by the number of hours that I personally spent on the job — well, it's shocking. You wouldn't even believe how much money we make in an hour, but it's in the tens of thousands of dollars. That's God's honest truth.

You can make a lot more than that. That's the point I want to bring to your attention here: **If you want to make millions of dollars like we have, all you have to do is the same things we've done.** That's it; just do what we've done to make millions of dollars, and you can make millions of dollars too, and you can be in the same place that I'm in. If you know you have the ability to develop products and services and the sales materials that go with them, and you're using the power of direct-mail like I'm expressing here, you could make tens of thousands of dollars an hour when you get the right promotion out there working for you. **This is a powerful**

way to make money.

I've talked about the printer, the mailing house, the list broker, the great copy. **The last thing you need is an experienced staff to handle all the other things, because it's what you do with those orders that's going to help customers feel better about you.** The secret to reselling to your customers again and again is to have a stable, competent staff of good people who know how to process orders quickly, and know how to handle all the customer service challenges, so the customers are happy. You're using direct-mail to attract thousands of new customers, and then using that same powerful medium of direct-mail, to resell to those customers, again and again. If you have a stable staff that's very capable and competent, they're going to help you make more money, because a happy customer is a customer who keeps buying from you again and again.

That sounds like common sense, but if it's really common sense, why aren't more people using the power of direct response marketing to build their fortunes? This is one of the greatest mysteries of the field, because even people I know who are very capable, very smart when it comes to marketing — they're still not doing enough. The reason that direct-mail worked so well for us in the beginning is because we were already on a good, solid foundation. We were already making a nice profit; then Russ came along and helped us take the sales promotion that was already working for us in space advertising, and expand it in this powerful new way. **Going from space ads to direct-mail was like throwing a 55-gallon drum of jet fuel on a raging fire for us.**

The bad news about direct-mail is it's expensive. We were already making a great profit, though, and that was the whole key for us. So my best advice is for you to start with space ads, just like we did; **if you're going to get into direct-mail, you'd better be using some kind of a proven offer that's already made money for**

> As long as you are a good student — then every person and situation you face is your teacher.
>
> > Remember this. Pull back. Distance yourself. Step back and see the big picture!
>
> > And keep your emotions out of it.

The power of the U.S.P. (Unique Selling Position):

How can we separate ourselves from every other competitor in the most important way for the customer/prospect?

Answer that question in a clear and dramatic way — And Get Rich!

somebody else, and you'd better have the back-end of your business solved first. With those kinds of challenges, you need what we call a "slack adjuster." You need something expensive, or a series of things that are expensive, to sell to your best customers once you extract them, so you can make your profit. Direct-mail is expensive — make no bones about it. This is the reason why a lot of people lose their shirts with direct-mail. You can cash in with direct-mail, and the key is right here: You put 80% of your effort into reselling your best customers, and 20% of your effort into attracting new customers. If you'll do that, you'll do well. Believe me, a lot of people know that — that's not a secret. You'll find that concept in marketing books and seminars all over. If you go to an experienced marketer and tell them about the 80-20 rule, they'll nod their head. But I know people right now who are very, very good marketers, a lot better than me, and yet they don't practice that principle, and I don't know why. Again, it's one of the great mysteries. This is the golden secret to making huge sums of money.

When it comes to writing copy for direct-mail, to put that offer out to your best customers, it's so much easier because they trust you; they have a relationship with you, there's a bond, and they'll buy from you. Your copy doesn't have to be too good; you can even write bad copy. When I go back and look at copy that I wrote 15 years ago, I'm ashamed at how terrible it is — and yet it made us money. The reason it made us money is because those direct-mail packages that I was creating were going out to people who trusted us, even though I wasn't very good at any of this back then. They liked us, they liked what we were doing, they liked what we sold them the first time. So the copy didn't have to be as good, and the direct-mail didn't have to be as powerful. I cannot express this enough to you. **It's powerful because it lets you develop your skills by writing to your best customers, by treating them as if they were friends — and, again, they *should* be friends.** The more you do this, the better you'll get, if you stay with it long enough.

We're grateful for Russ von Hoelscher for getting us started in this. **We want to be to you, and your business, what Russ von Hoelscher was to our business.** So, let's put some real time and focus into direct-mail. I want you to stop calling it "junk mail" from here on out. Just get that idea out of your mind: This is not junk mail, because if it's done right it's the most powerful sales medium on earth. **You can create money at will; when you do this right, you're never going to worry about money, ever again, for the rest of your life.** You'll never have to worry about where your next $1,000 or your next $100,000 are going to come from, because you'll be able to take great ideas and turn them into direct-mail packages that go out to your best customers, who love you and appreciate you, who value you and have respect for you. Those people will buy from you so fast that it'll make your head spin, and the profits that result can just be absolutely phenomenal. I want you to think very, very hard about all this.

Direct-mail is really such a simple thing, once you master it. **It may take you a little while to master it, but it's worth the time and effort, because the benefits are so great.** It's out there for you right now. It's the same secret that we used to go from $16,000 a month to almost $100,000 a week in nine months. It can be the same secret that makes you millions of dollars. So go back and read this chapter once or twice more, and think very carefully as you read. Remember what I've told you: **This is the greatest sales medium on earth.** It can make you millions and millions of dollars in the fastest time, in the simplest way, as easily as possible.

SECRET FIVE:

Put a Percentage of Every Dollar Back into Advertising

The fifth secret we've used to make millions of dollars is the fact that we constantly put a percentage of every dollar that we bring in back into advertising. In the beginning, we ran two different checkbooks at the company. We had one bank account that was just for advertising, and another that was for everything else; and every day, we made sure that we took 30% of every dollar that came in and put it into that advertising account. **It required discipline, but it became one of the foundations of our company.**

You need to have a way to constantly attract new customers to you, and to do that you've got to have money. It all takes money to make it happen. To make sure you have that money on hand, you need to discipline yourself and make sure you use our guideline here, our formula. **Every day you *must* take a percentage of every dollar that comes in, and make sure that you put it right back into more advertising.** Now, that may seem like common sense to you, and it *is* common sense to know where your next dollar's coming from. You've got to constantly ask yourself that, and yet most people really screw up in this area. I'm shocked at the number of marketers I know who are otherwise capable and competent but aren't doing this at all. They have no consistent message for attracting new customers and reselling to old customers again and again, and they don't bother to set the money aside to do it. It really confuses me, because this idea really does make sense if you think about it. **I want you to really grasp this principle, because this has made us more money than anything else.**

You've got to have a way to bring in new customers, and you've got to have a way to resell to those old customers again and again. This requires money. Now, I'm going to give you a very simple formula that we use. At first I thought, "This is too simple. I don't want to insult anyone's intelligence here," but then at the same time I know for a fact people I respect who are *not* following these principles — and they're not rich, either. That's one of my greatest personal mysteries: the fact that I know people who are smarter than I am, and yet they're not rich. There's no doubt in my mind, absolutely zero doubt, that these people have a lot more brainpower than I do. They were blessed with a higher IQ. They're more talented than I am. But I'll put my net worth up against theirs any day, and theirs will look pale by comparison to mine. That's not to brag — I know my weaknesses, and I know that I'm only really good at just a few things. **But I'm here to tell you that if more people would just realize that the secret to getting rich is to consistently attract new customers, and then to consistently resell them, they would be rich, too.**

The way to attract and resell to those customers is by advertising <u>constantly</u>. And it's got to be consistent; you've got to have a system. Now, what *is* a system? It's very simple. You build your business so that you constantly have some type of ad or direct-mail piece, some type of promotion, that's attracting new customers to you. Every week we send out 50,000 pieces of direct-mail, sometimes more, sometimes less; we've mailed as many as 100,000 pieces, and around Christmas we used to mail only about 20,000 pieces. Now, though, we're going full blast during Christmas — because we've noticed that our business doesn't slow down at all during the holiday season. There are too many people who are way too conservative about their mailings. For every reckless entrepreneur who blows their business up and goes bankrupt, there's got to be at least 10,000 who are playing it too safe. I'm going to tell you more about why that is, what the thinking behind that is, and why you shouldn't do that. It's all right here in this secret.

You've got to have a balance. **A good 80% of your time and effort and attention must go to reselling to your old customers, but the remaining 20% should go to attracting new customers.** Again, consistency is so important. One mistake that a lot of people make is that they're focused on bringing in new customers — and on one hand I applaud those people. We all need new customers; there's no question about it. We've got to do what I call constantly "replenishing the pond." Think about that. We've got a pond out in front of our house here, Eileen and I. It's a beautiful pond; it surrounds our house, and sometimes during the rainy season it'll be filled up to almost overflowing. We had to do some special construction, in fact, because the pond was actually running over the road outside our house. Then, at other times of the year, because we

MARKETING SECRET

The Slack Adjuster — Develop and promote at least one super high-profit item that helps build your overall net profits.

- This is crucial. You must develop this super high-profit margin to make up for all of the high expenses that eat into your bottom line margins.

don't get any rain and the heat of the summer comes, it practically dries up.

Think about your business as a pond; it constantly has to be replenished, or it will dry up. **The way you do that is, by having a constant front-end promotion out there that attracts new customers, and then you put a lot of emphasis on reselling to those customers, because that's where all your profits are.** Most people put too much emphasis on the front-end, and that means they're constantly chasing new customers — constantly. Or they're so focused on reselling to their established customers where they're not replenishing the pond. Both of these strategies are a mistake; though if I had to choose one of the two, I think the better mistake is to focus on reselling to your established customers. However, even that strategy is wrong. The people who focus on the back-end constantly do it because they realize that's where the profits are; but if the pond isn't replenished, then the best customers you have today could be gone tomorrow. Life changes, people change, circumstances change. You've got to constantly ask yourself, always, "Where's my income for next month going to come from?" Now, if you understand residual income you might say, "Wait a minute — what about residual? Why can't I build that into my business, so I don't always have to worry about where my next dollar is going to come from?"

Well, residual income can be a nice safety net or buffer, and sure, it's wonderful to have products and services that you sell on a continuity basis, where every month you've got money coming in because of something that you sold once. I encourage you to go for that, to experience what it's like to bring in $100,000 a month automatically. **But even that business will dry up if you don't replenish it.** Because life changes, circumstances change, people change; for whatever reason you can't just do something once, kick back, and expect money to come in automatically forever. That's a fantasy. There are things you can do to bring in residual income, but what you really need to do is strive to develop a system for attracting new customers, converting the largest number of those new customers to sales, and then working constantly on your back-end.

That's what we're doing. Our system is more like a money machine; and that's what you've got to think about your business as — a money machine. We've been doing this for years, and it works well for us. I don't know why more people don't do it. We have one or two front-end promotions that constantly attract new customers to us. Like I said, every week we mail 50,000 pieces on average, just to bring in new customers, and then we have at least one new promotion every week to resell to our established customers. **Almost all our marketing, both to attract new customers and to resell to old customers, is what we call two-step marketing.** Now, don't let the term "two-step marketing" fool you, because it actually involves more than two steps in all, and I'll explain to you why it's more than two steps if it's done correctly. Oh, and by the way, you've been exposed to two-step marketing all your life, though maybe you just didn't have a name for it. Think about every single time that you've sent away for a free audio tape, a free CD, a free CD-ROM, a free report, free information; that's two-step marketing. You make it very easy for people; you're not trying to really sell them anything in the beginning, you're just trying to show that you're serious about what it is that you sell, and that they've an interest in it, and you're just trying to get them to raise their hand by sending in some kind of a form or requesting something for free.

We call it two-step marketing because here's what it's designed to do: 1) to get interested prospects to identify themselves and 2) to turn them into conversions. Now, what is a conversion? Simple. Your prospects raise their hand. They acquire something from you initially for a small amount of money, or for free; they request something, and now you're trying to sell them something, which is the second step. **Your conversion rate is the percentage of the people who raised their hand initially who end up buying whatever it is that you sell.** That's your conversion, and that's the second step. One of the reasons we do two-step marketing is because we're very sensitive about the fact that people love to buy things, but they hate to be sold to — and I know that sounds ironic. It's almost like a joke; but that's how it is.

People want to believe that they're coming to *you*. Their perception is that they're asking you to send them something, that they're the ones that took the first step, and they really did, of course, in their minds; but the truth is, you took the first step by making an offer to them. You either had an ad in a magazine or you sent them some piece of direct-mail; so you're the one that made it happen, but in their minds they don't think that way. **People have the feeling that they're coming to you when you use two-step marketing, and that's one of the best reasons why you do it.** You don't want people to feel that you're pressuring them to buy something, or that you're trying to get them to give you their money. On the contrary, **the emotional feeling behind it all must be that they're the ones seeking *you* out, rather than you seeking *them* out.**

You might think it's a small thing, but it's really not, and it becomes even more important when you're going to your established customers again and again. **You always want people to raise their hands and send for something, so you can then separate the smaller herd of customers from the bigger herd.** You get a small group of people that you know are qualified and serious, or else they wouldn't have raised their hands. They've expressed an interest, and now you're simply following up with them. So when I tell you that it's called two-step marketing, there really are two steps; **but the second step is a series of follow-up mailings that go out to those people who raised their hands.** Now you're able to focus your marketing efforts on that smaller group of people who raised their hands by saying, "Yes, send me that information package," or "Send me the portfolio or the report or the audio CD or the DVD," or whatever it is that sells the higher-ticket product or service. We've had two-step marketing where we asked for one or two hundred dollars on Step One, because what we were really trying to sell them was something for thousands. We've had two-step marketing where we even asked for $1,000 on Step One, because we were trying to sell them a $5,000 package on Step Two.

This process is just too simple for a lot of people. If you ask them, "Hey, what are you doing to constantly attract new customers?" you might as well be speaking a foreign language, because they just don't think like that. This is especially true for these super-smart people I know who are always broke. They're really sharp marketers, but they're

focused on reselling to old customers. Now, they're not making the mistake that a lot of shallow marketers and fly-by-nighters make, where they're constantly trying to make a profit on the front-end. That's a terrible mistake, because **all the real profits come from the back-end — from reselling to established customers who trust you, who respect you.** They like you and what you're selling. They've already bought from you, so you've proven to them that you're a company they can depend on and that you're selling things they really want. That's where you're going to get rich, and the smart marketers all know it, so they put a lot of their emphasis on that — and they hate front-end marketing.

Look, I hate front-end marketing too, but it's an absolutely necessary evil if you want to keep your customer pool filled. It's not where the real profits come from, and in many cases we take an initial loss on the front-end, given the amount of money it costs to secure that initial sale or even just to get that customer to raise their hand. **But it's an expense towards future profits, if you've got your back-end business together.** If you have a wide range of products and services that you can sell to a customer once they raise their hand, and you've got a system in place that allows you to sell those things fast do that, then it may cost you $100, $500, or even $1,000 for every new prospect who sends for that free report — but what do you care, if you can immediately sell that person something on the back-end for a huge sum of money and make a quick profit? **Who cares what it costs, if you can then go to that same prospect and resell them again and again?** You want to keep customers for life.

Of course, you need to fill that gap between front-end and back-end immediately. The one time in my life when I really got into financial trouble was when I pushed the gap a little too far, and I didn't have other things going right with the business. Initially, we were asking people to raise their hands and send for a report: that was Step One. For Step Two,

MARKETING SECRET

Prepare for the worst possible outcomes, — Set up your company so you can still make money with terrible numbers.

- Set your margins high

- Keep your costs low

- Factor in low response rates...

- Plan for poor results. How? Figure out a way to make each promotion work — even if the numbers are bad.

we were asking them to pay $49 a month for a continuity program. For Step Three, we had a package to sell them for $2,500 that was related to what they'd bought for $49 a month. So it was more of a three-step campaign, and it was working really well, and it was making us millions and millions of dollars — **but the gap between our front-end expenditures and our back-end profits was wide, and it cost us a lot of money.** We normally mail 50,000 pieces a week at M.O.R.E., Inc., but at that time we were mailing more like 75,000 to 100,000 pieces weekly. At 60 to 70 cents apiece... well, you do the math. It was expensive, and it took time.

We use two different sequences. When somebody raises their hand, you don't just send him one offer once and say, "Okay, here's the product or service I have for you." That would be foolish — and again, it's a mistake that most people are making. Most markets just don't follow up enough. When somebody raises their hand for a free report, the marketer will send them that report, which is really a sales letter — and maybe they'll include a CD or DVD, or whatever supports it and gives their customer more information about the product or service they're trying to sell. But then they just drop the ball. If they don't hear from the prospect, they assume the prospect isn't a serious buyer. **The better marketers, the ones who are smarter, will go ahead and send him several packages.** They'll send him a second notice, a third notice, a fourth notice. The really sharp marketers, the ones who are making millions, build a sequence where they'll send as many as 20 to 30 different follow-ups. **They don't just give up on the people, which is something that's going to be more and more necessary in the future.** You can't give up on people. **Your job is to try to take those prospects who raised their hands initially and convert them into sales as fast as you can.**

The one time when I almost took the company into bankruptcy, we had a promotion that was leveraged out too far and took too long. It took an average of 3 to 4 months from the time the prospect raised their hand to bring them through to the initial stage, which was to convert those $49-a-month service buyers over to a $2,500 sale for a related product-service combination we had. **It took too long.** I knew then what I want to teach you here, which is that the companies that make the most money are the ones that don't worry about how much money it costs to get somebody in on their front-end. **They don't care about that, because they're in the business of converting those prospects into buyers and multi-buyers.** But you see, a lot of these corporations had more money than we had, and we weren't watching all our numbers on the back-end, and the whole thing bombed on us. It was too aggressive, and just about took us into bankruptcy.

But most people are not aggressive *enough*. They have unrealistic expectations and they're trying to chase new customers constantly, which is not profitable at all. New customers don't know you, they don't like you, there's no trust built up, there's no relationship. **It's terribly hard to make a profit selling to brand new customers once each.** Even those who do it are never able to do it on a large scale. People who make millions of dollars are the people who have a consistent large-scale campaign, or several campaigns that attract the largest possible number of the most qualified new prospects they can find to some type of initial offer. It could be a free or low-price offer, something to make it for the most qualified people to raise their hands. Sometimes you have to ask for money, because that's the only way to really qualify a prospect and know they're serious — and to help offset some of your high costs. Most of the time, though, it's better to have a free offer. **You give them something nice and you make a really good impression, and you show them how you're different than everybody else;** you blow them away, you surprise them, in some cases you shock them, because of all the stuff that you send to them. You make a great favorable impression. Before a young man goes and knocks on his date's door, he'll go to the barber, he'll take a bath, he'll put on some cologne, he'll put on his best clothes, and he'll clean out his car. He wants to make a favorable impression; and that's exactly how you have to do marketing, too.

You have to winnow your larger group of potential prospects to a smaller group you can focus on, whether that's by having them send for something or by sending them to a 1-800 number or a website. **Now you have a smaller group, but they're more qualified.** They've proven that they're serious, so you can spend more money to market to them. You can afford to do that, if your profit margins are good and you're selling them something related to what they raised their hand on. And that's what it has to be: **It has to be part of an integral campaign, so the front-end and back-end are closely tied together.** Do that, and you're going to make a huge sum of money, because your conversion rates are going to be good. You've got to follow up on them more than two or three times. **Stay on top of them.** We'll send our prospects as many as two different follow-up packages every single week, and we'll do that for twelve weeks in some cases, especially when we're selling an upcoming seminar, or some other product where there's a real sense of urgency. **The greater the pressure, the higher the conversion rates.**

All this does take a good bit of time to think about and master, and you may have to go back and read this chapter a few times before you really get the essence of what I'm sharing with you. **My best advice is to find the top companies in your market and study them closely.** Look for the ones doing the best job of selling and reselling to their established customers, the ones who are doing the best job of attracting new customers because of the ads they're running or the direct-mail packages they're sending out. **Find those companies, get on their mailing lists, see what they're doing, and start realizing the magic behind these tricks.** If people are making millions and millions of dollars in direct response marketing, they're doing it for this reason; and the more you're aware of it, the better. So get on these customer lists and start thinking like a businessperson rather than a consumer; get on the other side of the cash register.

SECRET SIX:

Focus on Back-End Marketing

The sixth secret we used to make $10 million in less than five years is the fact that **we focused on back-end marketing.** In the previous chapter, I talked extensively about the difference between front-end and back-end marketing. On the front-end, you're trying to attract new customers; on the back-end, you're trying to resell those customers again and again, for the largest profit possible. **As long as you make sure the value you're providing exceeds the dollar value of the money they're giving you, you can't go wrong.** Then the question becomes, "How can I sell my customers more and more?"

I feel very strongly about this; you have to think this thing through, and realize that **you absolutely have to develop long-term relationships with your customers if you want to profit.** Far too many people are self-conscious on this point, including me; for years, I felt that I was going to upset my customers if I went back to them too much. I honestly feared that my best customers were going to become upset and quit me if I tried to sell them too much stuff. **I didn't understand that both of us profited from that long-term relationship.** I understand, now, that most people overthink this point, and that's one of the reasons they never get rich; they tend to complicate things a little too much. But it doesn't have to be complicated. **I've always understood that business is mostly about retaining customers,** because when I had my carpet-cleaning business, I depended on repeat business; after all, I was operating in a small town. But a lot of people have never figured it out, so they don't have any kind of intimate relationships with their customers.

I've thought about why this is for years, and as far as I can tell, many of the people who are attracted to direct response marketing are simply people who want to hide out. They want to avoid contact with the entire world — and this is especially true for Internet marketers. I know that there are plenty of exceptions, and I'm really grateful that there are, but **I see Internet marketers in general as people who just want to sit behind the computer screen every day.** That's all they want to do, just as people who are attracted to traditional mail-order just want to get cash, checks,

▼▼▼▼▼▼▼▼▼
MARKETING SECRET

You must put as much of your time, attention, energy, passion, and skills into the specific areas that bring your business the largest profits. FOCUS! Identify these areas and put everything into these activities.

- Focus only on these activities — and let other people do most of the other stuff.

money orders, and credit card authorizations in the mail every day. They love the idea that they never have to speak to or meet with the customer, and that's part of what attracts them to the business. Hey, that's part of what attracted *me* to the business: the fact that you could get money in the mail, and you didn't have to deal with some of the things that other people have to deal with in traditional businesses.

My mother had a day-care center for 15 years, and every Sunday when I spoke to her on the phone, she would tell me about the pain and the adversities she had to go through with that day-care center. Twice a day, she had to see all her best customers — once when they came to drop their kids off, and once when they came to pick them up. There was still that constant contact with her customers, and that gave me a deep appreciation for direct-response marketing. This is a business where, in many cases, you'll never meet the people who give you the most money. **But that shouldn't be your main reason for being in this business.** We have regular seminars and workshops, and have for years — and I advise everyone to do that. **We like to talk about the fact that you should view the direct response marketing business as if it were a restaurant:** unless you're in a super-high traffic location you're going to go broke if you don't get the same clientele to come back again and again, month after month, year after year, and bring all their friends, family and associates, so their friends, family and associates can bring all their friends too. If you have a favorite restaurant, you know how that works. Eileen and I have a restaurant in Newton, Kansas, that we go to regularly; it's a Mexican restaurant, and when they opened up in 1988, Eileen and I were there. We were one of their very first customers. It was only a few blocks from our house, so we could actually walk over there. Their kids were just so cute and adorable; they used to bring us the chips and fill up our glasses and such — and now those little kids are running the place. We got to know the Mom and Dad and they got to know us, and there's a kinship there. Since then I've watched them carefully, because their business has grown and thrived and they're making so much money. I watch how they treat all their customers like they're special. They stop and talk to their customers, they get to know them, they make sure the food tastes good.

You know, they do that at Applebee's, too. One of the neat things about all those "neighborhood" chain restaurants, like Applebee's and Outback Steakhouse and Chili's, is that they try to focus on customer service and consistency. It's not the same thing as with a local restaurant that's owned by a family, where you get to know all the kids and aunts and uncles and cousins and brothers, but they try to instill that same attitude. They really focus hard on that, and that's one of the smartest things that they do with their marketing. **It's also one of the smartest things you can do with *your* marketing. It's hard to be intimate with a mailing.** It's easy to start thinking of your customers as numbers when all they are to you is a spreadsheet with some names on it. You lose that feeling that you had as a local businessperson, when you're face-to-face with your customers.

In the very beginning, when I started my carpet-cleaning business, I had customers who loved me and appreciated me; they looked forward to me coming, and they would have me inside their home to clean their carpets, just so that I could sit down and eat dinner with them, and they had cookies for me. I'm serious — milk and cookies. They just wanted a visit; their carpets weren't dirty. It's the same way old guys will go to the barbershop, even when they have no hair left, and spend a half-hour or 45 minutes in there. I'm thinking, "What is the barber doing? Using a tweezers for every hair?" But it's not about that. It has nothing to do with the haircut; **it has everything to do with the relationship.** So we think about all these old guys who go in constantly to the barbershop week after week to get their hair "cut." Their hair doesn't need to be cut anymore; there *is* no more hair. It's all about the routine; it's something they're comfortable with. They like doing business with that barber, they like going back; it makes them feel better about themselves. That's how it is, in general, for all of us. **It's an emotional thing that has little to do with logic.** There's no more hair to cut, but we keep going back to that same barber anyhow, because it's all about the emotional elements — and **it's those same emotional elements that will keep your customers coming back. It's up to you to figure out what those emotional elements are.** In the market that we deal with, there are emotional reasons that cause people to become insatiable, to continue to buy the same things over and over again. There's no logical reason for this; it just fills an emotional void they have.

If you're going to sell to people again and again, you have to understand that it's all about the emotions; buying often has nothing to do with logic.** To really comprehend this, you have to know your customers in the most intimate way. That was very easy for Eileen and me when we started in 1988. There are two basic reasons why we were able to turn our $300 investment into over $10 million in less than five years. The first reason is the most important one: We already intimately knew who our customers were, even if we weren't aware of it consciously. We were *exactly* like our target customer. For years I was what I affectionately call an "opportunity junkie." I just couldn't get enough of this stuff; I couldn't buy enough, and I was on every single mailing list. I had an insatiable appetite for getting rich, and I was sending away for all the plans and programs that promised miracles. The crazier the programs were, the more I liked them.

That's part of the insanity of it, because a lot of these programs didn't stand a snowball's chance in hell of making any money. Didn't matter to me; it was all about the emotions. I wanted to get rich, and I really believed that there was some secret out there that could make it happen. **As it turns out, there *are* secrets — but they involve good, solid business practices and a lot of good, solid marketing.** You know that cliché that says "it takes one to know one"? There's a lot of truth to that. The best advice I can give you is to do what they tell you when you take a creative writing course: **Write what you know.** Even a superstar like John Grisham was a lawyer first, so he started writing fiction books about the law. Then there's the late Michael Crichton, who was a medical doctor. You might have heard of him. He wrote a lot of books that had to do with medicine, and created a little TV show called *ER*.

So write about what you know; that's especially true if you're going to get rich in the information business, niche marketing, or direct-response marketing. **Stay in that marketplace and try to figure out ways to attract the thousands, and in some cases millions, of people out there who have something in common with you and what you know about.** When I started, I knew all about the opportunity market. When it came time to developing some of these ideas, I knew what was hot and what wasn't. I knew the places to advertise and I knew the companies whose ads were appearing over and over again, because those were the companies I was buying from. When it came time to decide on the first ad, I spent a whole weekend just looking at similar ads before

▼▼▼▼▼▼▼▼▼▼▼▼▼▼▼▼

E verything I do is <u>directly</u> connected to everything else I'm doing.

coming up with something similar. We copied from proven stuff that I had an intimate knowledge of, without even realizing it at the time.

This was our number one wealth secret for years, at all our seminars. Who shows up at these events? **People on our mailing list, of course; and who are those people? They're opportunity junkies.** They've been sending away for all the plans and programs, so they're on all the mailing lists; they have the insatiable appetite to continue to buy program after moneymaking program. For years, this was one of the things that I kept trying to beat into people's heads, because I feel so passionate about this, and I know it's true. I *know* it can help people make millions. I know without any doubt that the people who are already buying all these things are in heat for this kind of stuff. Heck, they should be the ones selling it to other people. But what do they want to do? They want to try all kinds of other ideas. It's always something else, some crazy, whacked-out idea that doesn't stand any chance of making any money. **They all want to do something other what they should be doing, which is sticking with what they know.**

The second secret is that we had a lot of help, of course. I've already gone over this one in detail. We had Russ von Hoelscher working with us from the time we were six months into the business, and that's what caused our income to really explode — because his shortcut secrets became our shortcut secrets, and we ended up getting a lot more done in a lot less time. That's how we went from $16,000 a month to almost

Write down your best ideas when they are new — and when you are first getting started and very excited!

- These ideas are HOT! And you'll need them later on when you are cold!!!

- Ideas are like slippery fish! Hard to hold on to! So you must capture them!

The best ideas come to you in the heat of the moment!

$100,000 a week in our first nine months of working with him. **If you don't have the intimate knowledge of your business that you need, you can get it.**

Now, for those of you that don't understand the opportunity market, it's easy to figure out. All you've got to do is start sending away for some of the plans and programs that are for sale in the tabloids, *Popular Mechanics*, and *Popular Science*. Pretty soon you'll end up on every single mailing list out there. You'll go to your mailbox, and it will be overflowing with offers; and there'll be a little card in there that says, "Come to the front desk, we have more mail for you" or "We have packages for you." You'll see that this is a rabid market. **There are a lot of people out there selling opportunities, and the good news for you is that most of them don't know what the hell they're doing.** There are exceptions, but most marketers don't understand the concept of back-end marketing, so they're not doing a good job of following up with their customers.

They're not building relationships with their customers, either. All they're trying to do is make some money by selling one product one time. They're shallow marketers, and they're missing the point I want to emphasize here: **People want to do more business with marketers they like and trust,** and so the more you do to stay focused on reselling to your best customers, the more money you're going to make. People will want more of whatever they bought from you the first time — assuming they didn't ask for refund, and assuming it's a hot subject. **It's all about variations on a theme; that's a lot of the secret, to continue to come**

up with something new over and over again. People will also re-buy a lot more than you think they will. People just can't seem to get enough; they're like I was.

When people get in heat, they buy like crazy. I used to worry that I was selling to the customers too much — that they were going to be upset and quit buying from me. **Now the only thing I worry about is that I'm not selling enough to them. The key to making that conversion yourself is to know your customers in the most intimate way.** We kept journals for years, and these journals were filled with customer comments from sheets that we sent out in all of our packages, where we offered a bonus, just some little free report, if they answered a few questions. At the bottom of the form we told them that they were giving up their rights if they accepted that report, so that we could use their comments in our promotional materials. **This was a great way to develop testimonials, but more importantly, it was a great way to get inside the heads and hearts of our customers.** We asked them for comments, and some people wrote the minimum, just chicken scratch that you could barely read. But about half of those comment sheets came back to us with some great stuff, and we typed it up and I studied it. I made it a science to know my customers better than they know themselves, and that made it so much easier.

I see a lot of people who are so confused and frustrated, constantly asking themselves, "What do I sell?" They can't seem to get beyond that one idea: "What do I sell to people?" Well, the one thing I want to say is, when you have a group of customers who have already bought something from you, the question of what to sell goes out the window. Now it just becomes, "What are the best things to sell?" **That's because you know these people. You know what they like, since they've bought something from you already.** Now you know that they'll continue to rebuy from you, if you just come up with variations on a theme. With our company, we're always coming up with new stuff, but people who don't understand how this works say, "My God! You guys are so prolific. How in the world do you keep coming up with all that new stuff?"

The truth is, most of it's just the same old stuff that's been given a new facelift, a new veneer. **We keep finding new ways to recycle the same materials,** and do you think our customers care? Absolutely not; they don't care at all. If they did, we wouldn't do it. We're in business to attract and retain customers, so why would we do something that our customers didn't like? We follow the money. Our customers like seeing new things — but they also want the elements behind those things to be established and proven. **So we sell old, established moneymaking ideas, with a new exciting flavor or twist on top.** Each product has that element of "new" which is the buzz, the draw, the jazz. It's this thing that gets them really excited, the "sizzle" that Elmo Wheeler, the great sales trainer, talked about; it attracts them to the deal. **But if it's too new, people get freaked out.** Nobody wants to be the guinea pig, so they love the idea that you've taken something that's proven and added this new twist to it; and the more exciting that twist is, the more they'll buy.

Product development is really the easiest thing for us opportunity marketers. I'm going to tell you more about product development later, but for the moment I just wanted to share with you the fact that you're going to discover better ways to sell more products and services at higher profits to your customers as you move forward. With a little bit of knowledge and experience, that confusion about what to sell goes right out the window. The same things that confuse you now won't confuse you a month or a year from now, because you learn. You just keep moving forward, staying focused on your customers. **When you stay focused on them and on how to give them more of what you know they already want, then all that confusion just goes right away.**

Everybody wants to make millions of dollars, but most have never stopped and thought things through in even the simplest of ways. Here it is: **All the profits that you'll ever need to run and build your business come from the back-end marketing.** They come from being focused on that small group of your best customers, reselling to them again and again, constantly making them new offers. I want to share with you one of the greatest secrets that we've learned over the years, and if you'll master this secret, it's going to help you make a lot more money — and it's so simple. I'll try to express it to you in the possible clearest way. It's what I call the pre-publication product development strategy. Got to call it something, right? **The pre-publication product development strategy involves using your best customers as the testing ground.**

If you'll just dedicate yourself to spending a little time every day coming up with new ideas, you'll have the foundations of new products. **You test them to your established customers first. You make an offer to them, and you tell them it's not even ready yet, that it's in the pre-**

publication phase. Then you have a deadline to meet. You've got a bunch of people who gave you money, so now you have pressure to perform; you've got a purpose. You've got a hundred or a thousand customers who just gave you big bucks and you don't want to disappoint them, so you'd better get off your ass and start working. The deadline helps keep you focused; it helps add purpose to your life, and you'll get a lot more done.

Once you've done all that, you take the things that sell well to your very best customers, and you start testing those to your new customers. Those products become part of your new customer acquisition. **Your best, most established customers are the testing ground for your front-end customer-acquisition program.** A lot of the secret to selling to your customers on the back-end has to do with constantly replenishing that supply of customers, so you need those new people. Put this secret into play, and you'll always have something on the front-end that attracts new customers on a continual basis, so that you'll always have customers on the back-end that you can resell to again and again.

You've got to think of your customers as if they really were your friends. You see this used all the time; every sales letter that you get says "Dear Friend," so maybe you're a little cynical about that. But your customers *should* be your friends, because they're the ones fueling your ambition. They're the ones helping your financial dreams come true. **They're the ones who are really building your company; why shouldn't they be your friends?** Think about all the elements it takes to be a good friend. First of all, there's some understanding. You feel that your friends understand you and you understand your friends; you have a shared interest in each other. There's some respect and trust; there's some appreciation. You look out for your friends; you try to do special things for them. **If you try to treat your customers like that, you're going to end up head-and- shoulders ahead of all those direct-response marketers who want to hide out, who want to avoid the world.**

I realize I'm speaking in generalities here, but it's almost impossible to feel any intimacy with names and addresses on a spreadsheet. **This is why I honestly believe that you should produce seminars, tele-seminars, and workshops on a regular basis.** You should talk to your customers; you should get to know them as more than just names and addresses on a list. **The more you do to develop this intimacy with your customers, the more money you're going to make.**

Consistent New Customer Acquisition

▼▼▼▼▼▼▼▼▼

MARKETING SECRET

A business is very similar to a living organism...

- The marketplace is its life and livelihood.

- It feeds off its market.

- It changes, grows, and adapts to the changes in its environment.

- Many outside forces can kill it. Some slowly. Some quickly.

- Keeping it alive for a long time can be a delicate thing.

The seventh secret that we used to make millions of dollars is this: **We disciplined ourselves to do constant front-end marketing.** I went over this to some extent in the previous chapter on back-end marketing, but I plan to hit it harder in this one.

Now, to discipline yourself means that you do something whether you feel like doing it or not. This is *not* the fun part of the business. **You're lucky if you break even on the initial sale; you usually lose money to get those new customers.** The people who make millions and millions of dollars don't even worry about breaking even on the front-end. It's not even a concern; nor should it be, since the back-end is where you make a profit. In fact, most companies go negative on the front-end. It may cost them $1,000 to bring in a customer who initially only spends $100 — and yes, some companies are willing to make that kind of sacrifice. Now, think about that; it's kind of scary. Admittedly, the people who are making the most money have the deepest pockets, and they can afford to do things that you can't afford to do; **but you *can* be more aggressive.** That's part of the secret to front-end marketing: to be aggressive. Do wild and crazy things; be bold and audacious, be outrageous, try to come up with things that wake people up and get them to pay attention.

The famous Tony Robbins has a wonderful story about this. He points out that you've got all these people who are so interested in the subject of meditation and self-hypnosis — and that's a joke, because most people are already hypnotized. They're already asleep at the wheel; they're already running around in an apathetic fog. **Nothing could be truer in the world of advertising, where we're living in an overly competitive marketplace.** There are all kinds of ads and marketing messages out there trying to lure customers in, all kinds of competition for the customers' dollar.

Now, that shouldn't be a negative thing. Some people use it as such, and it just ticks me off when I hear that. Here's an especially annoying example: the town of Hillsboro, Kansas is just six miles from where I'm writing this now. They had a store come into the marketplace called Alco; it's like a miniature Wal-Mart, which is about all the town can handle. Well, there was already a Ben Franklin store that had been doing business for 30 years in downtown Hillsboro, but when little Alco came in, suddenly the Ben Franklin store shut down. They just went out of business, because the owner decided they couldn't compete. That was it. I happen to think the owner of that company is a wimp; he's weak. I see other people who are so focused on the competition that they just let it scare the hell out of them, and that's not right. *Nothing* **is more wrong then letting the competition scare you or make you nervous.**

Sure, you should be aware of your competition — because if you're going to go out there to make millions of dollars you've got to be the lead dog. You've got to take that position right away. Even if you're not the lead dog, you've got to pretend that you *are*. **You've got to be bold and aggressive; you've got to do things that attract customers to you.** I don't care what it is, but you've got to do it on a consistent basis. **It's got to be part of your routine.** It has to be a systematic process of your business, so that every single week, every single month, you've got some kind of a new ad or direct-mail package out there, some type of offer that's designed to attract the very best customers possible. You want to repel everyone else. **You've got to see your front-end marketing as a powerful magnetic force that attracts only the specific type of people you want.**

Now, this won't happen overnight. **It's a process; the more you do it, the better you'll get,** and yes, some of these other marketers can be intimidating. They've been out there for a long time, they've got a lot of experience, they've tried a lot of things, they've got a lot of knowledge, and with that comes a tremendous amount of confidence or ego or both. There's a difference between egotism and real confidence, but it's hard to tell them apart because they look the same on the surface. It's easy to get intimidated by these experts who've been out there for 10, 20, 30 years. They've tested everything; they've got all these things figured out. Some of the things I'm going to talk about in this chapter they already know in the most intimate way. **What you don't realize is they had to stumble and fall to get there; they had to go through some adversity to learn these secrets on their own. You're going to have to do the same thing.** I wish somebody would've told me *that* 20 years ago! I wish somebody would have said, "Look, you can become great at this; you can become a master at marketing and making millions of dollars by selling and reselling to the same people over and over again within your marketplace — but it's going to take time, work, effort, energy, frustration, confusion, lots of anxiety, and lots of pain." **I had to go through a lot of pain to get where I am right now, and I know I've got further to go, too, so it's a process.** You keep moving forward, you keep figuring it out slowly but surely, and over a period of time as you do figure things out, the money does start flowing in; and the more money flows in, the greater the level of confidence you'll have. **The greater the level of confidence, the more aggressive that you're going to be.**

Being aggressive is very, very important when it comes to new customer acquisition. You've got to realize that your competitors are trying to get the same customers you're trying to get. They're trying to attract these people into their folds, just like you are. They're the enemy, they really are — though of course you can develop alliances with some of your best competitors. Some of those people will end up becoming your best friends. But there has to be a certain attitude in the beginning — almost a cocky attitude, some real bravado. You're going to go out there to get these people and bring them into your fold, and if you really have something that's good for them, something that can really help them, something that can make a difference in their lives, if you're selling products and services that really do offer tremendous benefits — **then you *should* be bolder, more aggressive, more outrageous, and do things that shock the living crap out of people.** It makes them stand up and notice you and say, "Who the hell is this?" **It breaks people out of that apathetic fog they live in.**

Most people are running around in a daze. A lot of new marketers don't realize that, and neither do some old ones. They're so much in love with their stuff that they really do think, in their heart of hearts, that people are reading every word of their copy, that people really care about it — and they don't. **Most prospects have built up an immunity to advertising.** My best friend has a pest-control company, and so in the last six years, I've gotten a chance to get to know something about the pest-control business. It's an interesting business, by the way. She has customers who, for the last 27 years, have been paying a monthly fee to let service people come in. It's a great business from a money/profitability standpoint, because once somebody trusts you to come into their home and spray for insects, it takes a force of God to for them to switch companies. One of the things that I've learned from being around her and her business, something that I've used as a metaphor to apply towards marketing, is the way these insects become immune to poison. When her technicians go out on a regular account, they have to use a different poison than they used last month — because what happens is, those insects build up a tolerance for the poisons. If you try to shoot that same poison month after month, eventually it won't kill them — and then the customers get ticked off and you have to keep coming back for free, because it's part of the monthly contract. I believe the people within a marketplace respond the same way to advertising messages. **It doesn't matter what you're offering, the customers still build a tolerance for it. So you need to constantly offer new things to your market** and, most importantly, you must be sure you don't fall under the delusion that people really care about any of this stuff, because they don't.

The more you know about marketing, the more cynical you'll become about people in general. **It's safe to say that people only buy for purely selfish emotions, and they buy the most when it comes to messages of**

> ▼▼▼▼▼▼▼▼▼▼▼▼▼▼▼
>
> Use MORE photos of yourself... your staff... customers... office events, etc.
>
> PHOTOS SELL!
>
> A picture may not be worth 1,000 words — but a combination of the right pictures can definitely let you sell more of your stuff.

Almost all profits come from the back-end...

- Spend more time, money, and effort — doing more business with your existing customers.

- 80% marketing to existing customers

- 20% to get new customers.

total greed. Some fear messages work really well, too. The more you're aware of the fact that there are a lot of competitors out there who are trying to get the same people you're trying to get, the more you're going to be bigger and bolder; you're going to do things that are more aggressive, and **you're going to do things that completely and totally separate you from everybody else out there.**

I'm going to go over some important questions with you here, and your answers to these questions will help you continue to get better and better. Now, some of your first answers to these questions may be kind of uninspired, so you should keep some journals and keep thinking about all this. See yourself as the general at war; see yourself as the architect of your company; try to develop a higher image of who you are and what you're trying to accomplish here. **The better you get at answering these questions and then implementing the right promotions based on the answers, the more money you're going to make, simple as that.** Some of these questions sound like common sense, but then again, if they were, then everybody would be doing certain things, and they aren't.

One of the greatest things I can share with you, at the risk of sounding like an egomaniac, is that **most marketers are weak. They're easy to beat if you'll just try.** Most competitors never think through the kinds of things that I'm going to share with you here. Their marketing is very feeble and ineffective. **They're not doing much at all to build strong bonds and relationships with their customers.** They're not doing nearly enough to ensure that they can resell to the same people again and again. **So you come along, and you just do the bare minimum sometimes, and that puts you out there in front right away. Here are some questions you need to ask yourself to do that:** "Who are the best customers I'm trying to reach? What are they really searching for? How can I reach them in the best possible way? What could people in my marketplace want that they're not getting anywhere else?" That last is a particularly good question, by the way. Keep asking yourself that question. Keep asking them all; the answers will come to you! At first there might be just small answers, but be aware that answers — including some great ones — are waiting for you out there if you'll just keep asking the same questions. Who are the biggest and best companies selling to the people you want to sell to? What are these companies doing right? What are they doing wrong? Where are they running their ads to attract new customers? They're all doing some kind of lead-generation, front-end advertising, or they wouldn't be the biggest and best competitors in your marketplace.

So you're looking for that. **You're constantly trying to get on the other side of the cash register.** Pay attention to your market, as if you were a consultant trying to help a client, and start thinking these things through for yourself — **because you're always going to care more about your business than any consultant you can hire.** Now, I believe in hiring consultants; I think they're very helpful, but they can't do it all for you, and that's what most people want consultants to do: everything. They hire consultants, and they want the consultants to run their companies for them. That's total nonsense. You've got to ask yourself: "What are these companies doing right, and what are they doing wrong? What are the top ten things that are most important to my market?" That's another great question, and the answer will evolve over time. **You should keep journals filled with your answers, because I promise you that the top ten reasons why you think your customers buy things from you will change over of time.** The answers will become clearer to you.

Remember, people buy for emotional reasons; they're insatiable. Often their reasons have very little to do with logic; and I expect that in the beginning, a lot of your answers to the questions I've mentioned will be logical ones. You've got to get beyond all that. I promise you that the emotional answers to those questions are more important than anything else, and **once you understand the emotional reasons of why people buy and continue to buy, that's when you start becoming a great**

marketer. *That's* when you get to the point where you know things that other people don't know. Because, you see, most people are real "surfacy" about this. **When I say that most marketers are weak, I mean it.** They may be very good when it comes to product development; they may be very, very good at providing certain services, and they may be extremely knowledgeable. But when it comes to marketing, they're wimps. I don't mean to sound like some egomaniac here; I just want to tell you the truth. It's an advantage if you see it as one. It becomes very important when you want to make millions of dollars; all this does, because **the more money you want to make, the more you have to turn up the volume.** You've got to use these principles in the maximum way; the less money you want to make, the more you can be just like most marketers out there. You don't have to be that strong, and you certainly don't have to do anything in any aggressive way, if all you want to do is make a couple of hundred thousand a year.

But some of us want to make millions — and if that's what you want to do, you've got to turn up the volume. **You need an appropriate balance between front-end and back-end.** As I've mentioned before, front-end marketing is a necessary evil; that's all it is. **Your real business is developing customers, getting them into the fold, doing things that establish relationships that cause them to think of you in a different way than they think about all the competitors.** You've got to build a friendship with these people. A friendship is based on mutual understanding and respect, but it's also based on other things. For instance, the quickest way you can become somebody's friend is to get a mutual enemy. Find out who their enemies are, what problems they face, and get more in tune with that than anything else. **It's about what they want — but it's also about what they** *don't* **want.**

Part of the way you separate yourself in the marketplace is you speak directly to their pain and their frustration; you've got to know about these things in the most intimate way. It was easy for Eileen and me in the beginning. Little did I know that we'd stumbled onto a multimillion-dollar secret here. It's based on the idea of the unique selling position, or USP. I learned about USPs from Jay Abraham back in the late 1980s or early 1990s. **You've got to have something about your company that completely separates it, in the minds and hearts of your prospects, from every other company out there;** and when I heard that,

I thought, "Man, that's a great idea!" So I spent a whole day just thinking it through: "What will be our USP?" I came up with a simple idea, and yet it's been the very foundation of our success. Our USP is the fact that for years, we were out there desperately seeking a way to make more money. *We* **were the customers.**

We established that as our USP, and decided we were going to be very upfront with the customer. We weren't going to play games with them. We were going to tell our story; **we were going to let them know that we've been in their shoes before.** We've traveled down that same road that they've traveled down, we've been lied to and misled, cheated and abused by all these other companies that promise all kinds of crazy plans and schemes that are based more on fiction than fact. We just decided, "No holds barred." **We were going to remove all the filters and be totally honest with people.**

Little did we know that we'd stumbled across an amazing secret. I would advise you to do the same thing with your customers: **Be honest with them. Don't play games.** Some of them are going to hate you, some of them are going to like you, some of them are going to love you. But even the people who don't like you, if they're good prospects in your marketplace they'll respect you, and that's the most important thing. They know that you're being real with them. **People are so unbelievably skeptical in this day and age;** even the people you think trust you probably don't. There's always something in the back of their heads that's saying, "Is that person for real? Are they telling it to me straight?"

With your new customer-acquisition marketing, what you're trying to do is to establish a relationship with somebody. **I call the front-end marketing a necessary evil, because it's something you have to do on a consistent basis to constantly attract new people into the fold.** You can't depend on your established customers being there forever. Life changes, people change, circumstances change. People get hot for something one year, and next they get hot for something else. **Emotions rule most of these markets, and emotions tend to be unpredictable.** If you had to describe the term "emotions" in ten words, one of those words would probably be "undependable." They are illogical by definition, and the most rabid markets, the ones that can make you millions of dollars, are the markets that tend to be most emotionally driven. So you've got to understand how to attract these people; you've got to look for things that

▼▼▼▼▼▼▼▼▼
MARKETING SECRET

Developing great selling messages is a process — not an event!

- It takes a lot of time, work, thinking, and re-thinking.

- The best ideas develop after a great amount of hard brainstorming and work.

- You must flush-out the best selling and marketing idea.

As *Einstein* said... "Genius is 99% perspiration — and 1% inspiration."

---

are bold and audacious.

That's some of the best advice that I can give when it comes to planning and trying to think things through. Ask yourself, "How am I going to attract the best prospects, the ones I know everybody else is trying to attract too?" That's really what's important. **The most aggressive competitors in your marketplace are consciously trying to attract the same small group of qualified prospects, the people who will end up buying the maximum number of products and services from them.** Here's another great question to ask yourself: "What's the wildest, craziest, most compelling thing I could offer to these prospects, the people who have the greatest chance of buying the most stuff from me?" Just think about it; you don't have to do it. This is just a tool to help you jog your mind to come up with some creative ideas; to think bolder, think bigger. Everybody's afraid they're going to think too big, and the whole thing's going to come crumbling down. **But the truth is, 99% of people don't think boldly *enough*. They're far too timid.** Besides, you can test on a small level the boldest idea that you have. You can come up with the craziest, most outrageous idea ever to attract the best kind of people to you, and then test it on a smaller group of people.

If you're using direct-mail, that's perfect, because you can control it completely. But even if you're using space advertising, you can just run one ad; and if it bombs, if you lose your ass, if you get taken advantage of, if you're doing some outrageous no-risk kind of offer, at least you've learned something. That's what you have to keep doing: **you have to keep learning by**

---

trying new things. The market will always change; it's constantly evolving. What's hot one year may not be hot the next year. **Think of it as a game, and then you won't be so freaked out all the time.** It's just a game you play; and if a lot of people saw it that way, they would have a lot more fun. Games are about challenging yourself; about having fun, about trying something new and then being so excited.

I love direct-mail, because with direct-mail you get a crazy, wild idea, and while you're in the heat of the excitement and the enthusiasm, you create some little campaign and you throw it out there — and within days from the time you got excited about it, you can see by the numbers whether or not it's something that resonates with your market. It becomes fun, and if you're constantly doing it, then your whole life is filled with fun. You think, "God, I can't wait to see what happens here!" Things move even quicker when you start using Internet marketing and start doing voice-blasting and tele-seminars. You can come up with an idea today, and by using voice-blasting to your best customers, you can have a tele-seminar two days from now — and **you can make tens or hundreds of thousands of dollars within just a few days of the time you come up with the idea.** Now, those kinds of things come with knowledge and experience. Some of what I am saying here just sounds like common sense, it really does — that you constantly have to have a way to re-attract new customers. But I'm surrounded by marketers that aren't doing it.

To me, that's one of the great mysteries of this business. People know they should be doing it and every time I spend time with them I ask, "What are you doing to attract new customers on a regular continuous basis?" And they mumble; they can't give me a straight answer because they're not doing it. **We've strived to do this on a very regular basis.** Every week we send out 50,000 pieces or more on a regular basis to attract new customers, to bring them into the fold. **We also have at least one promotion every week that goes out to our established customers.** It's so damn simple; I wish more people could get it. You can use this secret to make millions and millions of dollars for yourself.

SECRET EIGHT:

Become a Marketing Junkie!

The eighth secret that we used to make millions of dollars? We became marketing junkies! Yes, that's right, we became marketing *junkies*. **We became *addicted* to marketing.** Hooked on it — hook, line, and sinker. We became obsessed with this whole wonderful subject of marketing; and it *is* a wonderful subject. **It's something that can make you rich.** When you learn how to master every aspect of marketing, you'll never have to worry about where your next million dollars is going to come from. This is the key. If I had to narrow this book down to one secret, just one, it would be Number Eight, because it encompasses so much. I want you to think carefully about what I'm going to say in this chapter. **This is your meal ticket for life.** This is the answer to your highest ambitions. It's right here. **It's simple; it's all about marketing.**

Now, marketing is one of those things that takes a day to learn and a lifetime to master, because there are certain things that make it very complex. You can spend the rest of your life learning how to become a great marketer; there are certain skills necessary to do that, and most of these take some time to learn. I don't want to discourage you; **what I *do* want is for you to understand just how complicated some of this can be.** I'm going to reveal some specific secrets in this chapter that could change your life, so I encourage you to focus in on them as tightly as you can. Think carefully about what I'm saying here. **The more money you want to make, the more complicated it's going to be — and the higher the price you're going to have to pay.** Why more people don't tell you that is beyond me. They prefer to tell you that you those millions of dollars you want to make will all come raining out of the sky, that it's all going to be so easy and fast and simple.

That's nonsense, and there's a part of you that knows that. If you want to make millions and millions of dollars, especially if you have no knowledge, experience, or skills at the beginning, then you're going to have to work your butt off. You're going to have to sacrifice. **It's going to take a lot of focus.** You have to focus on the basics, and the basics of marketing are pretty simple. **Marketing is all the things you do to attract**

---

and keep customers. In today's competitive world, that can get kind of complicated, especially if you want to be one of the dominant players in your market.

When you want to take over a substantial market share, the things you have to do can get pretty extensive. **First of all, you need to set yourself apart in the minds and hearts of your best prospects and customers.** What is it about you that's completely different from all your competitors? The answer is: nothing, really. **There's really nothing different about you — so you have to create the differences. Then you have to make them real, and to do that, you have to know, first of all, what's most important to your best prospects.** Forget about the rest. The smartest marketers in the world know how to attract the very best prospects, the customers who are most likely to do the maximum amount of business over the longest period of time, for the largest amount of profit in each transaction. They're the customers who are going to spend the most money; but not only that, they're going to spend the most money with the most frequency, and they're going to be the ones who are happy to spend that money, even *proud* to spend that money.

Marketing is about knowing what's most important to your best prospects and customers, and then developing products and services that give these things to them in ways that no one else is doing. Think about that; that's pretty complicated. **It requires an intimate knowledge of the average customer in your marketplace.** You've got to know them in an intimate way, deeper than they know themselves. **You've got to know why they buy, and why they *rebuy*.** You have to understand the underlying emotional reasons that cause them to keep spending their money in an insatiable way. **You look for markets that are rabid, markets where people just buy like crazy, and then keep rebuying and rebuying.** Those markets are out there. I'm involved in one of them right now;

Develop educated-based marketing messages and strive to be knownas a trusted adviser.

Everyone wants to do business with an expert. Re-invent yourself to be seen as the foremost expert in your area and they'll stand in line with money in hand.

MARKETING SECRET

Test small — but aggressively. You can lose money or nine out of ten of your tests — and still make millions by rolling out your one winner!

• You'll never find your greatest winners — without aggressive testing.

it's called the opportunity market. The opportunity market is the one to be in. It's a marketplace that can make you rich, because it's rabid; people just keep buying and buying.

Your marketing should give people all the reasons why they should do business with you, instead of all the other companies who sell similar products and services; and to do that, you have to understand your customers at a very deep level. **This also requires knowing the biggest competitors in your market — knowing what they're doing right and, possibly even more importantly, what they're doing wrong.** This is where marketing gets complicated; you've got to learn to see things from the other side of the cash register. Get away from this consumer mentality that most people are bogged down in.

You've got to start thinking like an entrepreneur, thinking like a marketer, looking at this as if you were a consultant who was hired to examine the marketplace. **You're looking for the biggest competitors.** Now, the biggest ones might also mean just the most profitable ones, the ones who have been around the longest. Sometimes they're kind of hidden, because great marketers love to stay hidden. We use things like direct-mail to make sure we're always flying under the radar, and the only people who really know what we're doing are the ones who know where to look. **If your competitors are using stealth marketing methods like direct-mail, then you have to get on the company's mailing list and start buying from them on a regular basis** — or you're never going to figure out what exactly they're doing. The very best competitors will always remain hidden because of the things that they do to resell to their very best customers, and you've got to be one of those very best customers, or you're never going to see it. You almost have to be an insider to really identify the people making the most money. **But you *can* figure it out.**

Once you've done that, start looking for all the things those companies are doing wrong, since that's one of the most powerful ways you can differentiate yourself from them. **Marketing is about differentiation. What are *you* doing? Or, what *can* you be doing? Those are the most important questions.** What can you be doing that's different from the rest of those companies out there, serving the same prospects and customers that you want to serve? Take a look at all the companies that are really doing well: the ones that are making money hand over fist, the ones that have been in the business the longest, the ones that are the most successful from a financial standpoint. Put those companies under a magnifying glass — through eyes of an entrepreneur, not the eyes of a consumer. **Find all the things they're doing well, and develop products and services that have those qualities. Give people what they really want, without any negative side effects.**

That's one of the most powerful ways you can communicate to customers. Marketing is about communication, it's about relationships, and it's about all the tools and the techniques, systems, and processes you have to use in order to maintain those relationships and make them even stronger. I want you to think about marketing in the simplest of ways. **It's about developing thousands of relationships with people.**

What is a relationship? **It's a bond you have with someone.** It's the bond, the feelings they have about you. They feel you're their friend; or at least they feel that you respect them and really understand them, and you're trying to serve them in the highest possible way. **You have to do all you can to make sure that they *do* feel that.** You've got to let your customers know that you do care about them. Everybody says they care about the customers, and you know that's nonsense. Customers don't even believe messages like that anymore. Everybody's saying it. But since marketing involves doing things that separate yourself from everybody else, show those customers, in the ways that are most important to them, that you really *do* care about them, that you understand them, that you respect them, that you know exactly what they want. You've got to make them feel that.

So when I say that marketing takes a day to learn and a lifetime to master, realize that the ones who have mastered it are the ones who know how to create and maintain deep relationships with hundreds and even thousands and, with some marketers, tens of thousands of people. Think about all the elements it takes to form and maintain a relationship. It takes communication; it takes understanding; it takes the ability to express how you feel. With marketing you do this with many people at once. **It's also the creation and implementations of specific messages that attract the right people and repel the wrong ones.** It's knowing exactly what to say to cause the best prospects to seek you out — and we suggest that you use as much two-step marketing as you possibly can. **Use it in such a way that people are coming to you, or at least have the perception that they are.**

And it really is just a perception, because you're actually the one who ran the ads. You're who one that sent out the direct-mail package. You're the one who came to them first — but they don't even think about it that way. They buy in an emotional, unconscious vacuum. They see your ad, they get your direct-mail piece, and by their way of thinking and feeling, they're the ones who send in that reply card. **They're the ones that come to you, seeking you out. That being the case, now they've given you permission to sell them, and to resell them again and again.** They've also shown you by their actions that they're qualified. **You want to create special offers, where you're only looking for the right type of people while getting rid of all the others.** You want to make customers feel special; you know you can't be everything to everybody. **The more you're able to communicate your unique selling position to your customers, the more you make them feel special, because they're part of an elite group.** Now, all this takes years to learn how to do well, so I don't want you to be frustrated by what I'm saying. I want you to be *excited* about it. Once you learn how to do all this, you can make as much money as you want for the rest of your life. However much that might be, it's out there for you, and it's acquired by getting better and better at attracting and retaining the very best prospects and customers.

You're looking for prospects who stand the greatest chance of doing the most business with you over the longest period of time, so you need to know how to create ongoing systematic promotions that only attract these highly qualified prospects to you. **The more you know who these people are, the more intimately you understand them, and the more you have the ability to create products and services that are just for them —**

then the more eager they are to give you their money in exchange for whatever you're selling. People are happy to give you their money, they're even proud to give you their money; if that sounds like a pipe dream or a fantasy, it's not. There are marketers out there doing it right now. I've seen it; I've done it. **This is the end goal: to get people who are overjoyed to be your customers, because they like your products and services.** They know in their hearts that you're trying to do everything totally above the board, and you're trying to be the very best in your marketplace. You're trying to serve them at the highest level, whatever serving them means — because in each marketplace it means something a little bit different. **Good marketing is made up of all the things you do to build solid relationships with your best customers.** It's about bringing people into the fold, and then developing those relationships: building them, deepening them, just like you would with any other relationship you wanted to keep. Think of your best relationships. They came over a period of time, and time is the one element that does strengthen relationships.

If you break a relationship down to its essence, you'll see that there are a few things that are absolutely necessary: things like regular communication, understanding, respect, appreciation, and trust. The great marketers are wonderful about building all those things with thousands and thousands of their best customers. Do it right, and it turns them into raving fans for you and for your company. Make them feel bonded to you; make them feel they're understood and appreciated; make them feel great about their decision to keep giving you more of their money. All this is based on the creation and the implementation of certain systems and processes that automatically do this for you so that, on a regular basis, you're constantly attracting more of the people who are perfect for your company and the products and services you've developed. **The better you know your best customers, the more you'll be able to create these crucial processes and systems that let you stay focused on the best prospects and forget the rest.** Focus on the development of the systems that attract the very best, most-highly qualified prospects, then lead those first-time buyers through an orchestrated series of steps that causes them to rebuy the largest amount of products and services from you.

It does get complicated, much like the game of chess. When my son was nine, he taught me how to play chess. Now, I always thought you had to be genius to play chess — but the truth is, there are just 16 chess pieces

MARKETING SECRET

Your marketing Mantra: What are the 3 BIGGEST THINGS your customers want — and how can you give it to them?

a. Find the answer to that question

b. Tweak it — work with it — refine it — polish it

c. Then shout it as loudly as you can!!!

Let the people in your market hear it in the clearest and most compelling way!

on each side of the board, made up of six basic types. Each of those pieces can only move a certain number of ways. Within an hour after my son taught me how, we were playing chess. We were both feeling pretty good about ourselves, because he wasn't that good, and neither was I. We only knew the most basic strategies. Anybody who knew how to play chess could have come and beat us in about two simple moves. And it *is* simple. This piece can move this way, that piece can move this way and that way, and that's it. The end goal is very simple in chess, and yet there are chess masters who spend their entire lives studying every aspect of this game, keeping reams and reams of notes, thinking it all through very, very carefully.

My ancestors are German; my grandfather came off the boat. There were certain relatives who played chess with their friends and family back home, and they did it all through the mail, so they would have a way of staying in touch. Both sides would keep chess sets in their homes, and then they would think carefully about all their moves. The board is numbered, so when it was their turn they made their move, wrote it down on a piece of paper, and then mailed it back to their relatives back home; and then the relatives would put that move on their chess board, think through their moves very carefully, include it in a letter, and send it back to America. Sometimes it would take up to a year for one of them to come up with a move, because they would think it through so carefully. Every decision was weighed against all other possible decisions, so they'd spend months and months asking themselves, "If I moved it here, what would happen? What would they do?" They would try to think through all the various strategies that resulted, three or four steps in advance — so not only would they be considering each move, they would be thinking about the overall strategy of each. They would consider how it could affect everything else, and how they could ultimately win the game. That's the way good marketing is, too. **The people who have mastered it are thinking things through, and they try to stay several steps ahead. Every decision is weighed against an overall philosophy — a deep understanding of their customers, and an intimate knowledge of who those people are.** What do they want the most? What do they hate the most?

Eileen and I learned this by accident, really. It came as a result, first of all, of our desire to make millions of dollars. If it weren't for that desire, none of this would have happened. I became a salesman in 1984; that's how I learned to sell things. Some people think that marketing and selling are the same things, but they're really not. Selling is something that happens *within* marketing, but **marketing is more about building relationships with customers, and then knowing and understanding the tools and the processes used to strengthen those relationships.** Ultimately, you need to learn how to make people want to give you more and more of their money over the longest period of time for the largest amount of profit. Selling is something you do on a short-term basis; **marketing is more about the long-term effects of what it takes to keep people coming back again and again.** It's more about reselling them than selling them.

Eileen and I learned this by accident. Initially we were both trying to run the company at the same time, and then that simply didn't work anymore, and one of us had to go. It was a partnership that started creating problems. We would yell and scream at each other all day long, because I'm a control freak and she's a control freak, and I have my ideas that I'm very opinionated about and she has hers, and so I had to leave the office and start doing all my work from home. This was in 1992; four years into the business, and what did I do at home? **Well, I learned how to work *on* the business rather than *in* it, and I learned how to become a good marketer;** then for nine years, that's all I did. I simply focused on marketing: nothing more, nothing less. I became obsessed with it. I call it the "magnificent obsession." I bought thousands and thousands of dollars worth of seminars on tape. I bought newsletters; I studied this thing intensely. I ate it, slept it, breathed it. I thought about nothing but marketing. It was fascinating to me. It was the answer to all my ambitions. It became the thing I just couldn't get out of my head, and I surrounded myself with other people who were as crazy as I was, and we built this little group of like-minded entrepreneurs called the One Hundred Million Dollar Roundtable. Every year it's getting stronger and stronger, attracting like-minded marketers who are absolutely as obsessed about it as I am. I learn from them and they learn from me. I also spent six years with Eileen in Dan Kennedy's Platinum Group, where we met four times a year with the best marketers in the country, other people who were deeply committed to building companies that are solid and profitable. **The idea was that by building relationships with as many customers as possible, and causing those people to feel so attuned to what we were doing, that would make them want to continue to give us more and more of their money.** The more I subjected myself to this, the more I learned how to write copy, learned how to develop products, learned more about the customers and how to reach them in the deepest kind of way — well, the more money just started flowing in.

I'm assuming that you're the kind of person who wants to see that happen. You want to make millions of dollars — **and I'm here to tell you that that money is out there for you *right now*.** All you have to do is become a marketing master. You have to learn all the ways to attract and re-attract the very best customers within your marketplace, the ones who will continue to give you more and more of their money. **You have to lose yourself in this "magnificent obsession" I love so much.** I call it a magnificent obsession because it's actually so interesting. It's challenging, it's fun, it's exciting, there's a lot to learn, and the thrill of getting thousands of people to give you more and more of their money, every single year, is the greatest kind of thrill. It's the greatest kind of satisfaction you can have. It's the most wonderful feeling on Earth to have thousands of customers who love you; and if they don't love you, at least they respect you.

You know, some of my customers think I'm just a total jerk, period. That's okay; in some ways they're right. They think I'm egotistical; they criticize me for the way I repeat myself constantly; they criticize me for the fact that I fail to communicate in a professional way. But they still respect me, they still know in their hearts that I do give a damn about them, that in fact I really care deeply about them. **They know that, because I've done everything possible to express that to them. I'm trying to reach** out to my very best customers and give them more and more of what I know is most important to them. I understand them at a deep level, and so our profits continue to get bigger and bigger every single year. Our customers love us, they know us, they respect us, and they know we care about them. They know that we're striving to do everything possible to help them, and to separate ourselves from all those competitors in the marketplace who are basically ripping them off, lying to them, misleading them, and cheating them.

We've shared our story from Day One. We've reached out to the customers in a very intimate, personal way, just as I'm trying to do with

▼▼▼▼▼▼▼▼▼▼▼▼▼▼▼▼

An entrepreneur who never quits can <u>never</u> be defeated.

you right now. I'm trying to reach out through the pages of the book you're reading. If I could, I would grab you and shake you a little and get you to see that all the millions of dollars you want are out there. It's up to you to recognize that. The day that you do, the day you finally wake up and really see the potential and know that all of the money that you want is out there, if only you'll learn these techniques I'm trying so hard to express to you — that's the day your life will change forever, and it can all happen by practicing this eighth secret and becoming a marketing junkie.

SECRET NINE:

Develop Your Copywriting Skills

The ninth secret that made us millions of dollars is the fact that we learned how to write copy that sells, and then how to implement it in our overall marketing strategy. Now, this is arguably the single greatest wealth-making skill you can learn. Knowing you can write a sales letter that causes thousands of people to give you millions of dollars is one of the greatest feelings on earth. I want you to experience this feeling. It's just an amazing thing: to get an idea, write a sales letter, send it out to your best customers — and if you have enough of those customers, you can make millions of dollars. Maybe there are greater feelings than

MARKETING SECRET

The best selling messages and offers grow and develop as you work on them.

- You must take the leap of faith — and develop it gradually as you go.

- Whatever you focus on expands! So keep focusing on improving each offer.

- More often than not, your best ideas will come as the deadline approaches

that, but this is one of the top five you could ever experience.

So many people want to make millions of dollars... and they could, if only they'd just realize how simple it is to do it! You've got to have a group of customers who respect you, who feel great about you and who know you're out there to help them; and you've got to have the ability to communicate to them, simply by sending them a sales letter or a series of sales letters. You see, that's what it's really about. **One sales letter can make you millions of dollars, but the key is having a group of customers that you can send a series of sales letters to on a regular basis, so you build a business, not just a promotion.** That's what you're really after: a business, which is steady profits made over a period of time. **That's the key to overall profitability.**

Now, what is a great sales letter? **A great sales letter is something that replaces a live salesperson.** So if you have a thousand sales letters out there, you have a thousand sales people. **It's a salesperson in an envelope.** It does a complete job of selling for you. **It answers every objection in the minds and hearts of the skeptical prospect, and the fearful prospect, and the prospect who feels overwhelmed.** They're already getting a lot of solicitations, because the same people that are your best customers are also other peoples' best customers. Your sales letter answers all their objections, and it stands out from all of the other mail. **It's interesting to read, it's targeted to a specific person, it establishes the value of whatever you're selling, and it proves to them that what you have to offer is worth far more**

than the money you're asking for in exchange. It makes people excited about giving you their money. That's what a great sales letter is. It's exciting, it's interesting, and it's persuasive.

It's the ultimate way for you to stay in touch with your customers and to continue to resell to them on a regular basis, to give them more of what you know they want the most. **It's also the fastest way for you to make the largest amount of money.** They don't call it direct-mail for no reason. This is a media that goes straight to the prospect or customer, and it delivers a very direct sales presentation to them. It compels them to send their money directly to you, and it's the fastest way for you to make millions of dollars. **Direct-mail is a media that you have 100% control over, from start to finish.** You write it; you design it; you choose your printer. You choose the mailing house that's going to mail out your sale letter; you schedule it; you pick all of the mailing lists; you analyze the numbers as they come in. You have total control and total power over every aspect of this. **It's a media that you own, and that's the way I want you to think about direct-mail.**

Think about it as if you had your own TV station — or better still, think about it as if you had your own newspaper, and you control every aspect of that newspaper. You have regular subscribers who get it, and your job is to make sure that those subscribers stay subscribers. But even better, when you have direct-mail, your job is also to advertise in your own newspaper, and your job is to make sure that the largest number of your subscribers continue to give you money for all the advertising in your newspaper. It's a great metaphor; it'll help you think about this in the right way. Let's say you own your own newspaper, which you publish on a regular basis. It's a job; you just do it, and you send it out there on a regular basis to people that you know want it, because they subscribe. That's really what we're trying to explain here. **This is a media that you control. You call all the shots. You have all the power; you have all of the freedom and flexibility to do whatever it is that you want to do with it.**

That's the kind of control you don't have in other kinds of media, where you're totally dependent on the publication itself. They're the ones who set the deadlines; they're the ones to set the prices. If you want lower prices you have to negotiate, and it's often a painful thing. You're not in any position of power. But when you have a group of customers who have bought from you in the past, you know what they like and you know what they don't like; there's a trust that's built up between you and them. **You can mail to them as often as you want, and you control exactly what you want them to see, every aspect of it; you're in charge.** You don't have to ask permission from anybody. If you're not happy with the printers or the mailing house you're using, you can find new ones. If you're not happy with the mailing list broker, you can go out and find somebody else. You can mail as often as you want, as much as you want. If you've got a piece that's working and you know that there are more names out there, all you have to do is call your mailing list broker and say, "Hey! Give me another 50,000 names!" and then call your printer and say, "Print up another 50,000 pieces!" Then you call your mailing house and say, "Hey! We're going to mail another 50,000 pieces!" It's as simple as that.

You control it all, and it's a no-risk method if you use it correctly. Here's what I mean by that: You're constantly using direct-mail to test new ideas — and you can test *radical* new ideas, ideas that are totally bold and audacious. **You can test them to small groups of your best customers first,** and because the trust is established with those people, chances are they'll buy from you. You're looking for the things that make them most excited, the things that they buy the most. **You'll never lose money, because these are people who will, in most cases, buy anything from you if you've done your job right.** Then you take the things they buy the most of, the ones they're most excited about, and **start testing them to other groups of customers. Then, if your numbers are still high, you start testing to outside mailing lists, the lists of prospects your customers all originated from.** There are companies in your marketplace that sell the same types of products and services that you sell. If you're in a direct response marketing-friendly environment, those companies will be putting their mailing lists up for rent. At M.O.R.E., Inc., we rent our mailing lists out to all kinds of other companies. Our mailing-list manager picks the ones he wants; we're only renting our list out to companies he knows are honorable ones. Similarly, we rent names from other companies who have their mailing lists up for rent.

That's the way it is with the opportunity market; **millions of names every year are available.** These are proven buyers, folks who have bought other moneymaking plans and programs just like the ones we offer, so there's a buying history. **We can go to the people we know are interested in what we sell, and we can offer them the kinds of programs that we**

sell to bring them into the fold; and now they become our customers.
There are plenty of markets out there just like the opportunity market,
where you can rent, in some cases, millions of names every year.

The big secret is that, by the time we get to the point of sending an
offer to those outside names, we've already tested the product to our very
small group of best customers. **Think of your customer base as a
pyramid: it gets smaller as it goes up.** We test to the very best of our
customers at the top of the pyramid. We take the offers that work the best
there, the ones that produce the most sales and profits, and we slowly start
testing to larger groups of customers, working our way down from there.
Then, when we go through our entire customer base and the offer's still
good, we take that offer and we start testing it to the outside mailing list.
By the time we use it for our new customer acquisition, it's proven.
We know it works. The only question now is, how well is it going to work
with people who don't already have a relationship with us?

I just love direct-mail. Direct-mail and the ability to write copy:
together, they're such a powerful thing. It's absorbing; it's interesting. You
can spend hour after hour absorbed in this, and it becomes more a hobby
or an art than anything else. That's the way I think about it. Sure, it's work;
it's a lot of work. This is, again, one of the great things about it. I don't
say this to dissuade or discourage you; I just want to say that it's taken me
a lot of time and work to master my skills at writing copy that sells millions
of dollars worth of products and services. To some extent it's been a labor
of love, but in a whole other way it's just been an awful lot of work. There
are parts that are more interesting than others. Some parts are very relaxing.
Every night my wife and I sit on the couch, and I'm half-watching TV
programs with her; but the other half of me is quietly editing sales copy
I've already written. To me, that's the most relaxing way to spend an
evening.

I'm always working on different sales letters, constantly. I always
have different projects out there, and it's the most wonderful feeling to
create these things that produce revenue. It's almost like alchemy. If you
study history, you'll see that up until about the sixteenth or seventeenth
century, there were people called alchemists, and their job was to try to
turn lead into gold — to try to take something of no value, basically, and
turn it into high value. That's what we're doing here. The copywriters like
myself, who know how to design and develop and create sales letters that

Emergency money-making generator...

- When times get hard

- When business gets slow

- When you need cash-flow to feed the monster...

All you do is:

a. Go to your best customers...

b. Make them an irresistible offer!

c. Have a special sale that will blow them away!

They'll stand in line with money in hand!

cause thousands of people to willingly and gladly give their money to us — **well, we're taking paper and ink, which has very little value, and making it high value.** Of course you can do it on websites too, but basically it's the same thing concept. You're creating a complete sales story from top to bottom, and you're causing people to get so excited that they just can't wait to give you their money. We've had people wire their money to us through Western Union just to get our product quicker. We've had many people who Federal Expressed their orders to us. A few have jumped in their cars and driven from three or four states away, because they wanted to get the product even faster.

It's exciting to create millions of dollars worth of revenue where no revenue existed before, and to know that you're the one who did it. Now, I've had a lot of help over the years, learning how to write copy; **and the best thing I can do is tell you that you have to just decide that you want to become a great copywriter.** Make that decision. For years, I could write sales letters to my best customers. They trusted me; we had established relationships, and quite candidly my copy didn't have to be as good because of the relationship. It's just like when you have a friend — you'll do more for your friend. If you have two people who ask you to do something and one of them is your friend, you're going to go with your friend every time. Your friend hardly has to say anything. They just say, "Look, I've got this great deal," and you say "Hey! Stop, stop, I trust you. How much is it going to cost me?" Whereas any other person is going to have to work on you quite a bit. They're going to have to keep bugging you, over and over again.

If you just think about it like that, you'll realize that when you have an established group of customers, you don't have to be as good. Even a beginning copywriter can start sharpening their skills, creating new offers, writing new sales letters to those people who have shown a certain level of trust because they bought from you the first time. So for years, I would write these sales letters to our established customers. **This is how I developed my skills as a copywriter. It was just to write sales letters to people who had already bought from us.** They knew us; they liked us. There was some trust there, shown by the money they had given us. People vote with their checkbooks or their credit cards, and so for years I crafted all of these offers that went out to people who had already bought from us, and it was great to learn how to write copy and send it out there to people. When we wrote "Dear Friend," we really meant it. We were trying to be friends with our customers; we were trying to befriend them in every way, and that's what I'm asking you to do, too. **Operate with complete integrity and complete honesty. Treat your customers very well and make all kinds of offers to them, and then take the best of those offers and use them for your new customer acquisition program.** There are plenty of mailing lists out there, but **only the very best offers and the very best sales copy will work for those people who don't know you.** They don't trust you yet; they're still very skeptical. You're just another company showing up in their mailbox now.

For years I tried to write copy for new customer acquisition, and I simply couldn't do it; I wasn't good enough. That used to just tick me off! I used to get so angry because I was dependent on outside copywriters, and I wanted to learn how to do it myself. That anger and frustration emerged every single time we were forced to hire a copywriter because my copy wasn't good enough. I would take sales letters or variations that had worked great for our customers, and I tried to make them work to the outside list, and the profits were just never there. Then these outside copywriters came in who had a limited amount of knowledge and understanding of what we were selling and who we were selling it to — and yet they could go out there and make the copy work.

That just made me so angry — and I used that anger in a positive way. I became determined that I was going to be able to do this. **I studied a lot of sales letters, I read a lot of books, I practiced a lot.** This is one suggestion from Gary Halbert — arguably one of the best copywriters ever: a true legend according to many, including me. **Gary said that the way to learn how to write copy is to take one of the best ads you can find, the long-form, full-page ads, or one of the best sales letters, and to write it longhand word for word, over and over, until you get so sick and tired of it you can't stand it anymore.**

I did that; I took the *Lazy Man's Way to Riches*, a full-page ad that Joe Carbo used in the mid-1970s that made him millions and millions of dollars, and rewrote it in my own hand, day after day. I don't know how long I did it; at least for a couple of months, to the point where I just about had the whole thing memorized. **I learned the language, the rhythm, the flow of writing good, persuasive, hard-hitting sales copy.** That particular ad caused so many people to get excited that they sent in their money; and subconsciously, over a period of time, with the determination that I was going to learn how to write sales copy that really was capable of making millions of dollars, I became a good copywriter. It wasn't easy; it's still not easy. It's painful work at times, and don't let anybody kid you. There's a quote that I love: it says, **"The secret of great writing is to re-write,"** and I'm famous for re-writing my sales letters a whole bunch of times. That's what I'm doing on the couch every single night.

So I want you to think about that tonight; think about me tonight. Whatever you're doing tonight, realize that if it's before ten-thirty in the evening Central Time, I'm on my couch next to my lovely wife Eileen, I've got a laptop in my lap, and I'm re-writing some sales letter. When I get up in the morning, I work on the copy. I work on sales letters all the time. I've always got about three or four of them going at once, because I get bored with them, and I want to keep shifting around. It's more like a job now than anything, but still there's moments when this is just the most wonderful feeling on Earth, and **one of my secrets is, whenever I get really excited about an idea, I just start writing like crazy.** Some of the sales letters that have worked the best have been those I wrote when I was higher than a kite on caffeine. I tend to drink a pot of coffee or two every day. So I get wound up, I get excited about ideas. **The time to write copy is when you're in the heat of the moment, when you're really pumped up and excited.** Now, that can change; over a period of time, your skill and knowledge will develop to the point where you can write powerful, persuasive copy whether you're excited or not. You can still make it look like you're excited, and that's the method used by freelance copywriters

▼▼▼▼▼▼▼▼▼▼▼▼▼▼

There is no such thing as 'hard sell' or 'soft sell.' There is only 'smart sell' and 'stupid sell.'

— Charles Brauer (1958)

who charge many thousands of dollars. They don't really understand what your products are and who you're selling to, but they can create copy that's compelling. It looks like they were excited when they wrote it, when the truth is that they hardly understand anything about it.

This is a skill that can set you up for life. It's your meal ticket; it's the way to riches; it's the single greatest wealth building skill that you'll ever learn, when you think about the overall picture. That's what I want you to do: think beyond just writing one sales letter or whatever. **Think about copywriting as a lifelong skill you can use to sell and resell to your customers again and again, and to attract new customers to you.** Remember: the secret is to take your best promotions, work them through your customer base first, then send them out as part of your new customer acquisition process. **That'll save you a lot of misery, because if your existing customers aren't excited, then you know that the people out there who don't know you won't be excited.** There's no differentiation in their mind between you and all the other direct-mail they're getting.

These are the brutal realities we're dealing with here. There's a lot of competition, and people are sorting their mail over the trash can. When it comes to front-end, new customer acquisition, it's really tough to break through that shell of skepticism. But when you're mailing to existing customers, it's so much easier. You should have new offers going out to them all the time.

We've been doing this since 1988, and I used to worry that I was sending too much too often to our established customers. I don't worry about that anymore, and I don't think you should either. As long as you're making great offers that are altruistic in nature, that really offer tremendous value, that offer strong money-back guarantees if people aren't happy; that strive to give your customers special deals — then you're good. **The perception is that other people aren't getting these things; you're offer's just for them. You should be in their mailbox constantly.** The beautiful thing about it is, if you structure it right, and if your customer base is large enough, you don't need very many people to respond to an

▼▼▼▼▼▼▼▼
MARKETING SECRET

From *Dan Kennedy:*
"Magnetic marketing is: The use of systems, processes, and tools combined with the careful selection of methodology — to attract to you ideally qualified prospects — eager for your expert advice, and assistance, and predisposed to doing business with you — and only you — so you can sell yourself in a competitive vacuum."

offer to make millions of dollars. The secret of making your customer base large enough is to have a steady stream of mail that goes out on a regular basis to attract new customers to you, so your customer base continues to grow bigger automatically.

We have one direct-mail offer out there all the time to new customers. Every single week, 52 weeks a year now; we used to stop around Christmas time, but we don't anymore. Fifty-two weeks of every year, we extend tens of thousands of direct-mail solicitations to new customers who have never done business with us before. We want to get them to buy once, or get them to take some minor action, so we can bring them into the fold. **Nowadays, I'm way beyond that fear that I had for years, the fear that I would tick off my customers if I sent them too many offers.** I realize now that I literally lost millions of dollars because I didn't market aggressively to our established customers, because I was always holding back, always afraid that we were doing too much to those customers. Now, we strive to have one new offer that goes out there to our established customers every single week. That's our goal. We don't hit it every week, but we try to, so we're in their mailbox 52 times a year. **To make a profit on most promotions, we only need a small percentage of people to raise their hands and say "Yes."**

The same can be true of your promotions, if you structure them correctly. You can make millions of dollars, and **you'll always make more money by mailing more often to your very best customers.**

SECRET TEN:

Master the Skills of Information Marketing

The tenth secret that we used to make millions of dollars is this: **We honed our skills in product development.** My entire life changed the day I created our first information product, *Dialing for Dollars*. I look at it now, and it looks like some kind of a joke. It was poorly written, filled with typos; it just wasn't a good program in any way. Yet that was product that got us started, and it was just a little booklet that we sold for $12.95. We ran a small ad in an opportunity magazine, using the last $300 we had.

But the program clicked with our prospects, because it was based on something that we had been using that was totally proven. That was the only great thing about *Dialing for Dollars*, and yet it got us started and the customers loved it. Then I started writing *Dialing for Dollars, Part II* just a few months later, and I started putting my heart and soul into a better program. The first one included some multilevel marketing aspects, and I just didn't like that; it was creating too many problems, and my wife was begging me to stop doing it. She wanted me to take all the multilevel marketing stuff out. So I started working on *Dialing for Dollars Part II*, which became our new and expanded *Dialing for Dollars* program, and with that program the multilevel stuff; it just went out of the window. It became a straight distributorship opportunity — and people loved the idea of making money with an answering machine. **It resonated; people were absolutely crazy about it.** This was in the late-1980s, when answering machines were brand new and technology was making them more affordable, even as they were shrinking in size and increasing in power — and people loved the idea that there was a way to make money with this new technology.

Ever since then we've continued to use that theme, as when we showed people how to make money with computer bulletin boards. When the Internet came around, we showed people how to make money with websites. **People love the idea of new technology.** They're just crazy over it, and they're always looking for some way to make money with new

---

technology. It s exciting to them, it's interesting, and we really did *start* with our last $300. This was all the money we had at the time. We sold a beat-up van we'd used for our carpet-cleaning business to get that little bit of money, which gave us an opportunity to buy a tiny ad in one of the best moneymaking magazines of the time. Now, the first *Dialing for Dollars* was a glorified brochure! That's all it was. It wasn't anything that we would produce today, and yet the customers liked it, and it really worked for them. It really made them money. That was especially true after we came up with *Dialing for Dollars, Part II*. We got away from the multilevel marketing aspect. **We showed people how to use their answering machine to sell the products we'd created, although we also showed them how they could use it for other things besides just our products. They found our honesty and integrity refreshing.**

Once we came up with the idea of tiny manuals that were designed to sell in newspapers, we took a couple of different opportunities that were working for us and blended them together to create this whole *Dialing for Dollars* concept. **The ideas are out there, folks; and we happened to hit on the right ideas at the right time.** Little did we know it, but our idea resonated and it actually made people money, and that's a great thing. **To be able to really, truly help people make money is wonderful.** We had distributors who were making $10,000, $20,000, $50,000 a month. We had one guy in Utah who was making $5 million a year before he cut us out (as all of our successful distributors ultimately do), and that was back when our company was barely doing a couple of million dollars a year. So we had a distributor who was doing more than twice as well as us, and that's a great thing! It makes me really happy that we helped people. **That's one of the things that a good information product can do: It can really make a difference in people's lives. This was the foundation of our success.**

Within six months from the time we ran that $300 ad, we were bringing in $16,000 a month, and the strategy we used was very simple. It's one that you could use starting tomorrow. **We ran that little ad; it did take about six weeks before it came out, but we used those six weeks as a way of gearing up and getting things ready to go.** During the six weeks we were waiting for that ad to run, we were frantically creating that little booklet. The kind of product development that took me a month to do back then I can do in a couple of days now. That's not to brag; **the fact**

is that you get better as you go along. I want you to think about that; you've got to get started, you've got to bloom where you're planted. So get started.

Within six months we were averaging $16,000 dollars a month, and Eileen and I were like two kids in a candy store. That was more money than we'd ever made in our whole lives. We didn't even know what to *do* with that money. **Then we met Russ von Hoelscher, and Russ helped us go from $16,000 a month to almost $100,000 a week within the first nine months.** In other chapters of this book, I've explained to you exactly what Russ did to help us achieve those phenomenal results. **One of the things he did was help polish our product-development skills.**

Our first product with Russ von Hoelscher was called *The $2,500 Weekend*, and for us it was a major breakthrough. **That was the first time we did over $1 million on just one product, and we did it *fast*.** Now, that product took one weekend of our lives to create, but we're still using it. The sales letter took me three months to write, but we're still using parts of that sales letter *right now*. People loved the idea of *The $2,500 Weekend*. It was such a simple idea, just like *Dialing for Dollars* was a simple idea, but it resonated in the minds and hearts of the people who bought it. Here's where we got the name: We were paying Russ von Hoelscher $2,500 every single time he came down to spend a weekend with us, and the whole time he was there, we were working on ideas and brainstorming. He was sharing his greatest tips, tricks and strategies with us, and so I said, "Russ, why don't you come down here next time, and we'll a have a recorder set up. Let's ask you a million and one questions and get all your answers — ask you all kinds of questions that we know our customers have about mail order and making money, getting rich, and that type of thing. We'll go ahead and pay you your $2,500 plus your airfare, and then we'll be very honest and direct with the customers and let them know this is material that cost us $2,500." **We sold the product at $295 — so our customers were getting $2,500 in real value for a little over a tenth of that price.** This product was real and it was raw; it was honest. All we did was put a little tape player on our kitchen table. **It was all unedited, unpolished, and genuine — and that's exactly what people want.** They don't want anything fancy. The more you can create informational products that are just for them, products that are perceived as having been created just for them, the better.

▼▼▼▼▼▼▼▼
MARKETING SECRET

People want "The MAGIC Bullet":

- The one product/ service that is going to make everything okay.

- It's going to solve some major problem.

- Or give them a miracle cure!

- An instant solution!

- And an on-going solution.

If they believe you can give this to them — you will get their money.

You don't have to be professional; you don't have to be polished. In fact, it's better that you aren't. As you may or may not be aware, this section of this book was adapted from an audio product, part of which I recorded in my basement studio. During that recording, I tried to express myself fully, honestly. I was surrounded with notes; I didn't just make all this up on a whim. I put a lot of concentrated thought into it, but at the same time, the original recording is just me trying to reach out to you, trying to help you understand the secrets that made *us* millions of dollars so they can make *you* millions of dollars. When I'm producing an audio program or hosting a seminar, I'm not trying to be a professional speaker; **I'm just trying to be me. And that's what people really want; they don't want you to play games with them. People want information that's going to help them.** The *$2,500 Weekend* made us more than a million bucks because it was targeted; it was designed to help our customers get the information that they wanted and needed. **It touched them emotionally, and they identified with us.**

We gave people what they really wanted, and they rewarded us with very quickly with well over $1 million. **It was a wonderful experience for us to realize that we could go down to a Radio Shack, buy a $50 cassette tape recorder, and record a product that brought us in a fortune.** These days, I record on a computer, using equipment that cost thousands of dollars. Back then, I was using equipment that cost $50, and there was no real difference. The product was valuable in the minds and hearts of the customers who bought it. It resonated with them; it gave them what they wanted; it gave them what they needed. They loved it. **I want to stress the importance of this to you, and how simple and easy it is for you to develop your own informational products.** You do have to think things through very carefully; you have to think about your customers. There are specific things you need to do, and yet it's very easy as long as your heart is in the right place — as long as you really do want to help people. **Information products are an extension of you.** They're a way for you to reach out to other people and try to make a difference in their lives, and try to share a part of who you are with them, and try to extend your hand and pull them up. In the process you pull yourself up; you make a lot of money. **The profit margins are incredible on these types of products, which really do give people what they want.**

In the opportunity market there are two basic types of products. **There are what we call soft products and hard products. A soft product is just like this one: It gives your customers great ideas and shortcut secrets, proven strategies; it gives them personal stories from your own life that will help teach them the things that you want them to learn.** It's an extension of you, and it lets you reach out and help people. **A hard product is a product like our *Dialing for Dollars*. It gives customers something to sell, either a product or a service or some combination of both.** It contains, number one, something to sell. Number two, it contains the sales material that you've developed for them that they can use to sell the product or service. Number three, it contains the marketing system you developed and put together for them, so they can use that sales material to go out and promote this product or service and sell it. It's some kind of a distributorship manual that puts it all together in one cohesive package. That's it! Just those three things.

Hard products are what sell the most in our marketplace. **The fastest way to become a millionaire in the opportunity market is to develop hard products and turn-key distributorships.** We have some of them, right now, which we make available for you to sell in this marketplace. **That's what people really want: hard, turn-key products that let them go out and make money right away.** All this gets easier as you go along, and your confidence and knowledge will develop. It's all about serving your customers.

Here are ten things that all great information products have in common. NUMBER ONE: **they speak to the person who buys them,**

just like I'm trying to speak to you right now; they're real, just like I told you about our *$2,500 Weekend* program. That program was real, and it was raw. Products like this give people something they really want. That's what I'm trying to do with you: I'm trying to show you how you can make millions of dollars. NUMBER TWO, these products are an extension of who you are. **They communicate things about you.** They let people know who you are, what you stand for, and what your company stands for. They let you express things to your customers, to help you bond with them; you tell your story, and you get a chance to reach out to people like I'm trying to do with you right now.

NUMBER THREE, **they help to establish your credibility.** In the beginning, we didn't really have any credibility — or so we thought. The whole idea behind our *$2,500 Weekend* product was to interview Russ and to let him share his tips, tricks and strategies with our listeners. Recently, we moved into the real- estate market. Did we know anything about real estate? Absolutely not, so we interviewed all kinds of experts, which helps make complicated things simple and easy. We went out there and found the experts, but we also established our credibility in the minds of the customers, because they knew we were trying to reach out, to give them the information they wanted, needed, valued, and appreciated.

NUMBER FOUR: Because of all this, **these products help you to create strong bonds with your customers.** When I meet my best customers at seminars, they all feel like they know me and I feel like I know them. We share a lot in common. They've listened to me on these programs. They know my heart's in the right place, and I'm trying to serve them. NUMBER FIVE: **These information products are perfectly matched to the customers you serve.** You're doing it for them, as I'm creating this product for you.

NUMBER SIX: **They make people want to do more business with you.** They separate you from the competition, and they really help bring people to you. People listen to you on your audio programs, they come to your seminars, they buy other kinds of information products from you, they like you; they know you're trying to help them, and they believe you really *can* help them, and naturally they want to do more business with you.

NUMBER SEVEN: **These products lead the prospect down the**

path you want them to take. I'm trying to give you the basic ideas here, but I'm also trying to take you to the next step; I'm trying to get you to do more business with us, so we can help you get what you really, truly want. **The things I'm trying to do right now with you, you can do with *your* customers.** Establish your credibility or your authority. You can break the ice with them. Start introducing them to more of whatever it is that you have to offer.

I'm going to keep continue to do everything possible to help you achieve your dream. Remember, Russ von Hoelscher helped

▼▼▼▼▼▼▼▼▼▼▼▼▼▼▼▼

If you can't dominate a niche, then create a niche you can dominate!" — *Al Ries*

us make millions of dollars, but we had to pay him hundreds of thousands to do it. However, for every dollar we paid to Russ, we probably made 50 to 100 dollars. What does it matter that we had to pay him hundreds of thousands of dollars? **He made make us money, and that's what I want to do for you, too.**

NUMBER EIGHT: **Your product helps the most qualified prospects and customers in the highest way.** It gives them the shortcut secrets, and that's what I'm trying to give you right now: proven strategies, insider knowledge. **How many people understand that the secret to getting rich in the opportunity market is to create hard products?** That's just one of the strategies that I'm sharing with you in this book. I'm reaching out to you, right now, to try to give you the insider knowledge that I've learned over the last 20 years.

NUMBER NINE: **A good information product separates you from all your competitors.** When it's done correctly, your information product has zero competition, because it's an extension of you. It's your unique thumbprint. It's also a great relationship-building tool that makes people feel that they know you. It deepens your bond with established customers, and makes new prospects want to do business with you.

And NUMBER TEN: **Product development is a highly creative activity that lets you clarify your thinking, lets you shape your thoughts, lets you learn as you teach.** See, you can never really help somebody else without also helping yourself. So I'm trying to reach out for you on this product, I'm trying to give you some of my best ideas; but

---

As marketers, our job is to fill the human desires.

- What do they want?

- Really want?

- And how can we promise to fill it as no one else can?

in the process, as I spent all this time writing and editing these chapters, thinking everything through very clearly, I'm learning things myself. **To teach is to learn twice;** one of the great philosophers said that thousands of years ago. So it helps you, but it's also something that's exciting; it's fun, it's creative. **The profit margins are also incredibly high, and the perceived value is very high for what you're offering.** In other words, developing products can make you millions of dollars. I told you about the $1 million we made with *The $2,500 Weekend*. That *Dialing for Dollars* program — it got us started, and eventually we made millions of dollars with it. But we've continued to develop more and more products, and that's the last thing I want to share with you in this section. You've got to do something every single day to develop products.

Ongoing product development is the secret to developing a ton of products, and you should discipline yourself to do a small amount of it every day. Every day, the first thing in the morning, my day starts out with product development. I'm spending one hour on product development each day, and it adds up to a huge arsenal of products. In doing this, you completely separate yourself from every other competitor, and it lets you attract and retain the largest number of best prospects and customers in your marketplace. Just do it a little every day. **Think about your customers and what they really want the most, and what they hate the most.** Think about what they're really seeking the most, and why they buy the things that they buy the most. **Study the most successful companies in your marketplace and figure out what they're doing right, what they're doing**

wrong, where the gaps are in your market, and just start developing products. It doesn't have to be perfect. I've been doing this for 20 years now. I told you what a joke our first product was; it was just some thin little piece-of-crap booklet that we came out with. **We give it away in our seminars now for free, just to show people what a humble beginning it was.** It's a joke to look at it now, and yet the customers loved it. It was raw, it was real, it was genuine, it really worked, and it was based on something that excited them. That's all that matters!

You don't have to be perfect to produce products that connect with your customers and sell briskly. I do face-to-face seminars and create audio products all the time, but am I a professional speaker? Absolutely not. I am, however, trying to practice what I preach here. **I'm very, very focused on you, the customers. I know what I'm talking about.** My wife and I parlayed $300 into $120 million in our first 20 years, and these are the secrets that did it for us — and so what do you care if I'm not a professional speaker or writer? You want somebody who's going to be honest and straightforward with you, who's going to give you proven methods to take you from where you are now to where you want to go. You may be saying, "Well, I don't have any expertise," **but I'm here to tell you that you *can* still create companies that provide all kinds of valuable information products.**

I've told you that we're doing it in the real-estate world right now. We're interviewing all these real-estate experts, and we ask each at the end, "Who else do you know that we should be interviewing?" One expert leads us to another. We did that in the world of eBay, and we've done that with computer bulletin boards for Internet marketing. **Eventually, you *do* become an expert. But I just want to get you on the path; I want to tell you that it's more than just making money.** This is a rewarding way of life that lets you develop products and services that truly can help people. The most qualified people out there, those who are willing to put in the effort to use the ideas you share with them — those people's lives will be transformed, just like my life was.

So I want to encourage you to think about everything I've said here. This tenth secret really is a secret, because most people just dream of it, no more. They would love to self-publish their stuff. They would love to produce books and audio programs, but they never do. They're always afraid, and part of that fear is that they've got to be perfect, that they aren't well qualified. **None of that matters. I promise you, if you want to do this, you can.** There are plenty of experts out there who have their own programs they want to promote. They want to develop clients and customer, so they're more than happy to spend 90 minutes or two hours with us on the phone, letting us interview them.

This is something that can make you millions and millions of dollars — and it can also provide a lot of joy and satisfaction. **It can help you completely separate yourself from every other company that's out there, because the products that you create are a piece of you.** They're an extension of who you are; they let people get to know you, and let you develop bonds with them so you can keep the same customers coming back and buying from you for many, many years. Start getting into the routine of creating some type of information product on a daily basis. If you'll do that, ten years from now you can have a huge catalog of products that you've developed specifically for your customers, and it'll give you a high level of pride and satisfaction, the joy of accomplishment that you did something that was so productive and so creative. **All you did was to discipline yourself to do a little every day and stayed focused on serving the customers.** This can lead to a lifetime of wealth and great satisfaction for you.

SECRET ELEVEN:

Constant Testing. What's Next?

The eleventh secret that we used to make millions of dollars is: **we tested as many different things as we could.** We're always asking ourselves, "What's next?" It's not work in the traditional way that most people think of work; this is more like a game. It's more like a hobby, an activity that you do for total enjoyment. **Work really does mix with pleasure if you do it the right way; you'll enjoy what you're doing and you'll make a lot more money.** The secret is to treat work as if it were a game. What you're doing is searching for the ultimate way to make millions of dollars, and if you'll do that, you'll have a lot more fun; it won't just seem like work, and even the things that are difficult will become easier because you're totally focused on finding those one or two ideas.

You can make a lot of money if you'll do this. It's simpler and easier than you can ever imagine. **You'll see that it's just the way of life for you.** It's about serving your customers in the highest possible way, and then going out there to new prospects and offering them the same types of things you offered to your best customers.

The secret to earning the biggest profit is just to stay focused on your best customers. Who are they? What do they want the most? What do they *buy* the most? The better you're able to answer those questions, the more money you'll make. That comes with experience and knowledge; it doesn't happen overnight, and the ideas you get today aren't going to be nearly as good as the ideas you'll get tomorrow. **Sometimes it takes months or years to intimately know your customer.** But once you do, you've got the golden key in your hand to making millions of dollars, and that's a great feeling. It's more than just the money and all the material things you're going to buy. That stuff is nice, but it has its limits. Money's a great thing to have, but you can only sleep in one bed at a time, eat one meal at a time, live in one home at a time, drive one great car at a time.

There's only so much joy and satisfaction that comes from money, and you need to get that out of your system. **The joy is in the acquisition of it all; it's in the hunt, it's in the chase.** That's what's going to give you the greatest pleasure when it comes to getting rich. **It's looking for those ideas that are going to be your next golden winners.** I think about it as a metaphor of a huge bank vault: we don't know what the combination is, so we're safecrackers in this metaphor. We're searching for that combination. We've got our stethoscope pressed against that two-foot-thick steel door. All the money we'll ever want and need is on the other side of that door, and so we're carefully trying different combinations, looking for just the right combination to cause the tumblers in that safe to come into complete alignment so the door will swing open and all that money is ours. I think about that often when we're testing new ideas; and you really do need to have that whole sporting attitude going, because when you find what works the best, when you have a promotion that's working and all of a sudden hundreds of thousands — and in some cases millions — of dollars are flowing in in a very short period of time, that's great fun; and **that's the part I want you to focus on.** It's nice to have all that money, but what's even nicer, and **what will give you the most satisfaction, is knowing that you have the ability within yourself to**

MARKETING SECRET

MARKETING MAXIM: You can tell everything about a person — by simply paying attention to what they spend their money on.

- People reveal their true selves — by the way they spend their money.

- "It is where a man spends his money that shows where his heart lies."
— A. Edwin Keigurn

- This is why 2-Step marketing is so powerful.

create it anytime you want to. Anytime you want to make another fortune, you know exactly how to get it. **The key is to go to your best customers first.** Stay totally focused on them, and start testing from what I call the top down. Every new idea is tested to your very best customers first. Those are the people who know you, respect you, and trust you; and because of that, the selling resistance is lowered.

A few years back, we got involved in an interesting opportunity. This guy came to me with an outrageous idea; it almost sounded like some scam. He came at me with, "Hey, T.J., if I said I had a proven way to make $750,000 to $1 million this year and all you had to do was a work a little to get it, would you be interested?" If anybody else had said that to me, I would have said, "No thank you," or I would have sent them to one of my staff members. But because this is a guy I've known for a few years, and he's somebody I want to continue to do business with. Because I trust him and I like him, I was open and receptive. I want you to think about that. **Your best customers will buy almost anything from you, especially if they know they can get their money back if they're not happy.** Those are the people you should approach first; **it's what I call your "warm market."** And then, of course, you have other groups of customers within your customer base, because of the way that you pre-qualify them.

You can (and should) segment your customer base by the amount of money they spend, or how recently they spent things — because sometimes people get into emotional heat for a certain type of product or service. While they're in that mindset, you'd better sell them everything you can, because you never know when they're going to settle down. **So you segment, sometimes by the frequency of their purchase; you know they're excited about your type of offer.** You know that they're hot for it. You've got to use that knowledge to go after them in a more aggressive way than you would the rest of your customers. Or, you segment them by what it is they bought from you the first time. Remember the general answer to the question: "What do people want?" That's where a lot of marketers are confused. They run around in total bewilderment, thinking, "I don't know what to sell!" **The answer is to sell people variations on the theme of whatever you sold them the first time.** It's really very simple. When you look at everything in a holistic way and examine it from the top down instead of the bottom up, it becomes easier to figure out what's going to make you the most amount of money.

First of all, stay totally focused on your very best customers. Forget about all of those other people out there, and do what you have to do to make profits in the first place — which is serve your customers. **Do very special things for them and create all kinds of opportunities for them, because you're using them as a testing ground;** but you're also doing everything possible to serve them in the highest way, and to look for the things that excite them the most. You want more people like your best customers. That's the whole goal of your marketing. You want to attract the very best people and repel the worst people. I always run into these great customers at my seminars, and I know their buying history; I know that they've been with us for years, and they've spent thousands and thousands of dollars. Sometimes I'm able to build enough of a rapport with them enough where I'm able to ask them face-to-face, **"Where do I find another thousand just like you?"** If I don't have enough rapport built with them, I at least think it. That's the question you should be asking too.

You're looking for people who will spend a huge sum of money with you over a long period of time, because they have such a deep interest in what you're selling. It causes them to buy and rebuy because they trust you and like you, you've built a real rapport with them, and you've expressed yourself enough to them where they know that you care for them. **Your best customers will forgive you for not being perfect,** because they know you're striving to reach out to them, to give them more of what they want the most. **You end up knowing your best customers better than they know themselves.**

For years I kept journals, and every time I learned something new about a customer, I would write it down. Those journals got filled with all kinds of things, and we had testimonial sheets that went out disguised as surveys. We would reward the customer with a free bonus if they filled out a survey and sent it back to us. They'd give us permission to use their comments in any way we wanted to, and we'd give them a free gift. **Well, I had those transcribed, and I saved all the best ones.** Sometimes people just wanted to fill out the bare minimum so they could get the free gift, but about one out of three was really good. I transcribed them and took notes and did a lot of careful thinking, until I got to the place where I am today, which is a high level of confidence that I understand my customers better than they understand themselves. **I know why they buy. Ninety percent of the time, it's for emotional reasons.** I've also done a lot of heavy reflection on all of the reasons that I personally used to buy those moneymaking programs, because that was our entry into the marketplace.

Little did we know it at the time, but we had a lot of insider knowledge — because I was buying them all. I was obsessed with buying the same kinds of plans and programs that we sell now, and when I say obsessed, I mean it. **Now, succeeding with most of these plans involves a lot of work — unfortunately or fortunately.** It's unfortunate because people want to delude themselves that they can make millions of dollars with no effort. It's a fantasy. It's what I call lottery mentality: you just know you're going to buy a ticket and win the grand prize. **The fortunate part for you is that because there's a good bit of time, work and effort involved in succeeding with these programs, it levels the playing field.** The desire to make millions of dollars is the most important thing, because through that desire, you'll hopefully be willing to do whatever it takes — and there are a lot of people who aren't. The good news is, yes, all this *does* take some time, work, and effort to learn; but if you're willing to go through what you must and do whatever it takes, then you're going to be part of a small minority. This makes it all that much easier for you. When you develop the skills and abilities of all 16 of the areas I discuss in this section, it does become easier; and there's the irony right there.

People are looking for a simple, easy way to make millions of dollars. **That way does exist, but *only* after you develop these skills.** Then it becomes quite easy. When we first met Russ von Hoelscher, one of the first things he said to us was vital. I'll never forget; we'd known him for a little while by then, and had talked on the phone a bunch of times. He's a likeable, friendly guy who really does care about other people, and he had more than 20 years of experience at the time. In the course of a conversation as I was driving him home from the airport one day, he said the words that stuck in my mind and have dominated my thoughts ever since. He said, **"All it really takes to make millions of dollars in this business is just one idea."** I just about drove the car off the road, I was so excited. I was so thrilled at that, and I still am, and since then we've proven it to be true. It's not just some concept that I'm throwing out because it sounds good. It's true. All you need is just one idea. That's one of the reasons why you should continue to experiment with as many new ideas as possible, so you can find that one idea. **Or it may be some combination of ideas, because sometimes the ideas that make you the most money are the ones you mix together with other things you've tried.** That's been a large part of the secret to our success. You continue to find new ways to mix different ideas together.

Often the secret you're looking for is a combination of other things that have worked for you in the past. **One of things we do is continue to find new ways to repackage the same, successful ideas that have already made us huge sums of money.** Why not? You're there to serve your customers. You're there to give them more of what they bought from you before.

▼▼▼▼▼▼▼▼▼▼▼▼▼▼▼▼

The ONLY people who matter are the people who give you the most money.

And the people who make you the most money!

Now, customers always want new stuff. New, new, new; everybody loves it. It's part of our thinking. **If you don't offer your customers new stuff, someone else will.** Either you get the money, or one of your competitors gets the money.

You've got to do it, if for no other reason than that you recognize and accept the fact that marketing is about attracting and re-attracting customers, retaining customers, continuing to do business with the same people again and again — as long as your customers don't get the idea that you're just trying to slam them all the time. No matter what you do, some

Our success is not dependent on the market we serve — nearly as much as it is in our ability to know how to continually give this market what they want.

- We have the power to influence the people to which we sell.

customers are always going to feel you're just trying to take advantage of them, that you're just trying to get their money. **So your messages have to be altruistic, and you really must have a desire to serve the customers and offer strong money-back guarantees.** Let your customers know that if they're ever unhappy, they can get their money back. That way, you're dealing with a lot of integrity.

The second reason you have to continue to test new ideas all the time is because **you never know where your next multimillion-dollar idea is going to come from.** Your biggest breakthrough could be right around the corner, and unless you're testing new ideas you're never going to find it. Make a game of it; have fun with it. **The next reason to test is that the secret to getting great ideas is to get *many* ideas.** More ideas lead to better ideas, and the more things you test, the more power you'll have. The very best, most profitable ideas are often a combination of many ideas — the themes, formats, and models that you've used before. The best ideas for you will often be a combination of many different things that you've done, the years that you've spent intimately getting to know who your customers are, what they want the most and why they continue to rebuy, and how to give those things to them.

Your biggest breakthrough is out there right now. One idea really does lead to another. It's an evolutionary process, and your biggest breakthroughs will be a new combination of different ideas that you've used before. The more ideas you test, the more wealth-making power you have. Again, it's all about selling to your very best customers, because you're doing what I call **testing from the top down instead of the bottom up.** You're constantly thinking about that smaller group of people who buy and rebuy from you the most. I recommend that you have seminars and workshops just so you can get face-to-face with these customers.

Too many direct response marketers, especially this new breed of Internet marketers out there, want to hide out from the customers. They're attracted to direct response marketing because they don't want to be face-to-face with people. One of things that really turned me on the most about this business in the beginning was that I could do everything from home. I was in love with the idea that I could do business with hundreds, thousands, even hundreds of thousands of people without ever meeting most of them. **But you can't really hide out from your best customers.** If for no other reason than that, have seminars constantly so that you can get up-close and personal with them. You can get to know them that way. **The most rabid markets out there, the ones where you can make the largest amount of money in the fastest period, are 100% emotional driven.**

You also have to think conceptually. **See the absolute simplicity of even the most complicated ideas; find the hidden secrets behind the ideas that are making other people money right now.** See it simpler, believe it bigger. Go to your best customers first, and then test through the rest of your customer base. **Take the ideas that make you the most money and use them for new acquisitions.** It's the most risk-free way to make money.

I also recommend that you schedule meetings on a regular basis. We've been having regular weekly meetings now for well over ten years. We're always asking ourselves what's next, and we're planning different mailings, and we number all of them, and we schedule them, and we make commitments to do new things before we have all the answers figured out. **Remember, your best customers will gladly buy almost an unlimited number of products and services from you.** I used to worry that I was trying to sell to my best customers way too often, and I was always afraid that those customers were going to leave me; and what I found is that nothing could be further from the truth. **They're going to buy and rebuy from other companies unless I'm selling to them.** Now I just worry whether I'm selling enough to them, and I'm trying to stay out there in front of my best customers all the time, offering them other products and services.

You'll do well as long as the products and services you're offering help them get more of what you know they want, as long as you're striving to serve them in the highest way, as long as you're not just trying to suck money out of people for no value. **You're trying to offer value for value; actually, you're trying to offer greater value than what you're getting.** So you're giving them more and more of what you know that they want. As long as you're providing tremendous value and running your business in an ethical way — where they can get their money back without any game-playing if they want it — you'll build their trust, and they'll end up buying more stuff from you.

Then, last but not least, **keep finding new ways to recycle and repackage the same products and services; the same models that you tried before, the same ideas, the same themes, everything that's worked great for you in the past.** Keep trying to find new ways to give products a facelift, a new theme. Try to come up with something that looks new but is actually just repackaged; and again, the more you do it, the easier it'll get. **People love new stuff, and they want new stuff; but if it's too new, it won't fly.** Nobody wants to be the guinea pig; and so what you do is find new stuff for your customers. But then you let them know that it's not *entirely* new. It's still based on something that's solid and proven and tested, and there's still that conservative element present; because if it's too new, people are going to freak out. If it's too new, it will arouse their skepticism. **So you're constantly coming out with variations on a theme.** The car companies do it all the time. The best movies are just variations on a theme of all the other best movies. People want proven models, again and again.

This is a secret that most markets never put enough time and effort into. They'll never go through the painful learning curve of testing new things and working all this out. **But if you'll do it, you'll become part of a small group that's making huge amounts of money.**

SECRET TWELVE:

Fall in Love with Your Business!

The twelveth secret that made us millions of dollars is the simple but powerful fact that we fell in love with this business. Now, when I say "we," I'm talking about my wife Eileen and me. But I can really only speak for myself; she has her own opinions, and to her it was always more like a business. It was an exciting business; it was a good business but to me, it was more than that. It really, truly became an obsession for me, and I believe that in my contribution as the marketing arm of the company, I was able to contribute at a higher level, and I know that I made the company millions of dollars. Now, it would never have happened without Eileen; I just want you to be very clear about that. **I'm not a businessperson, I'm a marketer.** I became very, very good at developing information products that the customers loved, and they showed their love because they continued to rebuy from us, again and again.

That's how you know that people love you in this business. **They vote with their checkbooks, their credit cards.** Customers stay with you year in and year out, and continue to buy from you. That's the whole secret to making millions of dollars: Just get enough people to rebuy from you enough times with enough profit margin on every transaction, and the question isn't, "Will you get rich?" The only questions are, "How rich will you get?" and, "When will you make that money?" Think about that: Business can be complicated, there's no question about it, especially when you go through some hard times, when you make mistakes. There are hard lessons to learn; and the more money you want to make, the more of those things you'll have to learn. **But you also have to stay focused on the basics,** because no matter how complicated it gets, if you always go back to the fundamentals and see the simplicity in all this, it will help you. It will give you greater confidence, and help you through some of the hard times that I know you're going to have to go through. That becomes truer with the more money you want to make.

If you want to make $10 million in less than five years like we did, or if you want to do twice that, three times that, that's fine — you *can* do it, and I'm going to show you why I believe that this is the best business

Never Fear
Objections.

- Don't hide! Be upfront about the skepticism you know they feel... Bring up the biggest objections yourself. Then overcome them one by one. You'll win their trust and respect — and you'll get their money.

- The best prospects have major objections that must be faced head-on and not skated around.

on Earth. **It's the ultimate way to make money, and you can use some of these ideas within any business that you choose** — these ideas of developing information products that go out to the prospects and customers, attract them to you, and keep them coming back for more and more. Any business can benefit from this. It's a business that's worthy of falling in love with. It's highly creative, it's fun, it's interesting, it's challenging, and it's stimulating. There's always something new, and you get good at it. The better you get at it, the more confidence you develop, and the greater feelings that you have for it. I just can't stress that enough. **I want you to fall in love with this business; if you do, you'll not only achieve a greater level of satisfaction, you'll end up making more money.**

I became absolutely obsessed and possessed by this business. I fell in love with developing and selling information products, and I still love it. In fact, I love it even more now than ever before. It's this intense love that I feel for this business that's caused me to do many things that other people would never be willing to do. **I worked harder, I put in more hours, and I've gladly taken on newer and bigger projects that would have scared others to death.** They do scare others to death; they just won't do some of the things we've done. We've taken on all kinds of major projects, based only on the smallest, haziest concept of how we were going to put it all together; and then we *did* put it all together. It's the fact that I've been literally consumed with this business, and totally absorbed by it, that has caused me to come up with some of the ideas I've come up with, that have helped to contribute to this whole thing. The result hasn't always been perfect; it hasn't satisfied all the customers. We do have customers who don't like us, and that's fine! **We're looking for perfect matches;** and the longer we're doing what we do, the more willing we are to tell certain customers, "Look, I'm sorry, you're not right for us and we're not right for you," and send them off on their own way. I **don't want to pretend we're perfect for everyone.**

If it wasn't for Eileen, the whole thing would have been destroyed in the first 14 years. She was smarter than me; she ran the company, but I absolutely fell in love with developing products and services for our customers. I absolutely became obsessed with marketing, maybe to the point that sometimes, I took it way too far — putting in far too many hours, working way too hard, being too absorbed by the business, living it, sleeping it, dreaming it, eating it, all of those things. **It's because of this passion that I had, this obsession and the willingness to try new things and take on new challenges, that finally I developed some very specific skills that helped us make millions of dollars.** Now, we also had a great team of people in place. Eileen had a great staff, because we needed an infrastructure to help us attract and retain our customers. You have to have that; you can't get away from it. **For every 1,000 customers you bring in, you'd better add some staff to support those people, or those customers will go away.** There must be people there to take care of them, after they buy things. **The bigger you want to get, the more money you want to make, the more infrastructure you need.** Nothing takes the place of that.

But you also have to have products and services that people really, really want; **you need products and services that they want so badly, they'll continue to come back for more and more of the same.** There's an art to it, remember — an art to creating products that look and appear to be new and different, and have unique slants or angles or themes to them, and yet are just basically variations on everything else you've done. There's that level of familiarity that you must have with the products and services you create, no matter how many of them you create. **There's enough of the familiar to make people feel comfortable and secure, and enough of the new to captivate their imaginations, to keep them moving forward.** Selling information products can make you much more money than the highest-paid doctors and lawyers are making right now. That's one of the things that captivated me about the business then, and it still captivates me today.

Think about that: you have people who go to law school for 6 or 8 years, like my Dad did, going through this tremendous learning curve just so they can go out there and make enough money to live in the nice areas of town. Now, I have a business that's made me millions of dollars. **I can safely say that it can make you millions too, if you're just willing to put in some time and effort.** The secret of our success is in large part due to this tremendous obsession, this hunger that I had, to learn everything possible about how to develop information products that would keep people coming back for more, and keep those customers spending more money, and keep them happy and continue to give them everything I know they want the most. **It's been painful; I've spent a lot of hours working very hard to try to understand all of this stuff — and it's been worth it.**

Now, you want to make millions of dollars too — or so I assume. Why else would you buy a book like this? The only people who would spend what I'm charging for this product, simply to read it and not take it seriously, are foolish. I'm going to assume that you're *not* foolish. **Clearly, you really do want to make the money.** Now, here's a perplexing thing: why would people go and spend 6 or 8 years of their life, or in some cases 12 or 15 years of their life, learning how to be doctors, brain surgeons, lawyers, nuclear physicists or whatever? I realize that it's about more than just the money for them. But come on, let's face it — nobody spends all that time in college without the understanding that once they arrive, they're going to live in the nicest areas in town, they're going to drive the nicest cars, and they're going to have the kinds of things most people don't have. I'm sure there are exceptions, but most people are more than willing to go through 6 to 15 years of putting up with all kinds of pressures and challenges, and the discipline of being a good student, passing all the tests and learning all they have to — if behind it all is the knowledge that no matter how hard they're working right now, there's going to come a time when, because of what they're doing right now, they can spend the rest of their life living the good life, having all the wonderful things that money can buy.

That's why they're willing to put in those long hours. That's why they're willing to work so hard, to learn how to become professionals in their chosen crafts or professions. **Yet this is a business that can do the same thing for you. You can actually earn money while you learn —**

unlike going to college, where you've got to pay to put in all that time, so that you'll eventually get out of school and the money will start flowing in. This is a business where you're making great money, as long as you have a group of customers who bought something from you once, and your total focus is on reselling to those people again and again, then taking the very best ideas that come from that process and using those to help you attract new customers who are similar to your best customers. In some cases, you're making huge sums of money, and you're still learning. **You don't have to be as good a marketer, copywriter, or information producer to sell stuff to your best customers. They love you; they respect you.** When I say love, I'm using the term very loosely; at the very least, they appreciate what you're trying to do for them. Selling information products is a great way to reach out to people and develop strong bonds with them, so they get a sense of who you are. They can feel you, especially if you're using a medium like audio or video, where they can actually hear or see you, or if you're doing seminars, where they can get up close to you and spend time with you. **This is the chance for you to build huge profits, to serve people in the highest way, and still make more money than most doctors or lawyers can ever dream of — but there's a learning curve.**

You've got to go through some pain to learn all this, unless you're just a whole lot smarter than I am — and you may very well be. I don't doubt that, **but you're still going to have to learn some new skills.** I want you to think of the benefits, just like those college students that'll spend all those years in college, and their eyes are bloodshot, and they're putting in all that time to cram for those finals. They know that on the other side of that, a whole new life waits for them. Most people are more than happy to put in the

> ▼▼▼▼▼▼▼▼▼▼▼▼▼▼▼▼▼
>
> What you want the prospect to say:
>
> "Holy crap! If I got all this for only $XXX — what is this guy going to give me for $XX,XXX?"

time — but it's tough! Every time they call home to their parents they say, "Mom and Dad, I just can't take it anymore! I'm studying 12, 14, 16 hours a day, and I'm just barely making it!"

There's a lot of pressure on those young, ambitious, beautiful children who are trying to do big things with their life, and yet their parents are always saying, "Now look, you're only 25, 26 years old. After this, you're going to be a top doctor; you can work in Boston, you can work in New York City, you can pick your own salary." The parents are telling them these things; they're helping them hang in there, and pushing them to expend all the time, work, effort, and energy needed. There are times when your brain is just so tired, you feel like your head's going to explode. **I've gone through all that to learn what I've learned, too.** And I'm still trying to learn more, because **the problem is that when you learn all of these things, you start making money, and now the money just comes effortlessly — and you get bored.**

There's nothing worse for an entrepreneur than boredom. We need new challenges; we need to take on bigger and bigger things, try to do more with our lives, and make more money and see how high is high. How high can we go, and what are we capable of doing? **This is a business where there are always new challenges and new horizons, if you're willing to take on bigger and better things.** Certainly, you'll have to undergo struggles and adversity to get there, but you might just be a whole lot more talented than I am. Your capacity may be greater than mine, and therefore you'll do it all even faster. If so, I envy you; I respect you if you can do it. If you can make millions of dollars without going through a painful learning curve, then God bless you. I had to go through a lot of pain, but I've been willing to go through it, and the longer I do it, the more I appreciate this business and think that it's a perfect way to make money.

The best thing I can do is tell you to get involved in the information business. So many of our clients, our best customers, are people who habitually buy all kinds of information products. They're spending thousands of dollars every year — in some cases, tens of thousands of dollars — on information. **The kind of people who buy these types of products, we're constantly in their faces, telling them, "Hey, look, you're already spending tons of money on all this other stuff; why don't you get into the business of producing it yourself?** You've got an intimate feel for the type of person who buys this material, and you need that if you're going to be a great marketer and you're going to sell information products. **So what better person to get involved in the market than someone who already has that knowledge?"**

And yet so often, our advice falls on deaf ears. We stress this over and over again at our seminars. If I could grab people and throw them against the wall, slap them and stress this to them that way, I would. If only I could just drill it into their heads that they need to get on the other side of the cash register, and start serving the kinds of people out there who buy this stuff. If I could just wake them up out of their trance, get them to think about the other side of the cash register, so they would get into this business, so they'd learn some of the things they need to learn, so they'd go on to make a fortune in this business — then I'd do it. **I see that so many people have the potential, and yet** *they* **don't see it.** That's the problem: they don't see what I see. I think if you're already a customer and you're buying lots of different information products and you have a hunger for them, and you have the knowledge for this type of thing, you ought to get involved in the market yourself. It's a great way to make money, and here's why. **First of all, the demand for information products is absolutely huge, and it's growing all the time.** There are millions of people out there right now who want, need and are happy to pay for the benefits that a good information product can give to them.

What does that mean? **It's simple; the general premise is that the amount of money you're charged for these products has nothing to do with the actual cost to reproduce the product, because the costs are low.** That's becoming truer all the time. We're able now to take an audio program, like the one this book section is based on, and compress 12 hours of audio onto a single CD-ROM that can be played in any computer, or that can be downloaded into any mp3 player, or even played in many cars.

When you're able to take 12 hours of good audio or programming that really helps people and teaches them and tries to reach out and give them the things they need to get whatever they want — why, you can make a fortune. Look at all the information products out there: there are many, many different information producers selling a wide variety of things, and when (for example) you're able to take 12 hours of audio and put it onto one thin little piece of plastic that costs you just over a buck, that's amazing. But do people care if it cost you a dollar? No! Not the people who really matter. **The people who want and need the benefits of what you're selling are more than happy to pay for those benefits; what do they care if it cost you a buck?** Do you think it matters to them? I don't. Not the people who really matter, who are in your market, who are hungry and have the need for whatever you sell. They couldn't care less about what it cost *you*.

So look closely at that huge demand and the low cost to produce these products, which very often is just your time. Now, you've got to value that time, of course, and you've got to structure it and discipline yourself. But when you've got a demand that's so powerful here, and when the absolute cost for the products and services that you create to fill that demand is so low, but the perception of value is so high — then you've got a recipe for making millions and millions of dollars. If that was all there was to it, that would be enough. I promise you, that alone spells major success: the fact that there's a huge demand, there's a rabid market, there are millions of people that are constantly buying these information products. **The perceived value is enormous, and the cost to produce these products is very low. That alone would be perfect.** We could stop right here, and that would be enough. But there's so much more to this business than that!

This is a fun, creative, challenging, and extremely lucrative way to get rich. It's rewarding in every way. **When it comes to packaging and selling information, the number of markets out there is almost endless, because within every niche market, there are sub-niches.** If you're producing these products out of your home, you're producing them for almost no money at all, except for the time needed to develop them. **That means you can serve small markets and still get wealthy.** You need fewer people, because you're able to sell things for high prices. You're able to take something that takes you a small amount of your time, put it into a product that you can sell, and make money with it for the rest of your life. **Think about how exciting that is! To take something that you do once, and leverage it for the rest of your life.** If you choose your market correctly, it'll mean a lifetime of profits for you — enormous sums of money. **This is a very personal medium where you're able to express yourself fully;** and I don't mean to sound overly-dramatic about this, but when I hand someone an information product I've poured my heart into, I'm giving him a little piece of me. It's a piece of my entire soul, the essence of who I am.

That's what a great information product is: it's an extension of who you are, what you stand for, what you believe in, what's most important to you. You're sharing your best ideas; you're reaching out to the people you're producing that product for, just like I'm trying to reach out to you right now. You are reading this book to learn these secrets that made us millions of dollars in just a few years, and I'm trying to express those in the fullest way that I can possibly can. **I'm trying to reach out for you, reach out _to_ you.** If I could crawl through those pages right now and come into your home, and we could sit down and drink a cup of coffee, and we could talk for hours — I would. I hope to meet you in person someday. Your goal is to help people in the highest sort of way; not everybody, but at least those who really want it the most, who are willing to take your ideas and use them. **You're able to develop relationships with those people, and that's another reason why I believe that this is a business that's worthy of falling in love with.**

The ideal in this business is to develop good information products that reach out to people, that form strong bonds with them — a strong connection that helps them get whatever they want. That's what you're really trying to do. **You're not just trying to make money for yourself: you're trying to make money through serving people. You're helping them get what they want.** The better you know your customers, the better you're able to help them. That's how you develop customers who respect and appreciate you.

Fair warning: it doesn't always work. If you're like me, trying to express everything in the fullest way with your heart in the right place, without thinking about what you're saying... well, you'll have a few people who can't stand you. They can barely listen to you. You drive them crazy, like in that movie _Jaws_, when the captain runs his fingernails along the

"Getting a new customer is like riding a bicycle uphill on a hot summer day. Doing more business with an established customer is like coasting that same bike downhill."
— Jay Abraham

- Re-sell to your existing customers more often.

- Sell more stuff — to more customers more often!

chalkboard. I have customers who hate my communication style. I upset them, because I say things that aren't politically correct. They wish I'd be more professional, polished. **They hate listening to me, but they know that my heart's in the right place, and they know I have things that can help them get what they really want — and they have a desire to learn those things.** So they come to our seminars, put up with the things about me they can't stand, and they learn what I have to teach. They move on, and take this information and change their lives with it — and that's what's important.

So even if your customers don't love you, they *will* appreciate and respect you. When you do it correctly, there's no real competition. You're producing products that are uniquely you. They're a piece of you; they're your ideas. If you're not the expert, find the experts. Right now, we're moving into the whole new area of helping our clients make money in real estate. What do we know about making money in real estate? Absolutely nothing! But that's not stopping us. We're developing products where we go out and interview all these real-estate experts — and there are a huge number of them, because the market is enormous. They're more than willing to let us interview them and capture their best ideas during the process, because they're looking for customers for their products and services. You have that in every single market. If you want to get involved in the health market (another multibillion-dollar market), you can create an information company that's uniquely positioned. **You don't claim to be an expert, you just go out there and find all the experts and do business with them.**

You can put on seminars, workshops, tele-seminars, or create all kinds of programs based on interviews where people freely share their greatest secrets, because they're trying to sell their own books and tapes. You become a toll road. You can develop many information products without really knowing much about the subject, simply by finding other people who do understand it; and then you simply work on developing new customers and create proprietary-based programs based on the interviews you do with these experts. We're doing it now with real estate; we did it with eBay. When it came to making money on eBay, which is a really popular subject, we didn't know anything at first. But there are experts out there, and this time we decided to interview them; and that led us to other things.

You could do this with anything, and I would encourage you to try. **This is a business where you really can separate yourself from every other customer, because you're creating products that are uniquely you.** You own them. They're proprietary, and you can keep customers excited and wanting to do more and more business with you. We've had customers who have been with us for 10 or 15 years; even a few who've been there almost from Day 1. They like us and what we're trying to do. They know we're trying to operate with integrity, and they're very skeptical of all these other companies, so they continue to favor us rather than try to do business with a new company. **People develop relationships with you as they get exposed to you through the products you create.** What that means for you is that, if you're using the marketing systems I'm talking about in this book, you end up with a huge customer base that keeps you motivated and excited about developing newer and better products.

Once you get this huge customer base, stay in touch with them on a regular basis. You know they're going to buy more stuff, if not from you from somebody else, so it might as well be you. You'll find yourself developing all kinds of new products and services just for your best customers, because you know they'll continue to buy, and you want to serve them in the highest way. With the information-publishing business, you can reach these marketplaces, and you can make money for the rest of your life — an endless stream of money, and in many cases far more money than any of your local doctors and lawyers make. You can be right there next to those people. I don't care how broke you are, you can't be much broker than I was when we first started. **This is the business that**

can do all that for you, and besides the money, it can give you a great level of joy and satisfaction; it's so rewarding. I want to help you get involved in this tremendous business.

SECRET THIRTEEN:

Schedule Weekly Planning Sessions

The thirteenth secret that we used to make millions of dollars is that **we hold weekly meetings where we plan all our marketing strategies.** These meetings are a form of discipline that keep us focused on where our next dollar is coming from. **They keep us moving forward;** and this is something you need to do if you're going to make the largest amount of money possible. You always have to ask yourself, "Where's my next dollar going to come from?" I'm shocked at the number of talented entrepreneurs I know who aren't using these strategies.

Even if you don't have staff yet, you've got to hold those meetings with yourself. I know that sounds funny, but it just means disciplining yourself, making the time to ask yourself, "Where's all of the money I want to make going to come from?" You see, many entrepreneurs get so lost in the promotions they're working on today that they never spend quality time thinking about two months from now. **Now, you probably don't have to think much more in advance than two or three months.** I never think more than a few months out at any given time — so forget all this long-term planning about where you're going to be a year from now, where you're going to be five years from now. All that's too confusing, so just stay on the path here.

Think about it as if you're jumping into your car in the middle of the darkest night of the year, where there's absolutely no moon; and now, you want to drive somewhere that's three or four hundred miles away. If you're a fairly competent driver and the roads are in good shape and the weather is okay, you can drive 300 to 400 miles in one evening, in pitch-black dark, and you'll never really need to see more than 150 or 200 yards ahead at any time. This is metaphor that I've thought a lot about over the years. As long as you're able to see ahead 150 to 200 yards, what do you care? Just don't outrun your headlights. It's the same thing with running a business. You don't have to worry about next year; you don't have to worry about two or three years from now. **Sure, you should generally figure out your direction; you need to know where you want to go long term, and what your company stands for.** Those kinds of ideas and general concepts about the marketplace you serve and your long-term commitment to that marketplace are important. But otherwise, you just have to think about what you're going to do in the next month or two months, and that's it.

▼▼▼▼▼▼▼▼▼▼▼▼▼▼▼▼▼▼

Y̶ou never get what you want — you only get what you expect!

High expectation is the key to taking your business to the next level.

Most entrepreneurs are lazy and undisciplined. A lot of the people I've gotten to know — very talented, super-creative people who really understand marketing — could be making so much more money than they're making right now. I even know some really smart people who are always struggling financially. They're great marketers, they intimately understand a lot of the secrets that I'm sharing with you in this book... and yet they're broke all the time. If they just applied some of these secrets to their businesses, they wouldn't have to be broke. They could make all kinds of money, but they're lazy, they're undisciplined, and they love to get lost in their projects. They love the work, but they hate all the planning and the organization; they hate going to meetings.

Many entrepreneurs are also very independent, so they don't work well as part of a team. **They're very undisciplined, and they don't like all the planning that's necessary to keep the ball rolling, to keep moving forward.** I can relate to that. You see, for years I absolutely hated meetings. I'm not going to tell you I love them now; I do one a week and that's it. It only lasts ninety minutes to two hours, and in that meeting we plan the new mailings, we come up with ideas for new promotions, and we keep the whole thing rolling. I'm going to explain to you just how simple it is before this chapter's over. But many entrepreneurs aren't doing

View the impossible as just another marketing opportunity!

- Believe so deeply in your ability to give your market what they truly want — that failure is not an option! Develop a missionary zeal for what you do! Then communicate your intense passion to your prospects!

this; they're not thinking ahead.

The money you want to make next month must be put into action *today*. It sounds simple, and you would think that this is just common sense, but most people have no method or no system to put this into play, so they're always disorganized. They're always frantically busy, and they're tired and they're too working hard, but they're never making the kind of money that should and could be theirs.

Remember, what you want to do is try to turn your business into a moneymaking machine. **Get it systematized, so the money just keeps rolling in.** Here's how to do it: You simply develop a marketing plan like ours, and our marketing plan is so simple that a twelve-year-old child can understand it. **First of all, during our regular weekly meeting, we plan mailings that go out on a weekly basis to attract new customers.** There are 52 of those mailings every year. **We only schedule them about a month in advance, so we're watching the numbers constantly;** we're not foolish about all this, we're looking at the numbers and making sure we're still profitable. **We're constantly testing new things on the front-end,** so in case one new customer acquisition promotion goes flat, we've got something to replace it with. **Every week we have a new marketing campaign, which is a series of direct-mail letters.** About 50,000 pieces a week go out on a regular basis; sometimes the number's 35,000, sometimes it's 75,000, and we're always experimenting to see what we can do to attract new customers who have never done business with us.

During our weekly meetings we look at all of this. How are our regular mailings working out? What's going on? What do our numbers look like? Our printer is at every one of these meetings, because he's looking for new printing business, and our mailing house representative is there at every meeting because *she's* looking for more business. These people are paid on commission. **My goal is to always make sure the presses keep rolling, to always make sure that there are mailings going out — because as long as we're watching the numbers and doing everything right, the more we mail, the more money we make.** For years we just weren't aggressive enough with our mailings. Now we're deeply committed to doing more and more mailings, so we watch our front-end, our new-customer acquisition mailings, and we make sure we've got something out there all the time, and it's working well for us. We're testing new things on the front-end. Next, we have regular new mailings that go out to our established customers to get them coming back. **All these mailings, and all the implementation of the products and services that these mailings or promotions sell, must be planned and kept organized.** All it takes is an hour to an hour and a half a week; that's it. You can do this even if you don't have a staff.

If you want to make millions of dollars, you have to get a big enough group of customers to rebuy from you repeatedly. **Do it long enough, at a large enough profit margin, and you'll get rich.** You've always got to ask yourself, "Where is that next dollar coming from?" Well, I'll tell you where's it's coming from: established customers to whom you make some type of an offer. Those customers give you their money in exchange for your offers, but you've got to plan these mailings. It has to be done in a disciplined, organized, regular way. **Consistency is so important.** I can't stress this enough, and I'm shocked at the number of talented entrepreneurs who never figure it out.

I was talking to a good friend of mine recently, and we were sharing the secrets that I'm sharing with you now. He's new to the business, and he asked me a great question: "Why don't more people do this? Because it really is simple." Develop a staff of employees who understand your business in an intimate way, have a regular promotion that goes out to attract new customers to you to buy from you the first time, and then have a series of systematic follow-up offers that go out to resell to your established customers. **It's so very easy.** You have a regular weekly meeting that keeps it all organized, that keeps the blade sharp; that's the way I think about it. But when my good friend Ray asked me why more people don't do this, I thought about it, and I could come up with only a few reasons.

First of all, I think they're really shortsighted; they're too focused on the moment. They get so caught up in what they're doing that they forget that the money they want to make next month and the month after that has to be thought through in advance. There has to be some planning there, some organization. But they never think it through in any long-term way. The second reason is what I shared before: **They're undisciplined, lazy, disorganized, too rebellious and too immature.** How do I know? Because that was me. For a number of years, that was exactly who I was. I hated meetings, just as entrepreneurs just hate meetings in general. We look at the way some of these big corporations are run, where all they do is go to one meeting after another, and it's the *appearance* of work. They feel important because they're going to all these meetings, but they're never getting anything done; and we know this. Non-lazy entrepreneurs are people of action; we like to be out there *doing* it, not sitting in some meeting talking about how we're going to do it.

But it's an absolute necessity to have regular meetings where you're planning and organizing things. This is a secret that can make you so much money, and it's so simple; and the benefits come from working with a staff who show up for these meetings once a week, who understand your business in a deep, intimate, way, and who can remind you of things and keep you centered. They can say, "Look, why aren't we doing this? Why aren't we doing that? Are we doing this? Are we doing that? What's going to happen here? What are we doing about that?" They help you stay sharp.

Number Three: most entrepreneurs just don't want to have an infrastructure. I talked about that in the last secret: They want to do it solo. They want to make millions and millions of dollars all by themselves. I think that's so wrongheaded. Of course, my friends have called me a kingdom builder, an empire builder, and have told me that I have a huge ego because I need such a large staff. **But I believe that the key to good customer service is making sure that for every thousand customers, you'd better have some staff there to support them.** It just makes sense to me, but granted, my critics have been sort of right about me over the years, too. We've had a hard time with this; often we've either been

FOOLPROOF SECRETS of Successful Marketers!

understaffed or overstaffed. Either we've had too few people, or too many people. It's been a constant struggle. There are so many people who claim that they want to make millions of dollars, but want to do it all by themselves, and to me that's a recipe for disaster. **You need to delegate your weak areas to people who are strong in those areas you're weak in, and you need to get good at the few things that it takes to make the largest amount of money, and put all of your time and all of your effort into those things.**

Nothing could be more important than that. If you're trying to wear all the hats, trying to do it solo without any infrastructure, you're never going to make the kind of money that you could and should make. So get rid of that idea. You need a good staff of competent people; if you have one, they can be a great asset, especially if they've been in your business for a number of years. **They can make you money, not cost you money.** Everything these people do to help you make more money will more than compensate the amount of money you're paying them. It's true, I promise.

It may not be simple or easy, but that's the secret to my success, and that can be the secret of your success too. It only becomes something negative when business gets bad, or you start going through cash flow problems; and if you'll use this secret, you don't have to go through those cash flow problems. For years, we lost millions of dollars by not marketing more aggressively to our established customers. Now, I couldn't have told you that then. Wisdom comes from hindsight; there's the old quote that "hindsight is 20-20," when after a number of years you're able to look back and see your mistakes. **I clearly see that this was a mistake, and I'm asking you to not make it.** You don't have to lose money.

You see, there are only two real ways to make money. Number One: everybody knows about this one. You look at all the areas you can cut. "Oh! We're spending too much here, let's cut this, let's cut that!" That's important, sure; you should always look for ways where you can cut expenses by doing something more efficiently, assuming you can still get the same quality with less effort or cost. **But what's just as important — and in some cases more important — is to look at all the things you could be doing to make more money.** These are things you should start fixing right now. **You need to make more offers to your established customers, people who have already shown that they trust you and**

▼▼▼▼▼▼▼▼▼
MARKETING SECRET

There's a lot of competition for your customers' money. Never forget this. If you can't answer the question — "Why should I give it to you and not your competitor?" then you don't deserve to be in business.

- Just like in sports: the team who wants it more than the other team — wins!

like what you're doing. If you'll do that, you're not going to have the cash flow problems that we've had occasionally. See, I used to worry so much that I was being too aggressive with my customers. My fears were that I was going to wake up some morning and all my customers were going to be upset because we were trying to sell to them too aggressively, and they were going to start thinking that they were nothing but walking walls, and they were all just going to go away. It was a completely irrational fear, as most fears are.

The truth is that if you're making your customers offers for products and services that really can help them, they'll respond positively. This is a service where, if you'll use my ideas and my personal help, you can make a ton of money. By the time you're done reading this book, and you know that I can really help you with these things, you'd be crazy not to use me as a personal coach and mentor. As long as you've got the same kinds of products and services you're offering to your customers, where what you have to give is worth far more money than you're asking them to give you in return, go out there and make them a ton of different offers. **Go out there very aggressively, and offer them more and more of the things that you know in your heart can really help them make money.**

Another reason I came up why so many entrepreneurs don't want to have meetings goes back to that laziness factor. **They're terrified of all the hard work. They don't want to plan things because they're afraid of commitment, responsibilities, and deadlines.** They don't want to put themselves under all the pressure it takes to achieve the maximum level of productivity. You see, that's what comes out of these meetings. Every single week, as we plan out our next mailings, we're always asking ourselves, "What can we do? What can we do? What can we do?" The printer's there — he wants more business, he wants to keep those printing presses rolling. The mailing house is there — they want to mail more stuff out, and we know that's the key to making more money. Our business isn't there to serve our printer or mailing house or our employees, **our business is there to make more sales to our customers and make more profits.** Those suppliers are there to help us make more money by offering more and different offers to our customers.

But here's what comes out of all of those meetings, and this is what all the entrepreneurs are afraid of: work, work, and more work. Somebody has to write the promotion, somebody has to put it all together, somebody has to do all the thinking; and that somebody is often you, if you're the one who's working on your marketing and you're putting all your focus in that one key area — product development, working on new sales copy, everything it takes to get those new products and services into the hands of as many people as possible. **That's work, and a lot of entrepreneurs are afraid of work. They're afraid of responsibility.** It reminds me of the quote that says, "What's the best thing about being self-employed? It's the fact that you're your own boss. And what's the worst thing about being self-employed? The fact that you're your own boss!" **A lot of people just aren't very good at being their own boss.** They want to lie around too much, they're not as productive as they could be; they're afraid of commitments, obligations, deadlines, and stress, and they never work as hard as they should. **These meetings are a format for you, so you've got to have them every week.** Your staff is going to show up, your suppliers are going to show up, and you've got to do something right during those meetings, besides tell jokes or talk about the football game last weekend. By the way, we also have fun at our meetings; I try to keep it lively. We make jokes, we crack up, we have fun. If it's not fun, why do it? **You've got to enjoy the people you work with, and so we keep it lively.**

But we're all there to make money; the staff is part of our revenue-sharing program, so they're getting a piece of every dollar that comes in. A rising tide lifts all boats as they say, so it's a win-win situation for our staff. They know that the key to getting a bigger paycheck is to do everything possible to make that cash register ring. So every week I've got to show up with three or four different things we can plan, because that's my responsibility. **I'm trying to practice what I preach and it keeps me on my toes, but I always walk away from those meetings knowing my to-do list keeps growing.** Many entrepreneurs are afraid of that; they want to run and hide from all the pain and pressures. **They don't want those self-imposed deadlines.** But if you'll do this, you'll keep your business moving forward; you'll get into the habit of realizing that all the money you want to make next month and the month after that comes from what you do every week in planning and preparing the mailings that will go out to your existing customers. Then there are the new mailings that are designed to attract new customers.

We use direct-mail almost exclusively, by the way. That's our favorite medium. It's just a wonderful feeling to be in total control over the media. But right now, today, after I'm done writing this chapter, I've got to get on the phone and negotiate with the publisher of some publications that we're going to advertise in; she wants us to sign a year's contract, and she wants to negotiate all kinds of things. God, I hate that. Once you discover the thrill of direct-mail, it's hard to go back. **Direct-mail is a medium you control completely.** You control the print, the mailing, the mailing list — it's just wonderful. But whatever media you use, you've got to plan; you've got to keep things organized.

Here are some of the ways to use this thirteenth secret to make millions of dollars. **First, plan new promotions on a regular basis.** Those plans can be kept in journals; that's all I do. I get up, drink a couple of a pots of coffee every morning, and get high on caffeine. That's when I do a lot of my great thinking. There's no phone, no fax machine, no distractions. It s just me and my journal full of ideas. I write a lot of different ideas down. **Many, if not all, are combinations of ideas I've worked on in the past.** It's always nice to have an arsenal of all kinds of ideas that you're working on, and just to think and to make the commitment to do new projects.

Once you make the commitment, figure out how to do it. What happens is, you create these self-imposed deadlines. Now, the deadlines are very stressful sometimes, but **I believe that deadlines are the entrepreneurs' best friend.** You're always going to do more when you're committed to your deadlines. You're going to show up in that meeting every week with your staff; you can't get into the habit of planning things, and then just erase them off the board. **You know there's an obligation here — that if you're in charge of the marketing of your company, which I'm telling you is the area you** *need* **to be in charge of, don't delegate that.** You may have people within your company who are working closely with you, but don't delegate it. That's your commitment to the company, that's your contribution to the company, and you've got to work your butt off and make sure you're planning all this stuff. **Then it's up to you to fulfill that stuff.** Now, here's one of the things we do that I just have to share with you, something that really can make you a lot of money. We do this all the time to help motivate ourselves to do more.

First, we plan a mailing and a basic promotion, and then we write some kind of small lead-generating direct-mail offer. It can be a postcard, or a small direct-mail package that stays under an ounce — a small package that's designed to just get people to raise their hands. **We plan that mailing, we get it out very quickly, but it takes about a week to ten days from the time we plan it until the time it actually goes out.** Now, during that period while it's going out in the mail, **we're busy working on all the fulfillment materials,** because we know we're going to get leads from a group of customers who'll raise their hands and say, "Yes, send that to me," **so we're obligated there.** We bring in a ton of leads from people who want the free report, the free CD or whatever; and now, we've got hundreds or, in some cases, thousands of customers who have raised their hand. The pressure we feel is out of a sense of obligation to our customers, knowing that if we don't get it to them quickly it's going to be a bad thing; **every day that you don't get it to them, you're sending negative messages to your customers.** You can't do that. When somebody sends for something you owe it to them right away.

> I've never been poor, only broke. Being poor is a frame of mind. Being broke is a temporary situation.
>
> — Mike Todd

So we scramble like crazy to put it together. We do this with all kinds of things. **Many are pre-publication offers where we make customers special deals on products that we tell them aren't** *finished* **yet, and**

▼▼▼▼▼▼▼▼▼
MARKETING SECRET

Do as much as you can each day to keep the selling-machine moving forward!

- Stay focused on your long-term marketing strategy.

- Always be working on the next project.

---

that's true. What they don't know is that many times the products don't even *exist* yet, so it's not that we're lying to people; we're saying, "Look, we're going to give you a pre-publication rate. You're going to get it for 50% off the regular price. But it's not finished yet." Then we get a bunch of people who order, and now the sands of the hourglass start dropping. **The timer's on; we've set a deadline, we've promised it to the customers in 45 or 60 days, so we've got to do it.** We do that with tele-seminars, seminars, and workshops, too. We offer things that aren't yet finish, and sometimes things that we don't even quite know exactly how we're *going* to finish. There are questions that remain to be answered, **but we go ahead and make the commitment, and there's magic when you do this right.** I know it sounds a little scary, but it comes with confidence and experience, and pretty soon it becomes a fun way to stay creative and challenge yourself to do more and go higher. You make promises to your best customers, which you only have the haziest of notions of how you're going to fulfill, then you scramble like crazy to fulfill them. **As you do this, you'll develop more confidence, and it'll become fun; it's more like a game.**

I've had this happen to me so many times now that I can speak with some real authority on this. All the answers of how you're actually going to pull it off and keep all the promises you've made — they come in the midnight hour. **Right before the deadline you start thinking about things where I am absolutely, positively convinced that, if it wasn't for the deadline and the commitment that you've made, you would never, ever have thought about.** Yes so many entrepreneurs are trying to run and hide

---

from pressure, responsibilities and obligations! **I'm here to tell you that the secret to making millions of dollars is to put more pressure on yourself, to take on bigger responsibilities, to set higher goals, to try to achieve *more*, not less.** Sure, there are going to be hard times, but you're going to get more done and you're going to end up with a feeling of tremendous satisfaction. You're going to make millions of dollars that your peers will never ever make, and you're going to feel so incredibly good about yourself at the same time.

SECRET FOURTEEN:

Rework Your Past Promotions and Materials

The fourteenth secret to making millions of dollars is to **rework the same sales letters, to keep redoing the same products, and to keep rerunning the same promotions.** Now, I've already talked about this a little, and I don't mean to sound like a broken record; I just want you to understand this. So many people don't get it. **They don't understand that you can keep reselling the same basic things over and over again.** It's a trick of the trade that a lot of people in the trade just never pick up on. **If you do, you'll have a major advantage over the other competitors in your marketplace, because most are simply not selling enough new things to their customers.** One of the reasons is that they just don't realize how easy it is to keep repackaging the same things and calling them new. Of course, there can be some element within your package that makes it look new; it has a new look, it has a new feel, there's some new angle to it. You're not ripping people off; you're giving them exactly what they want, which is old things with a new twist.

Look, everybody wants new stuff; there's no question about that. However, the newer it is, the more unestablished it is. Nobody wants to be the guinea pig, the first one out on the dance floor. **People need stability, the peace of mind that what they're buying from you has an established track record.** It's proven; it's not just something you dreamed up out of thin air. Customers like this; they like the message, in general, that what you have for them is established, it's rock-solid, it's proven, and yet they *also* like the idea that you've found some way to make it even better — and that's all you have to do. **Keep finding ways to put a facelift on everything, make it seem like it's new, and it** *will* **be new to some extent.**

If this sounds manipulative, I'm sorry; it's just something that everybody who's making the most money is doing. Maybe some of them don't want to tell you about it, because it does sound slightly manipulative, but really it's not. Look at the cars that keep coming out year after year. Every few years they may change the basic design of the model, but most years they're just doing tiny things to give it the appearance of something new. **It's just the same old stuff over and over, and that's what people want.** You've got to realize just how insatiable people are, and you have to realize the things I've talked about the emotional qualities in play here.

People buy for emotional reasons, so don't try to think all this through too much from a logical standpoint. There's all this irrational behavior that goes into the best marketplaces, the ones that can make you the most money in the shortest time in the easiest possible way. **These are markets that are driven by emotions; people are irrational in their behavior, and that's fine, it's good.** The only time any of this becomes bad is when you're not committed to delivering products and services that offer good, solid potential. When you're just out there selling crap that doesn't stand a snowball's chance in hell of giving people the benefits you're promising them, that's when it falls apart.

I think it's kind of funny how the same customers (and God love them all, I try to take good care of my customers) end up coming to our seminars repeatedly. People ask us, "What's the seminar about?" Well, it's just like the last seminar we had; and the next seminar we do will be just like the last one we had before that. And, yes, there's always the appearance of something new, and there's always something new we're introducing; **but the basic, core seminar continues to be the same.** We say the same things; listen to all the tapes of our seminars, and you hear the commonality woven throughout.

The same thing is true for all our major competitors. The reason we do this is twofold. **First, that's what the customers want.** All of us are in business to serve our customers, to give them more of what they want; and what they want are variations on the theme of what they bought from us the last time. **The second reason you do it is because it's easier to do it; it's faster.** You can keep coming up with new stuff again and again, so you can get all that pressure off your shoulders that it has to be somehow totally different than what you gave them last time — because I promise you, it doesn't have to be. **Once you have a library full of things that have worked for you in the past, it's easy to keep giving them variations of the same theme.** That should be something you look for towards the future. You work your butt off creating all this new stuff, finding out what works the best, experimenting, getting some things established; and then, after a certain numbers of years... well, it's not that you can just coast. I don't want you to even think like that. You can't just take it easy; but it does become easier, there's no question about it. Just keep pulling up the same old sales letters, rewrite them a little bit, and boom — that's all you have to do. **Once you understand at a core level what it is that really turns your customers on, it becomes so easy to do the things that used to be difficult for you.**

Once you get to that point, you can do in two days what used to take you twenty days. It'll be a whole lot easier, and it'll be a whole lot better. **Some of this involves simply pulling up old computer files and rewriting, and we do our share of that.** That can all be done while you're relaxing on the couch in front of the TV at night; it's no big deal. Rewriting is actually my favorite part of the job. The writing part is difficult for me, because I put so much of my energy into it. The rewriting part is easy: you've got your feet up, and there's the TV, and you're half watching some stupid TV program. In my case I'm with my sweetheart at night, and we're spending some good quiet time together. I've got my laptop, and I'm very quietly rewriting the same things we've done in the past.

When you're in the writing mode, you're able to get so much done, so fast, because you know exactly what your customers want. There's a power here, and you can acquire it. It's on the other side of that learning curve, so it'll take some effort, but you've got to know that it does get easier. There is a quote from the late, great Joe Cosman that goes something like, "What was once difficult is now easy," and when I first heard that I thought, "God, that Joe Cosman is such a wise man." And he is, but it turns out that he was rephrasing a concept that was already very old. Because I collect quote books, one day I ran into that quote. It was

▼▼▼▼▼▼▼▼▼
MARKETING SECRET

The greatest get-rich ideas come from a consistent state of activity. You'll never get them by sitting on your butt. They only come when you are moving forward.
The best ideas come when you are buried deeply in a blur of many different activities, projects, and actions.

- Focus on serving your customers.

- Focus on the road ahead.

- Keep looking for winning combinations and concepts.

from the King James Version of Bible. It wasn't said exactly the same way, but six hundred years before Christ, somebody expressed the same sentiment: that the things that are difficult for you right now are going to get easier and easier if you keep working through them. **Once you build up an arsenal of sales letters and promotions and products, they can make you money for the rest of your life.**

One of the things I wrote to myself a few days ago — because I'm trying to practice this principle myself, and I keep journals where I try to think these things through and I write notes to myself so I can go back and remember them — was "never create anything ever again; you've got so much stuff that can and should be recycled." I love to create new stuff, I honestly do, and I think a lot of entrepreneurs are like me. But the truth is, we've got all this other stuff that's worked for us over the years, and **you're a whole lot smarter if you'll rework the old stuff and try to incorporate your need to create new stuff into that, so that you blend it in with the old.** It's the best advice I can give you for making millions of dollars, and it all boils down to the same basic emotional reasons that cause your customers to buy and rebuy from you. Now, it's true that your customers do go in and out of emotional heat. **They get hot for things and they get cold, but the core reasons that cause them to buy and rebuy don't change.** The same basic selling messages keep working over and over again: the same themes, the same benefits, the same type of offers, the same types of products and services. You do have to get people while they're hot, and not all your customers are going to stay hot; **but the more you offer people, the more they'll buy**

from you in general, and I feel that you can't sell to your best customers enough. You have to keep going back to them again and again. As long as you're providing good value, there's nothing wrong with it; you're actually doing them a favor.

People are going to buy from you, or they're going to buy from your competitors. **They would much rather buy from you and from the people you recommend.** There's a trust built up there, so you might as well be there for them. **At the same time, they want old stuff with a new twist — and they trust you to provide it.** That means you can keep stamping out the same stuff over and over, as long as there's a new angle to it. Let me repeat: people want more of what they bought from you the first time; they want the same basic benefits and advantages in the items you provide. They'd rather buy from you and the people you recommend than anyone else. **Remember, a lot of this is emotional.** What you have to do is get a very good conceptual view; you have to think this through as much as you can from the top down. Keep swipe files of other people's sales material, and of course keep everything that you've done in the past. I have boxes and boxes of stuff that we've done previously, and it's nice just to be able to reuse it again; it's a fast, simple way to be creative. **You get leverage on all the hard work that you do once.** It's a great way to do something once and keep getting paid for it forever.

This is true especially if you're in the information publishing business; that's one of the greatest advantages that we have. **We do something once, and we can get paid for many years.** If I were to die next year or ten years from now, the people working within our company could just keep stamping out the same basic things, if they're smart — and I know they are. Of course, they suffer from the same thing most entrepreneurs suffer from. They want to keep coming up with new stuff; it's almost like we think there's something wrong with stamping out the same old stuff. But there's nothing wrong with it at all! **Remember, one of the reasons you do it is because that's what your customers want; all of us are in business to serve customers, to give them more of what they want.** If it's too new, they don't want it, because it makes them more skeptical; they want that old stuff with the new twist. **You've got to think conceptually, to look for patterns and themes, test as many new ideas as you can; and then you find out what works the best, and keep coming back to those things.** You keep incorporating those things in the new stuff that you're doing. You've got to always look at where your biggest sales and profits are coming from, the promotions that work the best, and keep asking yourself, "Why?"

Now, I want to tell you this: you'll never come up with a *real* reason. Remember, all this is driven by emotions, and emotions know no logic, so trying to apply logical answers to emotional questions just isn't a good idea. But you do develop themes and theory, once you understand the marketplace at a very intimate level. **You'll come to realize that one of the things about the opportunity market that causes people to rebuy so much is simply this: they want the fastest, simplest and easiest way to make the most money with the least effort, and if you can do it all for them, or promise to do it all for them, then so much the better.** This is one theory that I've developed. It may sound cynical, but I don't care; I know it's true. There are exceptions, and there are theories within the theory, but usually they want to get super-rich, even though most of them are like I was back in the 1980s. I could barely put a roof over my head or pay my bills, and I had no knowledge and experience; but I still had an overwhelming obsession to get rich. **That's who the people in the opportunity market are in general.** There's no logic behind it. It makes no sense. Certain skills and knowledge have to be developed to get rich, and although it's possible to get rich quickly, usually you have to put in some time and work, effort and energy. I stumbled around for years before it happened.

There is a compelling emotional reason why people buy, and I would suggest that you study your biggest competitors closely; forget the rest. **Study and identify the promises and benefits they're communicating to their customers.** Try to determine the general selling ideas that they're using; what are the promises behind the promises? Just identify these things, think these things through, and keep some journals. Look, all of this may sound easy right now, as I express it to you — and it is. For me this is easy, because I've been doing it for twenty years. But there were years when it was all very confusing, and I kept lots and lots of journals, and I studied my customers intensely.

Until you develop your own style, you have to steal other people's style. **You have to copy what others are doing until you can get a feel for it yourself; it's like training wheels.** Training wheels are the best way I can think of to learn to ride a bicycle, because you get the feel of it

▼▼▼▼▼▼▼▼▼▼▼▼▼▼▼▼

Your ability to clearly get your message across to the prospect in the most powerful way is crucial to your success.

So memorize this principle: It's _not_ _what_ _you_ _say_ — _it's_ _what_ _you_ _convey_ that matters.

without falling, and then eventually the training wheels can come off. **Well, the training wheels that we have are all the great sales letters, promotions, products and services that other people are using.** Get on the other side of the cash register, and start looking for ways to steal an idea here and an idea there. **Now, you don't want to copy what somebody's doing exactly; that's plagiarism.** We've had people do it with us. Did we go after them? No, we didn't. We didn't want to spend years in court and waste our time; we're moving forward. We're willing to walk over a few hundred dollar bills as we move forward in the direction of our dreams. What do we care? **People who plagiarize aren't long-term players anyway.** You don't have to be afraid of them, because they have nothing within themselves that will allow them to become any type of threat to you. **So don't plagiarize, but model after ideas other people are using, and then find your own way to incorporate them and package it all together.**

There are shortcuts, simple secrets, and proven strategies that do give you leverage. Stealing a little from everybody is one of those things, and eventually you're just going to steal from yourself. See, that's the thing I want you to think about: you start off by studying the marketplace, looking for the people who are making the most money, finding out what they're doing, studying and identifying and quantifying those exact methods, benefits and the advantages they're offering, what's behind the basic pitches. **You have to look at it all from what I call the other side of the cash register, because if you're locked into this consumer mentality, you're never going to see it.** You almost have to think of yourself as a consultant, a consultant for yourself, and your job is to study all this stuff. So you're able to get into this mindset where you can start really identifying all this, and you'll see things; it does take a trained eye. Part of that trained eye is to not think like a consumer. _Think like an entrepreneur._

Once you see all this, once you study it, once you get a feel for it,

---

▼▼▼▼▼▼▼▼▼
MARKETING SECRET

True power is knowing your strengths and weaknesses.

- Don't lie to yourself about these two areas. Most people tend to overestimate their chances of success and underestimate their chances of failure. You must become stronger in the areas you are already strong — and delegate (not abdicate) your weakest areas.

then you start copying from the best people out there. You develop a lot of stuff, and you develop a sense of confidence, and you start making a lot of money. With that comes a feeling of confidence; your experience level starts increasing, your skills start developing, and after a while you'll have so much stuff that you've done that you'll wake up, like I did. I've lost years of my life, because I was so absorbed in my work, and so absorbed in creating all kinds of new products and services for the customers. I wake up and look in the mirror, and I'm ten years older. **What happened was, I created such an avalanche of different products and services that now I can just spend the rest of my life, if I want to, reusing ideas.** I'm striving to do that more and more, because why work harder if you don't have to? If you can get so much more done faster, you're a fool to spend a lot of time doing something you know you don't have to. I'm practicing what I preach here. **After a while, you're not really stealing from competitors anymore at all; you're just stealing from yourself.** You just continue to find a way to hone it down more and more, and boil it all down. Pretty soon you develop this confidence that comes from knowing exactly what your customers want, and you know exactly how to give it to them, and you can just keep taking the same themes, the same things that you've done over and over again, and find new ways to give it a new spin, a new look, a new feel. **There's always something new that you can incorporate; and then that becomes your new theme that you develop.**

People wonder how in the world you're able to get so much new stuff out there; but you'll know the secret. You'll know the trick of the trade here, which is Secret Number Fourteen. **You'll know that all you're doing is reworking your past sales letters, products and promotions; and if you do this, you can make a huge sum of money in the easiest way for the longest period of time.**

SECRET FIFTEEN:

Join a Coaching Program

The fifteenth secret that we used to make millions and millions of dollars is the **five years that we spent in a great coaching program, Dan Kennedy's Platinum Group.** This is something that changed my life forever, and I want to share some ideas with you here that I know can not only put millions of dollars in your pocket, but can also help you experience a lot more of the joy and satisfaction that can come from making money.

Dan Kennedy is a marketing genius. **He's brilliant when it comes to his ability to teach people the things that can turn small sums of money into a lifetime of huge sums of money.** He's dedicated, he's committed, he's passionate, he's knowledgeable — a very, very smart marketer. In 1995 or 1996, when we'd already been his customers for a few years, he invited us to join a new group that he was thinking of starting. He was putting a meeting together just to see how it would go, and of course a bunch of people showed up, and most of us ended up joining right then and there. It was called the Platinum Group, and it was a decision that changed my life. **Just the fact that Eileen and I said "Yes" to being a part of that group made us millions of dollars; and it taught us some things that I want to teach you right now.** Again, some of this stuff sounds like common sense, but it's not. There are so many people who never ever figure these things out, and I'm going to tell you why that is. I really believe I have the answer to this, because some of this isn't that difficult; but as Mark Twain said, **"common sense is a very uncommon thing."**

Now, here's how being a member of Dan Kennedy's Platinum Group changed my life forever. **First of all, it helped me become the marketer**

I am today. It sharpened my skills. I learned from all the other members. I became much more serious about marketing. I got some of my biggest wealth-making ideas for our company. Eileen and I sat in those meetings for five or six years. Many times, right during the meeting itself, I would come up with some revolutionary idea that I never would have had had we not been sitting there, had we not made the commitment. First of all, **it let us break away. Whenever you break away a little, it always helps you — to just get away from the day-to-day grind.** It's a good experience to do that on a regular basis. We met four times a year, mostly in Phoenix, but sometimes in Cleveland and a few other cities. It was just an amazing experience for me personally to meet and get to know other marketers who were doing big things in their business.

There's a synergy created when people get together to help each other, and you can never pour your heart into helping someone else without helping yourself. Eileen and I tried to contribute to this group; we tried to encourage the other members, and tried to help them in their quest to make more money and build their businesses. The meeting was pretty simple. Dan would have some things to teach us in the beginning, usually, for a couple of hours; and then, just taking turns, we'd get up and make a little presentation that we'd prepared to teach the other members the best ideas that we'd discovered since the last time they'd seen us, just a few months earlier. Sometimes we would volunteer, sometimes Dan would hand-pick us. Nobody wanted to be the first, sometimes, and sometimes everybody wanted to be the first, just to get it over with — because you're under some scrutiny. **You got up and you shared your best ideas, you told the other members what you were working on, and then they'd offer you suggestions, both positive and negative.** There was some positive criticism, and there was some teasing. The group spurred us on, we spurred each other on, we gave each other a hard time. We tried to encourage each other to learn and do more and be more, and use some different secrets that the rest of the members were already using to make huge sums of money.

A lot of entrepreneurs just don't want to be a member of a group, and I can't blame them. We tend to be extremely independent; one of the reasons why we become entrepreneurs is so we can do it our way. We don't want to be part of anybody's team. We want to boldly carve our own paths, do our own thing, create our own destinies. I understand that, and I think it's a great thing. **However, things happen when you're involved in a group of like-minded entrepreneurs,** people who are trying to build their businesses just like you are, people who have the same goals you have, who are trying to do big things, who are equally as committed to becoming the very best that they can be so they can achieve everything that they dream of achieving. **When you're around those kinds of people, they'll inspire you, they'll motivate you, they'll persuade you to do better and to step it up a notch or two.**

That's one of the greatest things we got out of the situation — though admittedly, **just to be candid with you, not everything was great.** That happens to me at seminars all the time. I try to go to a few seminars ever year where I meet other marketers who are on their way up. Some of these people have been doing this a lot less time than I have, as far as years go. I've been doing this since 1988 — I've been self-employed since 1985 — and I'll run into people who've been self-employed just a few years. They're in the same type of business we're in, they've only been doing it a short time, and yet they're making huge money. It makes me jealous and envious in a positive way. Whoever told you jealousy and envy are wrong — well, they were right, and they were wrong. There's a good form of jealousy, a good form of being envious. **You meet people who are on the same path you're on, doing big things, and they'll help you realize you can do more.** It's one of the best things about being part of this group and other groups I'm a part of right now, like my One Hundred Million Dollar Roundtable group.

The friendships that you develop from people who are doing the same things you are can be tremendous. **You'll get ideas you would never have developed on your own.** There are all kinds of subtle variations here, and there's plenty to learn. You'll deepen your knowledge, you'll get outside your box, you'll broaden your horizons. **There's a whole world out there, and the danger of being too absorbed in your own work is that you can become provincial in your thinking.** You start getting locked into a certain way of doing and thinking about everything, and you actually close your world off. **You've got to widen your view; you've got to meet new people and experience new things.** Too many people attracted to direct-response marketing are what I call "hiding out from the world." One of the reasons they're attracted to direct-response or Internet marketing is because they want to be left alone. They're stubborn, independent,

MARKETING SECRET

Testimonials sell!

- What you say about yourself is not nearly as important as what others say about you.

- "Any fact is better established by two, or three good testimonies than by a thousand arguments."
  — Emmons

egotistical, and want to do everything through e-mail. **They want to avoid a lot of the headaches and hassles that most business people have to go through, and that's one of the cool things about direct response.** It can be a perfect business in terms of the things that most business people have to do, because you don't have to do them. You don't have to meet with people, you don't have to go face-to-face with anybody, and you don't have to do any personal selling.

But what happens is, you become so addicted to this kind of business that you close yourself off from the rest of the world. You become socially retarded, difficult to work with. Other people around you are doing big things, and they're moving in big directions, and part of the reason they are is because they're affiliated with a group that's helping them do, become and have more. They get new opportunities they would have never been exposed to, new ideas they would have never thought of on their own. **This is one of the greatest secrets I have to teach you.** I understand what it is to be an entrepreneur: you want to do it all yourself. I understand how difficult it can be to be part of any group. Lots of entrepreneurs, including myself, can be anti-social. You spend hour after hour behind a computer screen, day in and day out. **You get absorbed in your work; and ironically, you lose some of the skills that are essential in helping you make money!**

Too many entrepreneurs are too independent; they're small-minded and paranoid. They're so worried about other people stealing their ideas that they don't want to share them. They're afraid of competition, they're afraid of opening themselves up to others, they're afraid of getting cheated or ripped off. **I just want to say that you** *do* **have to open yourself up.** Yes, you'll get lied to and cheated and misled; there are people out there who are total jerks. **That's one of the reasons why when we find good joint-venture partners, we stick with them.** We try to do everything we can to keep doing more and more business with the same good partners, because good partners are hard to find. Sometimes the only way to find them is to go through a bunch of bad partners.

I want to emphasize that being part of a group of like-minded entrepreneurs is a powerful experience. It can make you rich, you'll learn more, you'll sharpen those skills for making money and marketing, and you'll experience a deeper form of knowledge. **You see, there's a difference between just knowing something and really understanding it at a deep level.** When you're working with a group, you're sharing your ideas with them and they're sharing theirs with you; this will help you understand things at a core level most people never get to understand. It's hard to do that on your own; it's hard to pick all the stuff up in books. You'll discover new ideas; you'll find yourself going in new directions and into new areas you would have never gone into if you were just by yourself. **You'll find yourself wanting to do more.**

I've shared with you the good part about being jealous and envious. We can see all these other people out there, and they're just kicking butt. One of the benefits of being part of Dan Kennedy's group is that we were all supposed to be totally honest about the amount of money we were making; we were supposed to share numbers that normally you don't share with other people. Now, I'm sure some of the members did hold back; it's only natural. **We didn't. We were just out there, very vulnerable, and the group responded to that; people saw that in us and they liked us.** It was a good experience, and these are people that I respect. The helped me a lot at a very deep level.

Among them were people like Reed Hoisington, whom I'll never forget. My wife is a smoker, and at that time Reed was too, and so during meetings I would go out there to be with my wife while she was smoking her cigarettes, and there would be Reed. He's a seasoned veteran; he's got about ten years on me as far as business experience goes. He's already made millions, and he'd already made all the mistakes I was making at the time — **so he saved me from some future mistakes, and he helped**

shape my thinking a little. Some of the things he told me while we were outside helped me a great deal.

You know, there are so many people who have already gone where you want to go. They've solved all the problems you're trying to solve, all those things you just get so overwhelmed with. **They can help you out of those things; they can show you answers that you would never come up with on your own.** They can support you, they can guide you, they can help you shape your thinking. That's what the members of this group did. I had a great opportunity to get to know Joe Polish, Kendra Murphy, Bill Glazier, Rory Fatt, Ron LeGrand... the list just goes on and on. Man, it was just such a positive and powerful experience in my life — and I recommend that you get involved in something like this. Too many people are locked up in their own little world, and there's such a big world out there for them, with all kinds of newer and better ways to make money that are faster and easier than you can imagine. By opening yourself up to a group of like-minded people moving in the same direction that you're moving, folks who've got the same high goals that you have, you're going to find things that you would never, ever have found on your own. **You're going to discover shortcut secrets that they're using that will become your shortcut secrets.** You're going to deepen your commitment to your business, and deepen your commitment to the development of your marketing skills.

Now, if you look in the dictionary under the word "power," you'll that see it means the ability to act. **It's your capacity to take action.** When you're trying to do everything by yourself and you're locked into your own little world, totally absorbed in your own thing and not realizing that there's a wider world out there, not trying to connect with others who are also moving in the direction you're moving in — well, you actually limit your ability to solve problems. You limit your ability to latch onto new things and strengthen your skills, and you become limited. **One of the ways you get more power is by networking with other people.** One of the reasons I love going to seminars has nothing to do with the stuff they're teaching. Now, every once in a while, I'll pay very close attention to what a speaker at one of these seminars is saying, and I do take notes. Some sessions are more important to me; **but mostly what I'm doing is hanging out in the hallways, meeting people who are on their way up.** I love that more than anything else. I love the look in the eyes of a newcomer who's ambitious and excited about the business, because it helps me connect with that part of me that was the same, back when it was new and fresh. It's a great experience, because there's a chemistry here that we all have as people; **and if you get it right, you can have a lot of fun and you can make a lot of money.**

Of course, if you get it wrong, it ends up being a waste of time for you and everybody else. Other people had an opportunity to join Dan Kennedy's Platinum Group.

> **K**nowledge is <u>not</u> power. The *correct application* of knowledge is where all the power is.

Remember, Dan had the first meeting where a whole bunch of people showed up, and many of them joined the group — but some didn't. We had other members who came in and out; they were just in it for a year, and then they were gone. They thought they were too busy to be part of the group. They saw the group as something that would cost them money rather than *make* them money. Now, Eileen and I spent about $10,000 a year to belong to this group — it costs more now — and that included the travel expenses. We thought it was kind of pricey, at first. But at the same time, there was something inside us that told us it would be good for us, and it turned out we were right. **We made literally millions of dollars because of the new ideas and directions we got from our participation.**

Now, this is going to sound bad, but it's the truth, so I might as well tell. **As part of our commitment to the group, I was forced to sit there in those meetings for two or two and a half days.** Now, if you knew me, you'd know that I'm energetic. I can't sit down, I can't stand still, I've always got to be moving. I'm just that way; maybe I've got attention deficit disorder, I don't know. I just know that I constantly have to move, and I can't stand it when I'm standing still. Even when I'm writing copy, I'm walking around with legal pads; I write and walk at the same time. That's how I write some of my best sales letters.

Well, when you're part of something like the Platinum Group, you have to behave a certain way. During those meetings, while I was trying to be a good member and contribute to the group, I was forced to sit there and be still. It drove me crazy. I was always scribbling away on my legal pads, and I'm sure the other members of the group thought I was just taking notes. But here's what was really happening: **I was coming up**

In lead generation,
the more you tell —
the less you sell!

- Just give them
  enough
  information to get
  them interested
  and excited
  Make them an
  irresistible promise
  and get them to
  send for more
  information.

with all kinds of ideas for making money. Some of them produced millions and millions of dollars for us in a short time.

So find yourself a great group of people to hang around with — people who are trying to do big things, who can coach you and help you learn how to dream bigger yourself. Most of the folks you know aren't going for their dreams; they're not doing big things. They're coasting through life, asking for very little. They're the employees of the world, working only for money or security. Even if they're attracted to business, too often they just want to do little businesses in tiny markets. If you want to get rich, you need to find a better group of people than these to work with. You don't have to let all those other people go; they provide certain levels of support and guidance, **but you've *really* got to be around people doing big things with their lives**. You've got to meet with them, and get to know them over a long period — **and you *can* do this.** There's no excuse not to. There are plenty of seminars you can attend. **Once you get involved, you'll realize that there are lots of shortcuts these people can point out for you.** As a member of the right group, you really can learn more and sharpen your skills, and experience a deeper form of knowledge and create all kinds of new ideas that can help you make huge sums of money for the rest of your life. **As you do, you can experience the tremendous satisfaction and joy of getting to know other people — good people who are doing the things you want to do.**

SECRET SIXTEEN:

Concepts First and Details Last!

The sixteenth and final secret I have to share with you is very simple, like everything else I've shared so far — and yet it's very profound at the same time. I call it "Concepts First and Details Last." **You've got to think it bigger, and yet you have to see things as simpler than ever before.** You must develop a strong personal philosophy that keeps you moving forward at full speed, no matter what the obstacles are. **This philosophy, which is made up of your core beliefs, will help you achieve bigger results in less time.** Too many people get bogged down in the details. Concepts First, Details Last; don't even worry about how you're going to do things. Instead, spend your time thinking about the "why" to the thing; spend your time working on your goals and developing all the reasons why you want to make millions of dollars, and think about all the previous other wealth secrets I've shared with you in this book.

Much of what I've covered here is conceptual in nature. **You still have to figure out a way to do all these things, but the more you focus on the details, the more you're going to get bogged down** — the more you're going to become overwhelmed, frustrated, and confused. **If you keep going back to the reasons why all these things work, or the general nature of the basics of what we talked about, you're going to be fully empowered.** You develop your belief system, the things that help to guide you; and one of the things that I hope you've gained from all of this is an understanding that none of this is easy. There are people out there who want to totally mislead you when it comes to getting rich; they want to tell you that it's a snap. But they're liars — and surely there's a part of you that knows that you can't just make money that easily. **There's a price to pay for it.** Now, the point is that once you fall in love with the ideas I've shared with you on this program, and once you become passionate about marketing, once you become passionate about product-development work and all the things you do to attract and retain customers, *then* it **becomes fun or challenging.** It becomes interesting and exciting; it becomes a way of life, so you're willing to do more than the average person. **And when you are, that's when you're going to develop the skills necessary to make millions and millions of dollars.**

That's when it becomes more like a lifestyle or a hobby. Some of the things that are very difficult for you to learn will give you a tremendous sense of pride and satisfaction, once you learn them, like you can't even imagine right now — a feeling of confidence and power because you've mastered these things. People tend to place the largest value on the things we pay the biggest price to gain, and some of these skills can make you millions of dollars, just as they have for me. If everybody had these skills, then everybody would be making millions of dollars, wouldn't they? And if everybody was rich, why would *you* want to be rich? **Part of the attraction of getting rich is the fact that it's the trophy, the prize, the catch, the goal that we set out for; it's the way we keep score, the way that we rise above it all.** It's not just egotism. You can always look at your net worth and know how well you're doing, but what I've have done is kept journals over the years. I've thought through my own personal philosophy, my own concepts and my own beliefs — and I want to share with you some of the core ideas that have helped me achieve my success. I've got 39 powerful, core ideas that have served me and have helped me to be, do and have more of what I really want. **I'd like for you think about these 39 ideas, and maybe some of them can be part of your core philosophy as well.** These are part of my belief system and part of my guidance, the things that help keep me moving forward.

NUMBER 1: Go as far as you can see, and when you get there, you'll be able to see even farther. So many people are confused because they're trying to figure it all out too fast; they want all the answers *now*. They want to try to figure it all out before they get started. Forget that: go as far as you possibly can, take it as far as you can take it, and when you get there you'll be in a better place. You'll be more knowledgeable, you'll know more, and you'll be able to see even farther. So don't think that you have to have it all figured out; you don't. **You'll figure it out as you go.**

NUMBER 2: "He who flies the highest can see the farthest." That's what conceptual thinking is all about. When you're detail-oriented, you tend to see everything from the bottom up; you get bogged down in the minutia. When you think conceptually, you're thinking from the top down; you're able to see it bigger and think it simpler. **So set your goals very high, and see the simplicity in everything we've shared here.**

Making millions of dollars doesn't have to be that complicated when you stay focused on the basics, when you don't worry about how you're going to do everything. **When you set your goals high and keep it simple, that's the one thing that's going to separate you from all the other people who are working with you.** You're going to be able to see things from the top down and know just how simple all this is. So fly high, and always answer that question, "How high is high?" What are you really capable of doing; how far can you go? Set those high goals; don't be afraid to do that, and you'll see even further than most people.

NUMBER 3: You must develop the heart of the lion and the mind of the fox. For years now I've had a little fox and a little lion, and I keep them where I can see them at all times. I've thought a lot about that: the heart of the lion, the mind of the fox. The fox is a cunning animal, and you've got to be a bit like that in business; you're always on the edge, you're always aware, you're always looking around, you're always watching people's actions instead of just listening to what they say. You realize that people are self-centered by nature; the more you have, the more people want to get it. So you've got to be on guard; you really do. I've talked a lot here about working with other people; well, you've got to be careful too. **And then you've got to have the heart of the lion: the lion is bold and audacious, the king of the jungle — and it does take a little bit of audacity.**

One of my greatest stories is the story of Solo Flex. The guy who founded that company was a jet pilot who flew high rollers back and forth to Las Vegas, mostly to and from L.A. or San Francisco. Over a period of time, he got to know some of the regulars. They'd get up to the cruising altitude, he'd flip it over to automatic pilot, and he would go spend forty-five minutes or an hour talking with these people. They got to know each other well. So here he is, at age fifty or so, and he's making pretty good money; he has a six-figure income coming in, he's a chartered jet pilot, and one morning he just seized on this powerful question: "What makes these people any different than I am?" **The answer to the question was: audacity.** These people were just audacious; they were bold. That's it. They were no smarter than he was, they were no better looking than he was, they had no more special abilities or talents; **it was just audacity.** They each had the heart of the lion, and that's what some of this really does take. **You've got to suspend all of your fear and go for it.** Don't be afraid to fall, and just keep getting up every time you *do* fall.

NUMBER 4: In every business deal, always assume there's something, or a series of somethings, that the other party is holding back from you. You have to be careful — that's sort of like the mind of the fox. **Always be careful; always.** I've tried to hold nothing back from you in this book, but I promise you, in every deal you have to assume that there's something that they're not telling you. Just assume it, even if it's not true. It'll help you stand guard; it'll help you be very careful. Here's an example: once upon a time, Eileen and I needed the help of an attorney. I'll never forget this: he was asking us to sign this contract that would have made him many, many thousands of dollars, and he was trying to scare us a little. We were in trouble; we needed some fast answers, and he was, I remember, using high-pressure tactics on us. Eileen and I were in his office, and I recall watching him very carefully — and I saw a little bead of sweat start rolling down his face as he was waiting for us to sign this contract. I got up and left his office, and Eileen followed me; and we didn't sign the contract. Pretty soon, we drove off and we found another lawyer who turned out to be a great person who worked with us for a number of years. The other guy was trying to use a number of tactics on us, trying to manipulate us, trying to scare us. **Look, you've always got to watch people, watch them carefully.** Always think that they're holding something back from you; then you'll be on guard.

NUMBER 5: You've got to work on yourself as hard you work on your business.

MARKETING SECRET

Learning is a process — not an event!

- All skills must be learned.
  Education can be a slow and painful process. You can increase your knowledge through books and thinking. But there is no substitute for hands-on experience.

- You have to get out there and do it!

These ideas are simple, really. If you go back and reread this book, you'll see that there's nothing all that complicated about what I'm sharing, and yes, a lot of it's redundant. That's because a lot of these ideas are really simple by nature. **It's all about working through the fears and the insecurities, and all the false and limited beliefs that have held you back.** That's going to be the challenge; that's going to be the determinator of how you use these secrets, whether you go full force and use them to make millions of dollars, or whether you hold back. It's about dealing with yourself and it's setting higher goals; it's about working through your fears and insecurities; it's about deciding that you're going to go for it, even if you don't have it all figured out. **So work on yourself; write down a list of all of the things you're afraid of, all the things that have held you back up to now, and be completely honest with yourself.** There are plenty of good books out there that can help. One of the best books I can recommend was written in the late 1980s by Susan Jeffers; it's called *Feel the Fear and Do It Anyway*. I would encourage you to get that book. You've got to work on yourself constantly. If you're not making the kind of money you want to be making, then there's something that's stopping you; and until and unless you work on yourself, you're never going to figure it out.

NUMBER 6: **Work *on* your business, and not *in* it.** You've got to be the architect of your business; you have to be the general of the war. You can't be on the front lines. **I would advise you to find other people to manage your business, so you can focus all your time on all the things that are necessary to attract and retain customers.** Work on it, look at your business in a conceptual way, and you see the simplicity of it.

NUMBER 7: **See everything from the top down, and not the bottom up; that's what concepts are all about.** They let you see how simple everything is — and it really *is* simple. I've tried to share that with you throughout this entire book.

NUMBER 8: **Self-discipline leads to self-confidence.** You've got to force yourself to do the things that are necessary, that will make you the most money. **You have to force yourself to learn these new skills of being able to write copy, develop product, do things that make you a great marketer.** A lot of times it doesn't feel good, and even when you get good at it, you still have to force yourself to do it. You'll have moments when you're on fire, when you're so excited, when it's not work at all.

You'll have moments when it's fun, it's interesting, it's challenging, and the energy is there and you just want to do it all, and it's easy. Then you have other days when it's very, very difficult.

Remember: the professional does it when they don't feel like doing it. You don't just do it when you feel like doing it, you do it all the time. You discipline yourself, *force* yourself to work. I got up at 5:00 this morning and wrote copy until my hands hurt, finishing up a sales letter. Some days, it just comes flowing out of me; today it didn't. **Today I had to work at it.** I've been doing this for twenty years now and it's still work, although sometimes it's a great pleasure. **So, you've got to take the good and the bad, and the more you do to force yourself to do the things that you know are in your best interest, the better you're going to feel about yourself — and that does lead to self-confidence.**

NUMBER 9: This Jim Rohn quote became my mantra, and I want it to be yours: "Don't wish things were easier; wish that you were better." So many people want things to be easy. When life gets tough, they fantasize about an easy life. Jim says, "Look: just wish you were better, because if you were, you wouldn't be faced with such obstacles." That's one of the cool things about growing and developing, and it's one of the ways I can see true growth in myself. I meet entrepreneurs who are on the path I've been on for 20 years, and I see them struggling with things I used to struggle with. I see them going through problems I used to live with — but they're not problems for me anymore. I see them getting upset about things that used to destroy me; but those things don't bother me now, and I know it's because I've gotten better. I've practiced what I've preached, I've put in the hours, I've done the work, I've developed the skills. You've got to do it too. **Wish that you were better, because if you *were* better, you wouldn't have such problems.** You'd be able to solve some of the things you can't solve right now.

NUMBER 10: It's always better to have a valuable resource and not need it, than to need it and not have it. That's true with so many things. A valuable resource can be great people in your life, or it can be money in the bank; it could be products that you've got waiting in the wings, all kinds of promotions that you can rework. It can be certain things that you've learned. It's always better to have that resource and not need it, than to be in a position where you need something and don't have it. Just think about what that can mean for you, and think about what a resource is: something that offers you value.

NUMBER 11: All that glitters is not gold. That's one of my most important concepts. There are all kinds of distractions out there, all kinds of things you can get into, and there's lots of different kinds of glitter; **but you've got to think about what's most important all the time, and realize that some of that glitter is just fool's gold.**

NUMBER 12: A quote from Robert DeRopp, a great philosopher: "Seek above all else a game that's worth playing, and then play it as if your entire life and sanity depended on it, for it does." I think the greatest game on Earth is the game of business: the money acquisition game, learning all the things I've talked about in this book that have to do with developing product, attracting customers, separating yourself from every other competitor in your marketplace, continuing to do business over and over with the same clients, who continue to give you more and more money for larger profits every time. This is a great game, so play it like one!

NUMBER 13: One day at a time; let go, and let God; this too shall pass. Yeah, I've had to learn that. It's easy to get overwhelmed; but all you've got to do is just worry about today, and let tomorrow take care of itself. If you're putting everything you can into today, you're fine. Think of it as a brick wall, a solid brick wall that's your whole life, and each day is one of those bricks, and think about what you're doing with it. Most people are just heaping those bricks outside; their lives are directionless. They're going nowhere,

> ▼▼▼▼▼▼▼▼▼▼▼▼▼▼▼
>
> People spend so much of their money buying things they want, that they have <u>no</u> money <u>left</u> <u>over</u> for many of the things they really need!

they're achieving nothing, they're not doing anything big with their lives. They're taking that brick everyday and just throwing it onto some great big pile. **I want you to think about this: Don't worry about the future, take care of today, let the future take care of itself, and don't get overwhelmed.** There were things, back in the early-1990s, that used to cause me to almost have a heart attack. Here I was, in my late 20s, early 30s, and my chest was hurting and I'd get so angry — but now those things don't even bother me. **I've learned to let it go, and you've got to, too.**

▼▼▼▼▼▼▼▼▼
MARKETING SECRET

Keep your cash flow flowing!

- Keep your money in motion! Always moving! Always flowing back into the plans, systems, marketing, and promotions that sell the largest number of products/services to the largest number of people — for the largest profit!

That's one of the things I see in all these up-and-comers who are on the same path: I see them getting so bothered about things that used to bother me, and there's no need for that. **Just let it go.**

NUMBER 14: You must be willing to lose a few (or many) battles so you can win the war. You have to decide what war is to you, but be willing to lose a few battles; be quietly effective. Don't worry about fighting every battle; you're going to wear yourself out. **Just be willing to stay focused on your goals.** Nothing else means anything.

NUMBER 15: The "why" to do something is always more important than the "how." That's where concepts and goals come in: knowing why you want to make millions of dollars. I *know* you want to make millions; only a fool would invest in this book if they didn't. You've got to ask yourself why. **You'll figure out the "how to do it" if the "why to do it" is big enough.**

NUMBER 16: "Selling is serving" — that's a Ray Kroc quote. Well, a lot of people don't want to be salespeople. Salespeople have a bad rep. A salesperson is somebody who's offering something that's worth so much value that the money they're asking for in exchange should pale by comparison. **Their whole focus is on serving, whatever serving means to your marketplace;** focus on that. That's what selling really is.

NUMBER 17: A successful life is a series of successful days. Take care of today and tomorrow will take care of itself. Everybody's worried about the future; **well, you don't have**

to be, as long as you're taking care of every single day, right here and now.

NUMBER 18: You've got to be willing to do what nobody else wants to do. You see, a lot of this is difficult, in the beginning especially, and that's not popular. If you want to go out there and buy some, well, there are magic programs where people are trying to tell you how simple and easy it is. And it *is* simple; that's part of what this last principle I'm sharing with you is all about. **You've got to *keep* it simple. But you also have to be very disciplined;** you have to be willing to put in the time, put in the work, put in the effort, and you've got to be willing to do the things most people aren't going to do.

NUMBER 19: Keep your eyes on the stars, and always let your reach exceed your grasp. You've always got to be pushing for more to answer the questions, "How high is high?" and "What are you really capable of?" Set your goals high; keep dreaming big dreams. **When you keep your eyes on the stars, you're willing to endure the problems and challenges that stop some people.** There are going to be speed bumps on your road, so keep dreaming those big dreams. Don't be afraid to do that.

NUMBER 20: Don't drive down the road with one foot on the gas pedal and the other on the brake. Too many people are trying to be so cautious all the time that they're afraid to drive. Look, race car drivers will tell you that the secret is to just stay totally focused on the road ahead. That's it; that's all you've got to do. **Keep your eyes right on the road, and just go for it.** Just drive; don't hold back.

NUMBER 21: The things you tell yourself about yourself are the most important things. You're better and stronger than you think you are. Keep telling yourself good things about yourself. **Don't listen to your inner critic; don't listen to the exterior critics in your life.** Write down all the things you're the best at, that you're strong in; and that goes back to what we talked about in Number 5. **Work on yourself as hard as you work on your business.** Be your own best friend. Life is too short to go through it by second-guessing yourself, criticizing yourself and tearing yourself down.

NUMBER 22: Business is a combination of art, science, sport, politics, and war. Think about those concepts. It's creative, it's artistic;

it's also scientific. There are principles at work here, and I've tried to share them with you in this book. **These are the same principles that have made us millions of dollars.** It's also a sport, and there are ways of keeping score. It's somewhat political; sometimes you can't always be direct with people. It's like war too; it's a battle. Try to keep that in your mind all the time. It's not just about making money. **You noticed I didn't use the word "money" in there at all.** It's art, science, sports, politics, and war; those are the concepts to keep you moving forward.

NUMBER 23: Marketing is like chess. The masters of marketing are always thinking three steps ahead at all times. Remember, chess is pretty simple; there are only six basic pieces, and a few basic moves for you to learn. Once you have those moves down, that's it. Marketing is like that too.

NUMBER 24: Making money is the greatest game on Earth. Play it, and keep playing it. It's not just something you do for the money, it's something you do for joy and satisfaction; it'll fill your life up. You'll keep wanting to go for bigger and better things; you'll keep trying to improve yourself and your game. **You won't just make money so you can sit on your butt and do nothing.** There will be no such thing as retirement to you. There may be semi-retirement, but your business will be about things that you truly enjoy. It's your passion; it's your skill set. It's the greatest game on Earth; play it, have some fun. Remember what DeRopp said: "Seek above all else a game worth playing and then play it as if your entire life and sanity depended up on it, for it truly does."

NUMBER 25: "Fear destroys more people than any other one thing." The brilliant Ralph Waldo Emerson said that. If you really knew you could handle anything and everything that happens to you, what would there be to fear? Absolutely nothing. We're only afraid because there's something inside us that doesn't believe we can handle it. **Well, I'm telling you — you *can* handle it. You handle it one day at a time, one brick at a time.** You handle it by continuing to go as far as you can see; and then when you get there, you'll see further. You don't need to take it all in at once. Remember that fear is the enemy; you've got to conquer it.

NUMBER 26: This is the thing I say to myself a lot of mornings — like today, when I didn't want to get out of bed. It's a Shakespeare quote: **"To thine own self be true."** You've got to be true to yourself, true to your goals, what you're trying to accomplish in life. **Keep moving forward, in spite of whether you want to or not; just keep doing it.**

NUMBER 27: In everything that you do, think it bigger and see it simpler. That's what Concepts First and Details Last is all about. Everybody else is getting bogged down in details; everybody else is focused on all of the little complexities involved in every major project. You can't do it. You've got to think bigger and see it simpler.

NUMBER 28: "You can have everything in life you want, if you'll only help enough people get what *they* want." This is a Zig Ziglar quote. And notice I said "want," not "need." There's a big difference here. You're helping people get what they want. Well, sometimes, what people want and what they need are two different things. That's one of the underlying principles I want to share with you here. It's all about serving. That's where this whole "selling is serving" idea comes from. **You're giving people what they want; you're serving them, and if you do that for enough people, you're going to get rich.**

NUMBER 29: Keep giving your customers more of what they bought from you the first time. You've seen me say that throughout this book. It's all about variations on a theme. What do people want? More of what they bought from you the first time.

NUMBER 30: Find just a few people you can really trust, who are super-talented in the areas you're weak in, and do everything you can to keep those people on your team. Grab them tight, give them whatever they want, love them, take good care of them, don't let go of them. These people are the most important people in your life and your business.

NUMBER 31: Express yourself fully. Don't hold back. If there's one thing you can say about me with this book, and the audio program it's based on, it's that **I've just tried to be myself.** I haven't tried to show off. I'm not a professional speaker or writer. I am what I am. Too many people are playing games; they're trying to be perfect, they're trying to be too polished, and they're not being real — and everybody knows that. **Whether you like me or not, at least you know I've been real with you.** I've been sharing things from my heart; hopefully you'll at least respect me for that. I want you to do the same thing, when it comes to everything that you do in your life. Just be yourself and express yourself fully, and

▼▼▼▼▼▼▼▼

MARKETING SECRET

Your highest priority is to spend your time on the activities that stand the greatest chance of making you the most money.

- You must determine which activities are high priority and which are low priority.

- Then spend most of your time focusing on the highest priority activities.

don't hold back. It's the people in this world who really don't give a damn about what anybody else thinks of them that we end up respecting the most. It's the people who are trying to be perfect and polished, who are trying to go through their whole lives pleasing everybody else, who end up getting no respect. **I just want you to just take off all the filters; that's what I've tried to do with this book.** Express yourself fully.

NUMBER 32: Everything is difficult until it becomes easy. You've got to be willing and even eager to pay the biggest price possible for the things that you want the most. We always value what we pay the most for — and the skills that it takes to make millions of dollars, like product development, copywriting, good marketing skills, everything I've shared with you that has been responsible for the millions of dollars we've made, has come with a price. You'll pay that price and you'll feel good about it. **It *will* get easier, but you've got to be willing to pay the price and understand that there's a learning curve involved.** I love what Ray Bradbury says: He says that to be a good writer is real simple. What you have to do is write 20,000 pages, and by the time you write those 20,000 pages, you'll have put in the time and work necessary for your writing to be where it needs to be. After you get past those 20,000 pages, you're a good writer. I love that quote, because it expresses what I've been trying to share with you. It's no accident that the greatest direct-response marketing copy writers, the ones who write sales letters that generate millions of dollars, are usually those who have been doing it for at least ten years, and quite possibly twenty years or more. **Experience is important; there's only one way you can get it, though. You've**

got to pay the price and get started today.

NUMBER 33: Fall in love with the few things that make you the most money: product development, marketing, and copy writing. Fall in love with doing those things. They're challenging, fun, rewarding — and the more you love them, the more you're going to get lost in them; and the more your skills are going to develop along with your knowledge and experience. **You'll gain tremendous confidence.**

NUMBER 34: At any given time you've got to know what the five most important things are in your life. I've got a list right here in front of me; and it's my five things. I know what they all are, and when I read that list I can see if I am on target, if I'm moving in the right direction. It helps you to stay focused.

NUMBER 35: Stay hungry. Remember where you came from, where you are now, and where you want to go. Never lose that desire. I'm just going to assume that you're hungry; you've invested in this book because you got a hunger inside you. It's a good assumption on my part, I think, and I want you to keep that hunger. Sometimes you'll get the success that you've longed for, and you start coasting. You can't do it; stay hungry. That's where playing it as a game helps.

NUMBER 36: Get really good at a few things that make you the most money, then delegate everything else. That's related to Number 33. Just stay totally focused on just those few things that make you the most money. Let everything else go. **Find other people you can work through who have skills that can help you fill in all the other gaps.**

NUMBER 37: Direct response marketing is math and psychology; that's all. You've got to really understand people — that's the psychology — and then, with every promotion, you need to understand the money math. It's really easy to do.

NUMBER 38: Business is an accelerated lifestyle. You get more of the good and more of the bad. For me, it's been a major roller coaster ride. I've experienced so many wonderful things in business, and it's challenging; it really is. **But it's also rewarding and exciting and depressing, and there are things that will break your heart.** There are problems and obstacles and difficulties, and it's the best of everything that life has to offer. You get more of everything; you get more of the good, you get more of the bad. It's a wonderful way to live, but keep that in mind; it's an accelerated lifestyle. That will help you deal with some of the pressures you have to deal with.

NUMBER 39: Money and material things are great, but true confidence doesn't come from having things; it comes from handling things. I've got to say that to you one more time. The reason you've invested in this book is because you want to make money. That was me, too; I wanted to become a multimillionaire, and that's all I cared about in the beginning. But money and material things... well, they're great. Enjoy them; they're your trophies, and the more you work hard for them, the more you can appreciate them. **That's why it's good to pay the price you need to pay.** You hear about people who win the lottery; their whole lives are destroyed, because they're not prepared for the wealth. But once you've paid the price for it, you'll really feel good about it. **You'll know you deserve it because you worked your ass off for it.** But true confidence, and true happiness also, doesn't come from having things; **it comes from your ability to handle things.** That's a good place to wrap this book up, one related to the ninth concept I shared. That's the Jim Rohn quote that says, "Don't wish things were easier, wish that you were better."

A lot of people want to make a fortune because they're looking for a perfect life. They've got this image in their heads that they're going to make millions of dollars, and then they're just going to kick back on some sandy beach, somewhere exotic, and everything's going to be perfect. **Well, I have my fantasies too, but at least I know that they're fantasies.** I want *you* to know that they're fantasies, too. Look, the greatest thing about business and reaching all of your goals is just what Jim Rohn suggested: **it's who you become in the process.** Life here is limited. All of our lives, we don't know how much longer we have here. This could be your last day; you could have another decade; you could have another five decades. It's who we become in life, through the process of working towards our goals, that's the most important thing, and having confidence means that you're facing all the adversity that comes your way, all the challenges. **You're taking charge of your life, you're willing to do the things most people are unwilling to do.**

You can make a lot of money, sure, and that's great. But true confidence comes from your knowing, just that knowing, that you have the ability to handle anything that comes your way. **Fear is a real enemy of success,** but if you knew you could handle anything and everything that comes your way, there would be no fear. I've dealt with a lot of fear and a lot of insecurities; I've had a lot of challenges in my life, and I've tried to share them with you in a very open and honest way throughout this book.

The greatest feeling is *not* just having millions of dollars, it's knowing that you overcame all that crap that was in your way. You've developed some real skills and abilities, and you've tried to focus on serving people and helping people. **In order to get your money, you've tried to offer tremendous value to other people, and that's a great, great feeling, especially when those people will use your ideas, your help and support and guidance, to do big things with their lives.**

There's no better feeling.

▼▼▼▼▼▼▼▼▼▼▼▼▼▼▼▼

B esides money... what's the #1 thing that wealthy people have over others? STAYING POWER! People with money can wait! They can say "No!" to all kinds of deals. They are never desperate. They can ride out all kinds of storms that destroy or limit others. They have many different choices that can all lead to making even more money!

In short, they have real power! At least from a business standpoint. If you enjoy business — then money can definitely lead to more happiness!

SECTION TWO:

SECRETS OF THE BLUE JEANS MILLIONAIRE...

AND HOW YOU CAN USE THEM TO GET SUPER RICH!

14 Wealth-Making Secrets That Can Make You A Multi-Millionaire In <u>No</u> <u>Time</u> <u>Flat</u>!

SECRET ONE:

The best way to get someone to give you $3,000 is to get them to give you $300 first.

This marketing secret is oriented toward the fact that it's very difficult to ask a new customer for $3,000 — or in some cases, even $300 — right off the bat. The way to build your relationship and trust with them is to sell them a low-cost offer on the front-end, with your very first sale. You do that by selling something for $30, or $40, or $50.

As long as it's a low-entry price, this will work well — especially if you under-promise and you over-deliver. The reason you do that is because you don't really care about the profits on the front-end. **You're not going to get rich with your front-end sales profits, and anyone who believes otherwise is doomed to failure.** Ultimately, the purpose of that front-end sale is to build a strong relationship that will lead to lots more sales. Your customers really have to take a leap, that first time, even when there's a very low-end product involved. When they get that product and it's more than what they expected — and they believe it's worth ten times what they paid for it — you've started that relationship in the strongest possible way, you've locked it in, and now they're ready to go with you to the next step and purchase that $300 product, or that $3,000 product.

Here's an example of this principal in action. If you watch infomercials (and as a student of marketing, you definitely should), you'll see that almost all the products advertised are very low-end items. For example, there's one marketer I know who sells a product on TV for about $40. When I asked him about how much money he was making selling that product, he said, "I don't make any money on it. In fact, I lose millions of dollars every single month selling that product. The infomercial alone costs hundreds of thousands of dollars to create." But, he said, "I don't sell that product to make money. I sell that product to get the people in, to qualify them, to build that relationship, and then I have my people on the telephone sell them a $2,000 product, then a $4,000 product, and then a

---

The purpose of a business is to find and keep customers.

- You must do all kinds of things to get them to come and keep coming to you, instead of your competitors.

- What is your competitive advantage?

$7,000 product! That way, **I don't have a problem losing millions of dollars on the front-end because I'm building up my customer base, I'm building those relationships, and I'm making $10 million to $30 million on the back-end."**

That idea of getting the people in, building the relationship with a low-cost front-end product, and then making your big profits on the back-end with higher-end products is a perfect strategy. "First you must win their trust, and then you win their money." The infomercial example is a powerful way of illustrating that. **You may not know this, but many marketers lose money on the front-end. All of their profits are made on the back-end.** A lot of marketers don't understand this at the beginning. One of my friends is a good example. When he was starting out, he once saw a full-page ad in a magazine that sold a $10 book. He said to himself, "I can write better copy than that! I'll put out my own ad." What he didn't know was that money wasn't being made at the front-end with that $10 book.

But that's how you have to start out in building that buyer-seller relationship. <u>Look</u> <u>at</u> <u>it</u> <u>in</u> <u>terms</u> <u>of</u> <u>a</u> <u>romantic</u> <u>situation</u>. When you invite someone to dinner, what you're really doing is hoping to form a relationship, so you might eventually invite them to your apartment. You can't say, right away, "Why don't you come to my apartment?" You might get a few takers, but not many!

SECRET TWO:

Never forget that Direct-Response Marketing is supposed to be a personal medium.

You may be writing to ten thousand people, or even a million, but you've got to do it on a one-to-one basis. This is easy to do in Direct-Mail because the number one reason Direct-Mail is so popular, even in this Internet age, is that it's a medium based on one-to-one communication. **You're addressing your customer directly, appealing precisely to their needs.**

But that's not all. Never forget that you can also get personal with print advertising and on the Internet, especially if you target a niche market, and if the people who get your communication believe you are offering them something they really want and need. In other words, it's a personal message: you understand their hopes, their fears, their desires, and then you can be communicating personally. You must "get inside the gray mush." By that I mean the mind of the person who you're aiming your communication toward.

Always remember that a customer is wrapped up in his or her own self-interest. This is a basic part of being human, so you can't blame them. **Your customers want to know the answer to WIIFM: What's In It For Me? They don't give a damn about your company or how much money you want to make.** They want to know how much money *they* can make, how much younger *they* can look, how much money *they* can save, or a thousand and one other reasons why *they* should do business with you. So if you're going to get their hard-earned money, you must come to them with a personal message that touches their heart. **Much more money is made by going after the emotions of an individual than by going after their intellect.** Get personal whenever you can!

When my mentor Russ Von Hoelscher started in this business more than 30 years ago and didn't have many customers, he used to write little personal messages to his customers along with his sales letters. Sure, it took time to write a little memo to them: *"Dear Jack, I want you to know this program really works. If you give it a try, you risk nothing with our money-back guarantee. Sincerely yours, Russ von Hoelscher."* But you know what? This worked like magic!

Of course, when you're sending out 50,000 sales letters you can't do that. But when you're first starting in this business, you can — and you should. Even if you're sending out 50,000 letters, get personal with people. **This is such an impersonal world that people are absolutely hit over the head by personal messages, and they'll respond to messages from people who they believe really understand them, who know what's inside them, and who know what their deep desires are.** To get rich, get personal!

Empathy is one of the most important aspects of any marketing campaign. You must show people that you care about them and that you feel their pain, so they can identify with you. At that point, you have the foundation for the sale. Plus, they want to always feel that they're doing business with people who are just like them, people who think like them and have the same views, outlooks, and convictions as they do. Don't be afraid to get very personal and talk about exactly what your product or service will do for them, and what it's done for you. Tell people, *"Even though we haven't met, chances are we're very much alike."*

This may all sound easy, but in reality, it's harder than it sounds. When writing copy, **it's easy to fall into the trap of talking to your customers as a *group*, rather than individuals.** This happens to us all sometimes. You have to watch your pronouns, or you'll be writing a sales letter and find that you're using terms like "people like you" or "people in your position," which is *not* what you want to do. When you do that, you've lost your focus. You have to go back through your sales letters and focus on the fact that you're talking to one person, and you need to use the proper pronouns to indicate that.

My friend Jeff Gardner has told me about one technique that's helped him quite a bit, and one that you can use if you're getting into copywriting. In any market where he's promoting a product, **Jeff tries to get a visual** idea of *one* person in that market who represents that whole market. He may even give them a name: Frank, Mary, or something like that. He visualizes their wants, their desires, and even what they look like, where they live, and what type of car they drive. Then, as he sits down to write the sales letter, he'll actually address it to them: "Dear Frank…" And then he tries to sell to just Frank or Mary, not the whole market for that particular product. Of course, after he's done he'll take out "Dear Frank" or "Dear Mary" and put in "Dear Friend" to make it more general. But by writing it to that one person it makes it a lot easier to focus on selling one-to-one, versus falling into the trap of trying to sell to the whole market. **If you do that, then you've distinguished yourself from the vast majority of people who haven't gotten that precision, and who aren't being personal.** By using that one little mental idea that you were able to hold onto, you've given yourself a tremendous advantage.

SECRET THREE:

Selling is finding out what people want, and then letting them have it.

When people start thinking about what they want to sell, or they realize they want to get in business and make money, they tend to start by coming up with an idea for a product or a service — and then they try to find a market of people who want that product or service. But starting with a product or service is the wrong way to go about it: in fact, it's exactly backwards. **You have to start by finding a market, and then flip it around and find a service that that market wants.** Even then, even if you think you've found a market or you *know* there's a market out there for your product or service, that market may be too small. You may not be able to make any long-term profits off that market. Since long-term profits are your goal, the way to achieve them is to find a large, starving market with a large amount of discretionary income. The bigger the market, the more money you can make with that product or service. Let's put it more plainly: **to do well in marketing, no matter the product, you have to**

If you want to go where you've never gone before — you must take a different road!

- "If you always think the way you've always thought — you're always going to get what you've always got!"
  — *Ron McFadden*

- "Most people who say they have 20 years of experience are lying. They really have one year of experience, repeated for the last 19 years."
  — *Jim Rohn,*
  Paraphrased

---

find out <u>exactly</u> what people (or more specifically, a group of people) really want, and then let them have it.

The opportunity market is a perfect example. There are millions of people who want to stay home and make more money. Same with the diet market: millions want to lose weight. In the sweepstakes market, there are millions who want to win prizes and money. I could go on and on, but I think you get the point — your best bet is to <u>start</u> <u>with</u> <u>a</u> <u>group</u> <u>of</u> <u>people</u> <u>with</u> <u>a</u> <u>common</u> <u>bond</u> <u>or</u> <u>interest</u>, and work your product backwards from there to cater to that market. That's not being cynical, that's reality.

Because I'm in the opportunity market and it's something I'm familiar with and study a lot, that's what I'm going to focus on here. Like I said earlier, there are millions of people who want to make money from home. They're not lazy: they just want to work for themselves. They've tried working for "the man," and know there's no future in it. That market wants useful, proven information products they can use to prosper and earn a living. When you start by focusing on that market, you can find something in particular they're looking for and develop products and services to match what they want.

Speaking of wanting, I want to make one brief distinction between what people want and what people need. Usually they're different: sometimes the two can go hand-in-hand, but often they don't. **So don't focus on developing products and services that the market *needs* — instead, spend your time developing products that the market *wants*, and more likely than not you'll have a lot easier time making money.** That's where the real money is.

People often spend twice as much money on something they *want* than on something they *need*.

A "want" is an unfulfilled desire. That unfulfilled desire creates the vacuum for the product or service you want to sell. It helps to visualize the situation, as my friend and colleague Jeff Gardner likes to point out. Let's say you have a group of people out in the middle of the Sahara Desert, and they've been out there for days and days. They're all sweating to death, and they don't have any water. Ultimately, they all know they're going to die — and the only thing they really have in their pockets is cash. Say you come along with one canteen of water. How many people are going to pony-up money because they want that water? You may say, "Okay, they *need* that water," and if you're any kind of human being you'll give it to them for free.

That was kind of an extreme example — very few wants are life-or-death needs. But here's how you have to look at it: **there are markets of people who are just as thirsty for products they want as for those people in the Sahara Desert would be for a glass of water.** If you go out there and you find the markets with that kind of a drive and a passion for something that they want — something they crave and have an unfulfilled desire for — you don't have to worry about coming up with product ideas because the market will tell you what they want, and what they're willing to pay for it. It's a very simple system, but it is making many people super rich! It's not about going out and trying to find products and develop products, but finding that key want or need, and then to find a way to fill it.

A friend of mine says something that's a little controversial, but it illustrates his point well: **he says he wants to sell donuts to fat people. He wants to sell heroin to drug addicts. He wants to sell porno to sex fiends.** Sure, these examples are metaphorical, he's not going to do anything illegal or immoral to make money by preying on people's addictions, and he's not suggesting that you do so, but you should look for markets with that kind of hunger. Find the people who are already hungry, who just can't wait to give you the money for what they want or need. He's also saying to make it simple on yourself. Go where the market is — don't try to create one where it isn't. Don't try to sell heroin to people as they're coming out of the church, go down to the seedy sides of town.

In short, my friend is saying that you should find the market first, and then serve it. That's important because **too many people fall in love with a product or service,** and they want to try to sell it to everyone, the market be damned. But let me make this point again: *you must find the market first and then serve the market.* Some of the best Direct-Mail millionaires I know based their products on existing products that they or someone else were *already* selling. Let's say they find a certain book that sold 75,000 copies by Direct-Mail; they study that book and write a manual or book or CD that's is similar to that, and they sell their version. People are insatiable! If a person is a horseracing fan, they're going to buy more than one or two gambling books on horse racing. If they want to make money, they keep buying moneymaking products. To use the porno illustration: the person who has two or three porno magazines or videos is the best candidate to buy a hundred more. It's a very sound marketing principle that can make you huge, never-ending profits!

SECRET FOUR:

"As long as it sounds good..."

One of the things we have to do as marketers is make things sound good. You have to make big, bold, dramatic promises to the prospective buyer. One of the things that Dan Kennedy taught me that I think relates very closely to this is the principle of selling people what they want, but then giving them what they *need*.

Let's look more closely at the principle of selling people what they want. Earlier, I discussed how, in the opportunity market, people want to make money. What they really want to do is to make money *without having to do a damned thing*. What people really want in the weight loss market is not just to lose weight, but to lose weight *without doing a damned thing*. That's why they flock to magic pills and other quick cures. **People want things that are simple, easy, fast, quick; they're looking for instant solutions.** Hey, I didn't create it that way! It's not my fault that this is what people want. And it's what they want.

Whatever you sell, you must make it *sound* good. Certainly, you have to be legal, and certainly you want to keep your customers satisfied because the first sale sets up the second sale. But **you have to make your product sound like the greatest thing since sliced bread, without going over the top** — and sometimes, it's really difficult to know if your claims are over the top. Sometimes you think something's really over the top, but the market doesn't perceive it that way. So how do you really know if you're making it too unbelievable?

▼▼▼▼▼▼▼▼▼▼▼▼

Selling money at a discount.

You are in the business of selling dollars for dimes — don't forget that!

There's a fine line between making your product sound good, and making it sound too good to be true. Don't go over the top, but you really do have to make it sound good, so it's very desirable and appeals to people's emotions. **It also has to appeal to the laziness that most prospects have;** this sounds cynical, sure, but the fact is that you're asking people to do a lot. Not only are you asking them to give up their hard-earned money, but you're also asking them to make a phone call or send a fax. You're asking them to respond to your ad in particular, when there are another dozen ads right there in front of their face that are *also* asking them to send their money. You have a lot of competition out there for the customers' money, and so it really is important to do what this principle suggests and really make it sound good.

One way to make it sound good is to make it sound simple. You can get bogged down in the details if you're not careful, **but an offer that's highly attractive and sounds good is invariably something that sounds simple. You take this pill and sleep, and you lose weight. Or you buy this product and it accomplishes "x" without you having to do anything.** Like I said before, most people want the benefit with the least expenditure of effort. So if you make it sound simple to accomplish, it always sounds good. Some of the most powerful offers are the simplest offers.

A marketer I know once told me, *"If you can't explain your offer and make it sound as great as possible in one minute or less, you need to go back to the drawing board."* Look at any of the great, successful offers out there — like those TV infomercials where they're selling real estate programs. If you closely look at it, sure, there are a lot of details. But the basic offer is simple: you can get rich buying and selling real estate, and we'll show you how. As long as it sounds good, **that can lead you into**

MARKETING SECRET

Creativity is dirty. It's a constant never-ending flux of activity. It's having the courage to move ahead and face the fear and uncertainty... It's the never-ending challenge of having enough courage to get started and commit to working on projects that you have no real idea (or only a hazy one) of how you are ever going to complete!

- These are the things that scare 99% of other people to death!

making an irresistible offer, where you just keep piling stuff on. Remember those old Ginsu commercials? "You get this great knife and also you get this paring knife and you get this scaling knife and, hey, we're also going to give you this free car!" They just throw everything in so at the end you go, **"Oh, my goodness! They only want $19.95? That's incredible! It's irresistible! That sounds so good I've got to get in on it!"** This is called **"the pile-on technique."** You stack up so much stuff, that in comparison to the amount of money you're asking for, the money seems inconsequential.

There are other techniques that will help your product sound good. Easy-to-read bullets that outline the advantages of your product are very effective. So are bonuses. **My friends and I sometimes buy information products — newsletters, for example — just because they offer five, or seven, or ten free bonuses.** Those free bonuses might be four-page reports that cost you a dime apiece to produce, but if the subject matter rings a bell in a potential customer's head, it might get them to subscribe to a newsletter that they would ordinarily have ignored. But you have to be careful with those bonuses! Marketer Ted Nicholas used to have a warning about freebies that I thought was especially cogent, since so many people will take things that didn't sell and add them as bonuses. He used to say, "That's always a mistake. **You want your bonuses to be so attractive and sound so valuable that people are willing to buy the product just because they want the bonuses."** So never, never add a bonus just so you can throw in things that didn't sell. That's shooting yourself in the foot, plain and simple.

SECRET FIVE:

Write down your best ideas when they're new, when you're first getting started and are very excited, because these ideas are hot — and you'll need them later when you're cold.

Ideas are like slippery fish. They're hard to hold onto, so you have to capture them and write them down. I know how true this really is because for much of my life, I've made my living by selling ideas. First, you have to know that ideas aren't flashes of inspiration that some folks have and some don't. **Ideas are inspiration that comes from perspiration. That's why most people never have a good idea a year: they don't work at it.** I can't tell you how many times people have said to me, *"You have so many creative ideas. I just don't think that way."* Well, they're partly right. They have the right tools and they're just as creative, but *they don't use them.* They operate under the mistaken assumption that ideas just come to you, which isn't true; <u>ideas don't come except as a result of effort. You need to *work* for them</u>! It may not appear that way sometimes, especially when you see someone come up with an idea instantly, right before your eyes. But I can absolutely assure you that that idea bloomed because of the work and studying they had previously done, or because of the time they'd previously spent thinking about a similar issue. It's more of a style of thinking than anything else.

If you say, "I never have any good ideas," then I can guarantee you that it's because you haven't tried hard enough. You've never just put yourself down at a desk or table and done the background reading on the appropriate subject, and then spent time trying to come up with ideas until you found one that worked. **For every great idea that works, there are**

---

dozens of bad ideas that have to be rejected. We tend to forget about all the bad ideas; that's reality. That's a part of the whole process. In any idea session, you want to <u>come up with as many potential ideas as possible, because most are going to be bad</u>. But you know what? It gets better with practice. The fewer times you sit down and do this, the more bad ideas you're going to have. In other words, **with practice, you're going to get a higher percentage of good ideas.** Your cerebral batting average will go up.

Frankly, <u>ideas are like photography</u>. Amateurs take a couple of pictures — maybe a roll — and then they compare their work to that of a professional photographer in a magazine. I don't know about your photos, but mine often have the red eyes, and they just don't compare favorably at all. In college, my friend Don Bice had an occasion to be on a project that was photographed by LIFE magazine. The photographer shot hour after hour, while his assistant changed the film. They went through more than 100 rolls of film that day. **They shot from every angle, bracketed every exposure, and they took a ton of pictures! They wanted to get the best picture possible. Out of all of those they took, the magazine ran one photograph, but it was an excellent one.** That's all you need when taking photos — the one that's a winner! It's the same thing with ideas. You go through a ton of them so you can find the one that's a winner.

Some people like to look at it as panning for gold — you end up with a lot of pebbles, and only a few are nuggets you can use. This is the point you should focus on: **you have to sift and sort through a lot of dirt and rocks and clutter and gravel before you find those gold nuggets.** I believe the one reason that people never find those gold nugget ideas is because they try to sit down and set their minds on finding that one, single million-dollar idea. They don't accumulate hundreds of ideas and then sift and sort to find that million-dollar idea. Heck, maybe it's not even there — maybe there are five or ten $100,000 ideas. You've got to be able to recognize them and keep them.

You shouldn't always be trying to get the home run all the time — in other words, don't go after that million-dollar idea to the detriment of all other ideas that might occur to you. Focus on just getting hits and getting on base — because **no matter how many ideas you have, you can never tell which ones are going to be home runs and grand slams! You can only discover that as you introduce them into the**

marketplace. As the market embraces the ideas, they're the ones to tell you whether your idea's going to be a grounder or a home run or whatever. You just focus on getting good solid hits — you don't always try to hit over the fence all the time. It's a numbers game. The more ideas you have, the more potential gold nuggets you have. You go for quantity, as many ideas as you can — good and bad.

Inspiration can strike anywhere, not just in a brainstorming session. I don't know many good marketers who don't always carry a notepad everywhere they go, so they can write ideas down. You can come up with ideas at 3 o'clock in the morning when you wake up to go to the bathroom, or when you're in line at Starbuck's, or when you're driving down the highway. When you do, **you write it down. Keep a log, and go back and evaluate what you've written later.** That's where the breakthroughs come: when you're looking at the material you've already written and then you go, "Oh, yes, *that's* an idea I can use!" Sometimes you'll be able to fit two or more ideas together into a profitable whole. Or you'll be working on something totally different, and you'll remember something or refer back to your notes, and you'll see another idea you can tie in. That's why it's important to write every idea down – even if, at first glance, you might think it's not such a great idea.

My friend and colleague Don Bice has a friend who creates illusions for magicians; he's the one who came up with the vanishing Statue of Liberty trick for David Copperfield. He puts his ideas down in composition books. He just comes up with an idea for a trick, and he enters it on a page in a composition book. Then he'll think of another one and put it on another page. Sometimes he has no idea in the world how to accomplish the trick, but then later he comes back and he says, "I've got an idea about this one," and he'll jot a few thoughts down. He does that on occasion, and the first thing you know, a need arises and he says, "Oh, I know where there's a great idea," and he goes into his composition books and goes through them. He finishes it and completes it or changes it at that point. He doesn't have to sit down and start from scratch every time.

Ideas don't just come at you from nowhere. There aren't little inspiration particles flying through the universe that just happen to collide with your brain occasionally and cause new ideas. You have to work at getting them. Don't wait for them to come to you; make them happen. My mentor Russ von Hoelscher gets up in the morning, gets a pot of coffee

Selling and marketing is the ultimate game!

- Show me any game or sport without ten tons of obstacles and challenges — and I'll show you one boring game! The only game worth playing is the one that lets you test your skills on a daily basis.

- Entrepreneurs thrive on challenges! We welcome the adversity. We need the problems, challenges, and obstacles. Without these things, the game is pretty boring.

going, then sits down with a yellow pad and forces himself to think. He writes down everything that comes to mind, regardless of how frivolous it might seem. *This* is how great ideas appear out of nowhere — by making those ideas happen, by giving them the time and the space for them to come to you.

And here's an integral part of that creative concept: **if you want better ideas, ask better questions.** I think, sometimes, you even have to ask yourself crazy questions. Ask yourself wild and outrageous things – impossible things! If you've got a company that's never done more than a half-million in one month, all of a sudden start asking yourself wild and crazy questions like: What would it take to get a million dollars a month? Other people would say, "Hey, that's impossible! You've never even done a half a million in one month. You've never broken that record, so what are you doing asking yourself what it would take to make a million a month?" Sometimes, **just by asking yourself hard questions about what it's really going to take to do what you want to do, all of a sudden you do come up with breakthroughs.** It opens up your horizon.

SECRET SIX:

Buckets of money on the back-end.

You can't get rich with one-shot offers unless you're selling something that costs many thousands of dollars. Therefore, most of your profits will come from the back-end. This is a message you'll have to learn and relearn in this business: in most cases, 99% of our profits will come from the back-end. If you're selling something on the front-end, you <u>want</u> <u>to</u> <u>get</u> <u>that</u> <u>"wow"</u> <u>factor</u>. You want the people to get it — whatever they paid for it, whether it's $10, $100, or $1,000 — and say "Wow! I can't believe I got so much value for my money! I got many times more value than I ever thought I would from this offer!" <u>You</u> <u>want</u> <u>them</u> <u>to</u> <u>be</u> <u>so</u> <u>impressed</u> <u>that</u> <u>they're</u> <u>ready</u> <u>to</u> <u>buy</u> <u>your</u> <u>back-end</u> <u>offer</u>, which can be much more expensive.

Of course, even your back-end needs a back-end. *Back-end selling never stops*. Constantly stay in touch with these customers because that's how you get rich in this business — by having back-end offer after back-end offer. **You should mail to them at least 10 or 12 times a year with new offers — and they should all be related.** Don't try to sell them a book on gambling, and then come back with a book on making money in mail order. You should always focus on the same product line.

It's also important to know **the lifetime value of your customer**. If you know a customer usually stays with you for 3½ years and spends, for example, $5,400 over that period, you know a customer's value, on average, is $5,400 over 3½ years. What you want to do then is some simple math about **how much you can afford to spend to get that customer.** I've already mentioned about how many marketers are willing to lose money, even substantial sums of money, to get a customer. **If you know a customer is worth $5,400 over time, you can probably double, triple, or quadruple the money you'd normally spend on the front-end just to get that customer.** So know the math of Direct-Response Marketing, and know that the buckets of money are always made by reselling to the customer over and over again.

Here's another principle that I happen to think is great: testing your new ideas and your promotions with your best customers first. If it won't work to your best customers, it's not going to work to anybody else. Let's take my pal Russ von Hoelscher as an example. His best customers are his 7,000+ newsletter customers. He makes offers to them, and within weeks he can tell whether he can send those offers out to the 20,000 or 30,000 other people on his customer list. <u>If</u> <u>your</u> <u>best</u> <u>customers</u> <u>won't</u> <u>buy,</u> <u>your</u> <u>other</u> <u>customers</u> *<u>definitely</u>* <u>won't</u> <u>buy</u>.

SECRET SEVEN:

Keep baiting the mousetrap with the same cheese that snared them the last time.

Many marketers are guilty of ignoring this principle. We make a sale, and then we say, "What do I sell them next?" I've spent a lot of time asking myself this. Well, the secret is right there in front of us: **we should sell more of the same type of thing that they bought from you the last time.** People new to this business invariably come up with the solution that keeps them from earning more money. They keep looking for something different to sell to their customers, while the successful marketer looks for more of the same thing. That always just seems to come as a shock to newcomers. They say, "But I just sold them that."

Well, good! It's time to sell them the same thing again. Sometimes folks will buy the same thing again in a different form. If they bought the book, they'll buy the audio CD. If they bought the CD, they'll buy the video. If they bought the video, they'll buy the CD-ROM. Look at it this way. Suppose you had an ice cream store, and I came in yesterday and bought a cone of chocolate ice cream. I came back today. Are you more likely to sell me chocolate, or vanilla? Well, the answer is obviously I will probably buy chocolate again, because I probably have a taste for chocolate. That's why you make money selling people more of what they've been buying **because when you know what people have an appetite for, then you can pretty well predict what they'll want the next time.**

Now, this doesn't necessarily mean you can sell them the exact same information, but often you really can. I can't tell you how many books, tapes, and manuals I've bought on direct marketing. I bet there's at least one subject where everyone reading this has bought about everything that they can afford. Most people have an appetite for certain types of information, with a craving for subtypes within that genre. **Once you've identified someone's craving, that's even better than knowing their appetite.**

FOOLPROOF SECRETS of Successful Marketers!

When you get someone to buy once, you can be sure they have an appetite for something, **but chances are that when they become a multi-buyer — when they buy something from you more than once — you've identified a craving, and you can sell them over and over again.** That's why, when you're looking for new customers and you rent lists, the list is important because it tells you what people have bought in the past. You go looking for people with an appetite for what you're selling. If people have paid $295 or $300 for a product, you can bet your life they have a really strong appetite. **If they're multi-buyers, then you know they're absolutely craving products.**

Then you know exactly what to offer them: something as close as possible to what they bought before, but with an added a twist or gimmick to it. **Something that will promise them the benefit they want, but give it to them even easier and faster than what they bought before.** If they bought a book about getting started in Internet Marketing, then maybe you can add a product about how they can sell better, or put together auto-responder ads they can run instantly. If it was a 30-day weight-loss diet that they bought last time, maybe you can offer them a 10-day lose-weight-while-you-sleep diet. You see? You offer them the same thing they bought before, but a version that's faster, better or newer.

It's the same for future products. At some point, people may get tired of the same thing. They've taken the same bait over and over, and they want something new. When I went to the ice cream store, I bought chocolate. I bought chocolate again and again, until finally I got tired of it. Well, the guy at the store's not going to say, "Well, why don't you take vanilla?" He's going to offer me deluxe chocolate with peanut butter, or something similar — **something very close to what I need, even when I wanted something different.**

> **Stop trying to change people's minds — especially your prospects.**
>
> **Once a mind is made up it rarely, if ever, changes.**

So, when your customers start to tire of the bait you're offering them, you can give them a couple of choices. You can sell him something slightly different, or you can sell him what he needs next to move him toward his primary goal, dream, benefit, or whatever he's looking for. If you sell a

▼▼▼▼▼▼▼▼▼
MARKETING SECRET

People buy for emotional reasons and justify their purchase logically. People often buy for strong unconscious emotional reasons. We can never know the real reason people decide to give us their money. America's first billionaire, J. P Morgan, said it wisely: "A man has two reasons for what he does — a good one — and the real one."

customer several manuals on making money on the Internet — well, when those stop selling, you can offer him what he needs next: a website. If you sell him a website, then what does he need? He needs traffic to that website. Now you can offer several ways of getting traffic: advertising, giveaways, contests, news release packages, and on and on. Did you change the bait? Somewhat. The dream is making money with the Internet. **You're just tweaking your offer to move the customer along by saying, "Here's what you need next."**

When the mice stop taking a bait of American cheese, you're not going to catch them by switching to worms. Try cheddar! *Cheese* is what they want, so all you do is change the variety. Your customer's no different. **You just need to identify the cheese, and be prepared to offer him as much variety as it takes to make the sale.**

Many years ago, my mentor Russ von Hoelscher did some critiques of sales letters from a guy in Brooklyn, New York, who was selling horse racing information. He got to talking about his customers, and said that over a 10-year period he'd put together about 45 or 50 different manuals on horse racing. *How to Speed Race Horses, Horses for Turf Courses, How to Bet Horses on What the Odds Are —Especially Prior to the Race,* and on and on. He said some of his best customers over the past 10 years had bought all the manuals that he'd produced. Russ said, "My gosh, that's incredible. You mean they just keep buying horse racing manuals with slightly different variations?" He said, "Yep. If I put out five new manuals this year, my best customers will buy all five." He was charging around $50 a manual, which back then was a pretty good price, but certainly not an exorbitant one. These people could not get enough of horse racing information.

That's the whole premise behind one of the more savvy marketing techniques that you see some of the more savvy marketers using. That is, they offer a newsletter or an Internet membership site to their customers. What goes with every transmission, of course, **is another opportunity for the customer to get happily involved with your products and services, and those are the best people you could ever sell to** — the ones who are already your fans, who trust you, and like your message. When you recommend something new, they're waiting to pounce on it.

You see, you don't just create a single product — **you create a line of products.** In this business, we always talk about the back-end, the items that backup that first sale you make. **Remember, you need to have lots of back ends.** This creates a line of related products that move someone from beginner all the way up the spectrum. Too many people, in the beginning, forget about the line of products that they need, and they just focus on a one-time sale. People also forget that consumers are insatiable. That's the one message Alan R. Bechtold drives home so successfully when he tells his story of *Playboy* and *Penthouse*. The way Alan explains it, when the publishers of *Penthouse* saw that *Playboy* was making money hand over fist, they went into business with their own skin magazine. The critics at the time (the early 1960s) said, "Oh, there's no room in the marketplace for two magazines like *Playboy*. It just won't work!" Well, they were wrong, weren't they? I know this is an extreme example, not to mention a controversial one, simply because of the subject matter. But the truth is, the pornography industry makes a good model to illustrate the concept of insatiability. **People are never satisfied with just one product: they want more of the same.** So *Penthouse* made more by giving them less clothes! And now instead of two magazines, we've got maybe 200 of these skin magazines selling regularly and making all kinds of money. It just shows you that the people who buy that kind of product just keep buying, from all the different publishers.

Once upon a time, my wife said something about pornography: "Don't men realize that if you've seen one, you've seen them all?" But the truth is, of course not! Not all men buy pornography, but those who do are driven by their emotions, however unpractical or difficult that would be to describe. *All* **customers are driven by emotion. People always buy for emotional reasons.** And those reasons are the driving forces that make them want to continue buying <u>MORE</u> of whatever they bought the last time... Who's the most likely to buy a diet book? Someone who bought a diet book last month. Who's going to want that new porno magazine? They guys who are already buying that kind of magazine.

SECRET EIGHT:

What people want is the magic pill.

What's the magic pill? **It's the one product or service that's going to make everything okay.** It's going to solve some major problem or offer your prospects a miracle cure. It's an instant and ongoing solution. I often use this metaphor of a magic pill because if people could pop a pill and have some great thing happen in their life, they'd buy it up like crazy.

For example, let's say you had a magic pill that, if someone swallowed it, would make them a million dollars overnight. Would they buy it? You'd better believe it. People would be lining up around the block for that kind of product. That's why <u>you</u> <u>need</u> <u>to</u> <u>focus</u> <u>on</u> <u>creating</u> <u>that</u> <u>kind</u> <u>of</u> <u>an</u> <u>aura</u> <u>around</u> <u>your</u> <u>existing</u> <u>product</u>. You need to look at it and ask yourself some really great specific questions: How can I take the existing product that I have and turn it into this magic pill? What can I offer? What can I add to that product? If I can't take the existing product and make it this magic pill type of an offer, what can I add to it to give it the aura of a magic pill deal?

Let me give you some examples of this. Remember how I talked about *wants* versus *needs* in another section? Let's look at weight loss. We all want to be healthier; we all want to be thinner. We all want to be in better shape. I can tell you in one second exactly what anyone in the world needs to do to lose weight: exercise and eat less. Boom! There you go. I've basically just taken all the information from of all those weight loss books and boiled it down to just a phrase. *But people don't want that.* Eating right is difficult, and exercising is difficult and painful. People want that magic pill. That's why all these companies aren't telling their customers to eat right and exercise. What they're saying is, "Hey, I've actually got a magic pill! If you take it every night before you go to asleep, you're going to start losing pounds. They're going to just magically melt away!" It's a magical, miracle cure.

It's the same way with hair loss. They have these pills out now that will cause your hair to stop falling out — and you actually may grow some back. They really work, too. Of course, in the ads they don't tell you the pills are going to give you terrible halitosis and you're going to become impotent, because that doesn't sell very well. But they do tell you if you take this magic pill, that's all you have to do. You don't have to do anything else. If you can pop a pill, you can get the benefits. *That's* what people want. **People don't want a lot of hard work and effort.** They don't want to put years and years into something to get what they want. Whether it's weight loss, more money, more hair, or a new house, they want that magic pill that will give them instant gratification. The more closely you can turn your existing product into that magic pill, the more you're going to be able to make more money by hitting the wants of your prospects dead center.

If you've got an existing product, you should really focus on turning it into that magic pill — or at least try to do so. But so many marketers just don't understand this principle. Why? Largely because they don't believe that they *have* that magic pill — so they don't bother trying to give it that aura. But you have to try. **I believe you can take almost any product, with the right type of marketing and the right type of an offer, and get that type of magic.** It may not be the absolute magic pill with no drawbacks and no side effects, but you could certainly move it in that direction.

Let's take a closer look at the hair loss product I mentioned before. If you really looked at the product and its side effects, then you really probably wouldn't call it a magic pill. It doesn't work for everybody. It has these noticeable side effects, like I mentioned. One of the crazy things about this pill is that they're selling it based on sex appeal. If you lose your hair, will your wife or spouse or girlfriend still love you? Well, probably, but they don't want you to consider that. Heck, the truth is that if you pop this pill, even if your hair stops falling out and actually starts growing back, well, yeah, you're going to have your hair — but you're also going to have bad breath, and you're going to be impotent. Oops! The sex appeal doesn't work

Spend more money to make more money:

- "In Direct-Marketing it's the cost to get the sale — not to make a mailing (or series of mailings) that counts."
  — Jon Goldman

- Many times, the secret is to spend more money, not less. This is especially true when you are making offers to your best prospects and customers.

in that case. But you know what? It's painted as a magic pill because it can save your hair, and to guys who really want to keep their hair that's exactly what it is.

Why does the magic pill approach work? Think of it as the Microwave Society Syndrome. **We want everything fast.** We want it sure. We want it right away, whether it's weight loss or making money. If you told people, "Now, here's a great way to make money: you work very hard and don't spend too much, and at the end of five years you're going to have a big bank balance." A lot of people would say, "That's crazy! Here's someone who has a book on how I can make $10,000 a day while I'm lazy as a mud rat! Why should I listen to you?" **People are looking for instant cures for all their pain, and they're looking for instant gratification.** As marketers, what we have to do is sell the sizzle — but we have to deliver the steak. In other words, we have to sell all the things that really push the buttons on our prospects, but at the same time we have to give them some realistic items that they really will have to do if they're going to achieve the goal they want.

Let me tell you how we're doing this for our company. **We sell Direct-Response Marketing distributorships and dealerships.** We supply our customers with a product to sell and the sales material they can use to go sell it. Our most successful distributors do a variety of things to achieve success, but of course we have a lot of other distributors who want someone else to do it all for them. **So what we're striving to do, more and more, is to create services within our company that offer to do almost everything for the customer.** We do web design. We do web hosting. We do all the typesetting on the postcards for them. We go out and find the best mailing lists. We print the postcards for them. Then we send them the postcards every single month along with the mailing lists, and all they have to do is lick and stick while they're watching television.

For some of our customers — not all of them — that's exactly what the magic pill is. We tell them, "Hey! You can do it in as little as five or ten minutes a day!" That's what they want: a way that they can be in the mail order business, when all they have to do is sit around licking and sticking. Actually, they don't even have to lick, because the mailing list comes on self-adhesive labels — and so do the stamps. Then they just go and drop them into a post office box, **everything else is done for them.** That way, in all of our ads we can keep that message in front of the prospects and customers: that we'll do almost everything for you. **We just keep driving that message into them over and over again, because that's their magic pill.**

Here's another example. Russ Von Hoelscher tells about a woman he knows who made $1 million last year. She first started out with a product where she told people that they could mail her program. She'd give them the sales material; she'd tell them where to get lists. It was pretty successful. But then she realized that thousands of her customers didn't even want to do that. Finally, she instituted a program where she not only produced all the sales material, the program itself, and everything else — she also shipped it for them. That's right: she actually did all the mailing for them. She told her clients, "You can send me anywhere from a $200 to $2,000, depending on how many pieces of mail you want me to send out with your name on it." The response was overwhelming. The money came pouring in. Because she was a good woman and tried to do her best for her customers, some of them actually made money. But the point is, **she did everything! Boy, did they love it.**

So there's a principle to consider. **The more we can do for our customers to make it easy for them, the better.** This doesn't just mean selling them information, it could work with anything. Whatever you sell, the more complete it is, the more thorough it is, the more it answers all the questions and is a complete system regardless of what type of product or service it is, the more your customers will love it.

SECRET NINE:

Develop the right offer, and you'll attract the person you're looking for.

The bait you throw out there determines the type of person you catch. Furthermore, **for every person there exists a bait that they *cannot* resist swallowing.** With this powerful principal, I have hit on one of the most important lessons you can learn as a marketer. I've nibbled at the edges of this principle in other sections, but this time **I want to focus on the bait itself: the requirements for developing the right offer, and therefore attracting the right person you're looking for.** This is important because your overall moneymaking strategy depends on you attracting the right kind of people.

Now, if you're attracting the wrong kind of people, you may make a little bit of money — but your overall marketing strategy will suffer. Do you want to attract a person who's dependent, or independent? Are you looking for someone who's rich, or someone who *wants* to be rich? The answers to those questions will influence the kind of offer you use to attract your customers. **It's very important that you know exactly who it is that you're trying to reach.** Your long-term marketing plan depends on you attracting the right kind of people, folks who are likely to purchase from you again and again. It's not just the front end marketing, that first thing that you sell, <u>it's</u> <u>also</u> <u>remembering</u> <u>that</u> <u>you</u> <u>want</u> <u>to</u> <u>attract</u> <u>the</u> <u>kind</u> <u>of</u> <u>people</u> <u>who</u> <u>will</u> <u>do</u> <u>business</u> <u>with</u> <u>you</u> <u>for</u> <u>years</u> <u>to</u> <u>come</u>.

In our business, we use **the fishnet analogy.** If your business services people who prefer fine fillets of some particular ocean fish, you obviously want to cast your nets where you'll catch the largest number of fish. It doesn't serve you any purpose at all to catch a bunch of other kinds of fish because that's not your market. You're not selling to people who need that kind of fish. In the business world, your offers are your fishnet. **You have to cast your fishnet** (or fishing lines as the case may be) **in the direction of the people you most want to do business with — the people who you** want to be your customers for the long-term.

For your market, **you just have to find out what that bait is that the consumer can't resist swallowing.** In the previous sections, I've discussed all kinds of unique selling positions, and things you can do to make people feel like they have to respond to your offer. That's the bait we're talking about. I can't tell you what it is for your product; you have to figure that out for yourself. Find out what that one bait is, that one thing that your customer can't resist swallowing, and give it to them. **Give it to them over and over again throughout your offer, and you'll find that more of your customers will respond to those offers.** That will build the kind of long-term customer you're really looking for.

A lot of people don't understand this principle at all. **Here's an example.** We had this guy working for us for about eight months. He saw our company mail millions of pieces of mail before he got fired. Now he's back to selling cars. I ran into him a few weeks ago, and he started telling me about all these Direct-Mail pieces he's been mailing out, pieces he'd spent a couple of thousand dollars on. I asked him, "What's your offer?" and he said, " I don't have any offer." I guess the idea is that because he saw us sending out millions of pieces of mail, if he did a bunch, he was going to make money too. I see this with other people all the time: they think it works like that movie *Field of Dreams* with Kevin Costner. "If you build it, they will come." That was the theme of that movie, but you know what? That was a movie. It was a fantasy. A lot of people have this crazy idea that just because they're obsessed with their product or service, just because they absolutely love it, they can introduce it to the world and all these people are just going to flock to them. That's a gross misunderstanding of the way the world really is.

> ▼▼▼▼▼▼▼▼▼▼▼▼▼▼▼
>
> Whoever said it was going to be easy lied to you.
>
> But maybe you needed to be lied to! I sure did! If someone would have told me the truth about what it really takes to make millions, I would have never even started!

You can have a product for sale, but that doesn't mean you have an offer to sell it; and if you don't, you're sunk. **There has to be a reason why people should respond right now, and that's all tied into your offer.** In the car salesman's case, just

---

SECTION TWO — *SECRETS* OF THE BLUE JEANS MILLIONAIRE
191

Major success in life comes from our ability to communicate to others in the most powerful way possible.

- Everything we want in life MUST come from other people. And communicating to their hearts — minds — and emotions is the secret to getting them to happily give us whatever we ask for!

thinking you can send something out in the mail without an offer attached to it is stupid; it's a bad marketing strategy. But that's the way a lot of people think. They haven't figured out that you have to have some kind of offer, some reason why people should do business with you. The offer's all part of a master scheme involving your overall marketing strategy.

An offer, as I see it, is something specific to get people to take action: a special sale that's going to expire on a certain date, or a special price, or a limited arrangement that really is only available now. **You need to look at the offer as the total package.** The price point, the payment terms, the bonuses that come with it, the reason for acting now, the primary benefit that's exploited when they purchase the packaged offer; all that together creates the final offer.

SECRET TEN:

Spend more money to reach fewer, more highly qualified people.

Another key to marketing success is to find the highly qualified prospects who are the most likely to buy whatever you have to offer. **This is what niche marketing is all about — spending more money to reach fewer but better qualified prospects or customers.**

First of all, **you should consider**

segmenting your customer list. If you haven't figured it out by now, **your customer list is the single most important asset in your business.** There are different ways of segmenting that customer list — by what the customers buy, the types of product that they buy, the frequency of their purchases, the dollar amount of their purchases, or how recent they made their purchases. Those are just the main ways that you can segment your list. The number one question always has to be, **"Who are my best customers?"** <u>Once you figure that out, set the criteria on a certain amount of money that they have to spend to qualify to get on a *different* customer list</u>.

Once you have these different customer lists, you can communicate to people a little bit differently, based on what they bought in the past or how much money they've spent or how long they've been with you. That's one really good way to segment your customers. If you have customers who have been doing business with you for years, you could talk to them differently because you know they're very familiar with you. **You have to build a bond with your customers:** that's key. You have to stay in touch constantly.

By segmenting your mailing list to find that smaller group of best customers, **you're now able to spend more money to reach that smaller group.** You're not as confined, now, to the mathematics. Normally there's the cost of printing and postage to consider, but it goes out the window when you have that smaller group of customers to deal with. You can spend a lot of money because you can afford to; **you know you'll get a lot more back if you prime the pump.**

This is something that I've known about for years, but it was my friend Jeff Gardner who **recently reminded me about its true power.** I saw one of Jeff's mailings. In that mailing, not only did he have a 22-page sales letter and an 8-page insert and all these other nice printed pieces, but he took a brand new crisp $1 bill and glued it to the letter. Then he packaged it all up into a really beautiful plastic envelope that's three or four times more expensive than most envelopes you'd use in a Direct-Mail campaign. To get something like this in the mail — and I know this because now we've copied Jeff's model with some of our own customers — costs about $3, especially when you count the labor costs, because you can't machine-insert this kind of package. They have to be done by hand. The dollar has to be glued on with a special expensive glue like the kind they use on Post-it notes. Your security measures have to be beefed up a little bit, to keep people from stealing from you. There are simply a lot of little things that have to be done.

So you're spending $3,000 per thousand mail pieces just to get the offer into the mail stream. But, the point is, if it's only going to your very, very best customers, who cares if it costs $3,000? Who cares if it costs $10,000 per thousand? Sell a few of your items, and you'll make all that money back. **The point is not how much it** *costs* **you but how much it** *makes* **you.** That's the only thing you should be concerned with. Now, in order to not spend too wildly, you should test a more expensive version against the less expensive version. But the point is you shouldn't be afraid to go out there and be very aggressive, and be willing to spend quite a bit of money in your communications and your different promotions to your better customers. **You'll spend more money to reach fewer but better qualified prospects.**

Keep in mind that **this works only if you have a niche market you know inside out: one where you're able to get a high response rate.** At the time Jeff was sending out his offer, he had a best-customer list of only 300 or so, but he was able to get literally a 25-33% response rate. That's one out of every 3-4 people on the list purchasing a product. I'm are not talking about a $5 or $10 product, where they don't have to think about it to make the order, I'm talking about a $1,000 product. It made sense to spend more money on this smaller market because Jeff knew them so well that he knew that he could get a very high response rate. Sometimes he'd spend $3, $4, $5, or more per mailing.

Jeff recently told me about a telephone conversation he had with a gentleman who was marketing to his own niche group. He was just building up his business. He said something that stuck in Jeff's mind, and he actually had to slap the guy on the wrist a little bit. The other marketer said, "I'm going to start out with small postcards because I want to do this very cheaply. I know it's a good niche market, but I'm always going to do it cheap, cheap, cheap." Jeff told him, "You shouldn't think that way because sometimes the best money you can spend is in putting out a slightly better package, putting in some grabbers, making it more attention-getting, making sure the envelope gets opened so you get that bigger response. If you're always thinking about your bottom line and not about what's going to get the best response and bring in the most sales, you're never going to reach your ultimate goals." So here's the gist of it: **you have**

to look at not just what your bottom line is on mailings, but what that marketing is going to bring you back.

I think some of that goes back to the principle that perception equals reality. If you're trying to sell something that's high dollar and it's perceived as something that's elite and ultimate, you have to put some bells and whistles into the package that are congruent with your pitch — that is, the message you're trying to put across.

Here's another example of that. There have been a lot of ads over the years saying "Send me $1, and I'll show you how to get $1 million!" The funny thing about most of those ads is that they look like they've have been put together by vandals, certainly not by someone who knows anything about graphic design. It certainly doesn't say, "Here's a millionaire placing this ad." You're supposed to send money to this person who obviously doesn't *have* a million dollars. Maybe they don't even have two nickels to rub together, and they're supposedly going to show you how to make a million bucks. That just doesn't work. **You do have to have a congruent message.** If you're going to be doing cheap, cheap, cheap all the time trying to sell anything — especially moneymaking information — you'll never make much because there's not a congruency between what you're actually putting out there and what you're selling. It's worth spending extra money, then, on elaborate and expensive mailings to people who've already demonstrated that they're good customers. Don't pull out all the stops on folks who haven't demonstrated their value to you as a customer. That's all part of segmenting your customer list and knowing whom your better customers are. There's something called the 80/20 rule, and it says that **20 percent of your customers are going to represent 80 percent of your profits.** In some of businesses, it's more like 90/10: ten percent of your customers represent 90 percent of your profits, and it's up to you to try and determine which 10 percent or 20 percent are the best. **You have to have qualifiers on their value.**

One way is to qualify people by how much money they spend. You'll find that a person who'll spend $200 is a better customer for you than someone who'll spend $29. First you get a responder, then you try to turn that responder into a buyer, and *then* you try to turn that buyer into a customer. **It takes about three sales before you have a real customer.** That's the 10-20 percent of your list you need to aim for. Those are the folks you need make test mailings to because you know that if they

---

respond, you'll get good response from the other 80-90 percent. Those are the customers who will tell you whether your offer is good or not.

SECRET ELEVEN:

"The Hand."

Every offer or promotion that you create must meet these five crucial criteria:

1. Is it the right offer?
2. ...to the right person?
3. ...through the right media?
4. ...with the right hook?
5. Does it fit together with some kind of long-term plan?

There are many different marketing methods, but only a handful of them are vital. **This simple formula lets you focus on the essentials.** I attribute this marketing formula to Bill Graham, one of the greatest rock-and-roll promoters who ever lived. Bill had five key areas that every concert had to fall under. He called it his 'hand' — so I created a marketing formula that did the same.

Let's get right back to the offer. Remember, **the offer is *not* the product. The offer is everything that surrounds it.** It's the bonuses. It's the importance of time because there's a limited quantity. It's given to you because you're a special person involved in this kind of thing. Is it the right offer? In other words, is the offer good?

▼▼▼▼▼▼▼▼
MARKETING SECRET

The greatest salespeople are MASTER COMMUNICATORS. Their sales pitch cuts through the clutter in their prospect's life. It cuts like a knife and goes right to the heart! It grips the prospect — and compels them to give up their hard-earned money, in exchange for the benefits the salesperson made them see!

Then there's the second "finger" of the hand. **Is it going to the right person?** Obviously you have to get the right person. If a magazine comes into our house and it offers beautiful, expensive clothing, if it's up to me that thing's going to find its way into the trash can because I'm digging through looking for Direct-Mail packages I can add to my swipe file. However, if it comes in and my wife's looking at the mail — well, she's going to pull out the catalog and she's going to throw all of the other stuff in the trash!

You also have to get your offer there though the right media: in the above case, I was talking about Direct-Mail. People who've bought from Direct-Mail are your best prospects to approach by Direct-Mail. People who buy on the Internet are the best prospects to approach on the Internet.

Next, you need to have the right hook because every buyer is motivated by a number of different things. As I mentioned in a previous section, everybody has some bait that they can't resist responding to. Our job as marketers is to find what that bait is. Is it the fact that what you're offering is so easy that it practically does itself, or is it the fact that it's going to make you feel special? I'm talking about that $75,000 convertible Mercedes I mentioned earlier. What will your audience respond to? Part of this is in the packaging. If you're offering to tell people how to make more money, don't send them a crappy mailing that looks like it's been run off on a photocopier 100 times.

Then there's the fifth point. **Does it all fit together with some kind of long-term plan?** Every action, every promotion, every marketing approach, every offer should be leading your buyers to the next market, to the next approach, the next sale. Let's suppose you do landscaping, and you're building decks. People who respond to that deck promotion can be given things in the offer that also encourage them to be proud of the fact that they're keeping their neighborhood clean, are building it up, and are being good citizens — because what do you want to do after you sell them a deck? You want to put up a fence for them, or you want to put in the Jacuzzi.

So again, you should work on these things as isolated events; **try to be as creative as you can, and act on every offer like it's the only offer and the last offer you can ever make.** At the same time, however, it needs to be fully integrated so that it's part of a whole deck — one of the 52 cards, even though we might be doing a trick with the joker or the ace. It's

---

SECTION TWO — *SECRETS* OF THE BLUE JEANS MILLIONAIRE   **197** part of the whole deck, and it's taking you where you want to go.

So my concept of the "hand" for business goes one better on Bill Graham's. One thing many people don't realize about Graham was that he only had a handful of ideas. If one finger was missing, then he could walk away from a project; **all five principles had to be there for it to work.** Everybody thought he was such a genius, but the truth was that he just had five good, solid principles that he used with every single deal. That doesn't mean his process was a bad one, quite the contrary. I think it's great when you can reduce your process down to five points because it's easy to memorize. Once you commit it to memory, you can commit it to action.

Modeling other successful people is important. Sure, we're all looking for creativity and that's good, but we should also recognize a formula that's working well for others when we see it. We get their mailing piece, we go to their website, and we find out through trial and error and investigation that they're making a lot of money, so we want to do something that's very similar — not to copy them word-for-word and design everything the same as them, but to capitalize on their success. **You can make a fortune just by copying success.** That's what I was doing with Bill Graham: I took that story and found a way to integrate it into Direct-Response Marketing. Some of the richest people in our business do that — they take ideas from other industries, just like that McDonald's exec took the concept of drive-in banking and adapted it for fast food. They adapt the idea to what they're doing, and the success comes.

That's what the great Broadway promoter, Billy Rose, used to do. He said, "Hell, anybody can write a Broadway show. All I do is look at the Broadway shows and find out what works. Every show needs an opening. Every show needs a dramatic piece, and every show needs an 'I'm down but I'm going to get back up' piece." He assembled shows by that formula, and it worked again and again.

Now, don't let the term "formula" put you off. Most people think using a formula takes away the creativity. The truth is that it's just the reverse. **A formula is a guideline for ideas.** It's a yardstick along the way to help you get along a proven path. So formulas are very useful, and they don't necessarily restrict creativity.

SECRET TWELVE:

What you really sell.

You must *never* fall into the trap of selling products or services; **you sell *concepts*!** You sell ideas, benefits, end results, and solutions. **Believe it or not, products are secondary.**

I've got the perfect story to go along with this point, one provided by my friend and colleague Jeff Gardner. He was recently talking to a copywriter, who was telling him about some of the people he'd worked with and some of the projects he'd done. There was this one person who did a lot

> **T**he richest and/or most successful people you know have the same 168 hours a week that you have.
>
> *What are they doing that you're not?*

of Direct-Mail, and he came to the copywriter and said, "Look, I need you to write this hot eight-page letter about a new program we've put together, one that will help people beat the slot machines in any casino anywhere in the world. I'll pay you $2,000 to write it this letter." The copywriter said, "Hey, that's great! It sounds like a great offer. Go ahead and send me the book and I'll get started." The guy said, "Well, there's no book." The copywriter asked, "There's no book? How am I supposed to write the letter?" The guy said, *"You just write a hot letter selling this program, and then I'll worry about coming up with the program itself."*

That's really the key to making money: **you have to have a great offer.** A lot of people fall in love with products. After they've developed a product and spent years and years honing it and polishing it lovingly, they decide that maybe it's time to sell it. They've thrown all this money into it, after all. But what if it doesn't sell?

The secret to avoiding this outcome is to do things the other way around. **First you come up the hot offer, the great idea, the great concept;** *then* **you decide what product can fit into that concept.** That's really the key to making money — not falling into this trap of starting with

---

Keep your business moving forward at all times...

- Complacency is like cancer. It's stagnant. It's like a river that turns ugly — muddy — a magnet for disease.

- To flow is to stay clean. To stagnate is to die.

the product. <u>Don't</u> <u>be</u> <u>product-centered</u>, where all your focus is on the product; <u>you</u> <u>need</u> <u>to</u> <u>be</u> <u>market-centered</u> <u>instead</u>.

Hot products are a dime a dozen. I get people calling me all the time saying, "I've got a hot product, and everybody wants it." That really makes me cringe because it's rarely the case. How many perfect products are there that just magically sell themselves? How many products are there where a person can stand on the street corner and say, "Hey, I've this hot product," and people will rush up with a handful of cash and want to buy it? **People have wants and desires, sure, but those are magnified by great marketing — by creating these great concepts and ideas and benefits, and the end results and solutions that go with them.**

Let's say you decide to target the weight-loss market. All these people are heavier than they want to be; they all have a problem, but they don't have a particular product in mind to fix it. They're not saying, "I want to have something that works my abs. I need a plastic product in the color red that straps me to the ceiling so I can do a flying motion!" See what I mean? They don't have any product in mind, **they have a *benefit* in mind. They have a *solution* in mind.** They want to lose that weight in any way possible — especially if it's easy. **So what you do then is create the hottest offer, the hottest concept you can, that will satisfy their desires.** In this market, <u>the</u> <u>hottest</u> <u>concept</u> <u>would</u> <u>be</u> <u>that</u> <u>magic</u> <u>pill</u> I've already discussed. With this famous magic pill you don't do any working out, you don't even change how you eat. You continue to sit on the couch watching TV, eating bonbons, and Ben & Jerry's Ice Cream, but every night before you go to bed you pop that magic pill and the pounds melt away while you sleep. Once you have the concept of the magic pill, then it's time to go to the scientists and the research department people and say, "Okay, now we need to create this magic pill."

That's the secret to making money. **You focus on the marketing and the concepts and on filling those wants and desires, and then you work backwards.** You reverse-engineer and then come up with the product. Using that type of a system, you can become incredibly successful a lot faster than the other way around, where you focus on the product and then you tear your guts out trying to find a way to market and sell it.

In other words, people don't want products at all. **They just want the benefits and advantages the products give them.** For example, the front-end sales letter we're using right now was written 12 years ago. When we wrote it, we had absolutely no product to go with it whatsoever. But we knew our market and wrote the sales letter to match it, and we tailored a product to fit it. Since then, we've changed the basic product several times, and we still use the same letter. The advantages and benefits of what we offer are what count — not necessarily the product itself.

Now, I realize that some people just have a real problem with this. They think it's almost a scam to create the ad copy first, and *then* create the product. I think one of the challenges with it is that a lot of people have, somewhere in their mind, that one product, book, idea, or invention that they know will make millions. Let's say you go out and stop ten people on the street and ask them, "Do you have an idea right now for a new product or book that would make you rich?" You're probably going to get seven to eight people who'll say, "Oh yeah, I've this great idea for this or that." They're product-oriented. They would never think of identifying a need and then creating a product to fill it; they think the product is supreme.

Obviously that's the wrong way to think, but it's just the way people are. We all come up with these great things and inventions that we think would sell like hotcakes, but we don't really think about who we're going to sell them to. I believe that if they think about it, most people don't have a huge problem with the marketing coming first. Sure, some will say, "That's not really genuine because you're trying to manipulate them. You're trying to manipulate their desires." But the way I look at it is that **you're fulfilling desires that already exist. You're delivering exactly**

what they want. I think the world would be a better place if, instead of us trying to push products onto people that they don't want, we went out and found out what people really wanted, and then worked our hardest to give them that. I really think that's the key to ultimate happiness.

SECRET THIRTEEN:

The Magic Pill, Part 2.

We're back to the magic pill again! Remember, people are looking for and willing to spend a ton of money for a magic pill in *any* market. The magic pill is very important because most of us forget that people don't want what we have for sale. They really don't. **They want the** *benefit* **we can offer them. So start with that benefit first, then build the product and offer around it.**

Let's take a look at the ingredients of that magic pill, and discover what we can put in it to make it as attractive as possible to the potential customer.

First of all, we want a pill that accomplishes the benefit effortlessly. That's is very important. Everyone wants to be rich, or at least have as much money as they desire, and they want it as quickly as possible. They want to get as much money as they can for the smallest expenditure of effort. We want to lose weight, but we want to do it without effort, without exercise. We want the fat to just melt away. A powerful headline is one that promises that benefit immediately, like "Lose weight without exercise." We want to master a skill effortlessly without pain and without failure. Whether it's Spanish or French, we want to learn it without studying. We just want to put a CD in the player and suddenly know it. A lot of education has been sold that way: insert the CD into your machine and master this material on the way to work. A few years ago, even learning while you slept was a popular idea. What could be more effortless than that?

Number Two: we want to achieve the benefit quickly. Speed is a very important part of the magic pill. Not only must it be effortless, but also it should happen quickly. The faster, the better. We're an instant society. We used to wait days for photos, then we got them in same day, and now we get them in an hour. Now I see 45-minute photos advertised. We want the benefit, and we want it in our hands immediately. It hasn't been too many years ago that the ad said, "Lose 10 pounds in 30 days!" Well, that's not fast enough. Those were successful ads then, but now we want ads that promise we can lose 10 pounds in 10 days. We want the benefits in our hands *right now*.

The third component is to increase the quantity of the benefit. In other words, **give your customers more results for the same effort.** For a book on speed-reading, that might be, "Double your reading speed in just seven days" or "Double your power to learn." Always promise a larger benefit for the same amount of effort.

The fourth component is guaranteed results. We all want to think the magic pill we're looking at is guaranteed to give us the results we want. Certainly we want to achieve those results at the lowest possible price, but if the pill is magic, low price isn't important.

I think those are the **key ingredients of that magic pill: no effort, quick results, larger benefits.** These are so powerful that you could chart the potential success of a product by how close you get to the magic pill. The closer you are, the more people are willing to pay for it. With a lot of advertising, that's exactly what happens. They move toward the magic pill until it gets to the point that it stretches our credibility, and then we go back and start going another direction, and we move toward the magic pill again.

So the magic pill is important for you to figure out. Let's just take a quick example here, and go back to my mention of the headline "Lose 10 pounds in 30 days!" To make it stronger we might say, "Lose 10 pounds in the next 10 days!" That would do it, right? It promises the benefit faster. Then we can move closer to the magic pill. "Lose 10 pounds in the next 10 days without exercise!" That makes it stronger and closer to the pill. "Lose 10 pounds in the next 7 days without dieting, while you sleep!" That's even stronger, because we've shortened the time and reduced the effort. What could be easier? The next step might be "Lose 10 pounds in 7 days while you sleep — while eating anything you want!" Now, that's even better — but here's the danger. When we started getting really close to that magic pill, we start stretching that credibility, and there's a very

The power of pressure: In the midnight hour — when the deadlines are closing in — you are forced to make decisions.

- The walls of indecision begin breaking down.

- And the answers, which were once very muddy now become clear.

fine line there — because what is the magic pill? In this dieting example, it's "Lose 10 pounds instantly in your sleep — tonight!" That's what they're really looking for, so we just have to get as close as we can and deliver. But we also need to know when to stop. **So look for headlines and titles and product benefits that come as close as is credible to being a magic pill, and your sales and your profits will both skyrocket.**

I've worried for years about hyping my products too much. It's been a major concern of mine. How close do you get to the whole magic side of the whole thing without it being too unrealistic? What we've tried to do — but not accomplished — is that whenever we have an offer that we feel gets real close to the magic pill, **we try to build tremendous credibility into the whole promotion so we can justify the hype.** We worry a lot about going over the top, but we hardly ever do. Because that's true, <u>80 percent of your message should be emotion, and only 20 percent intellect.</u> People make their buying decisions on emotions, mostly — but when you tell someone they can lose 10 pounds in 7 days while they sleep and still eat like a pig, a good percentage are going to say, "This sounds so good, and this is just what I want, but I just don't believe this person!"

That's when **you need to provide an explanation for the intellect:** "this is possible because of A, B and C," and give very good A, B and C reasons because all they want is a little nudge to their intellect. **The rest of the buying decision will be due to their emotions.** You need a gimmick to give them a reason that it will happen: "It's because of this secret ingredient or ancient herb that has been added." Give them some component that makes it happen, that gives them an explanation for the benefit.

Be honest with your explanation, but also tell them the truth about it. My friend Ted Ciuba has an offer where he tells people, "You can earn a $1,000 per hour with this business opportunity!" Well, that's the truth — but you can't earn $40,000 a week in a normal business week. There's an asterisk right next to the offer that leads to a footnote that says, "Beware! These results refer to the time that you actually spend in doing these deals. This will likely be the average that you actually earn."

Disclaimers are important, and not just because you warned them. You see, people are skeptical when they read our materials. No matter how much they want to believe, there's another part of them that has gotten ripped off before. There's always that little voice in the back of their head that says, "Yeah, right!" You've got to address that little voice. That's the whole secret here.

As I've said, I often worry about going over the top, making it all too "hypey." In my opinion, **it's fine to make the first draft of your copy over the top.** In fact, I think it's a good idea; you just have to go back and tame it later. When you edit, you can soften those claims and bring it more into line. If you're holding back because you're afraid you're going over the top, what I fear you'll do is reduce the enthusiasm and excitement in your letter. **If you let all that out, and get that enthusiasm and excitement in your first draft, then you can go back and bring your claims more into line with what you think people will believe.** You can have a claim that's valid but still sounds unbelievable. Sometimes it's better to scale it back a little and make it sound a little more believable — even though you can deliver more than you're promising.

One other thing to remember when you're writing copy is to **try to predict the questions that are going to pop into your reader's mind.** For example, you should directly address the point about people believing that something's too good to be true. You can say, "Okay, I know by now that you're probably skeptical. You probably think this is too good to be true — but let me tell you exactly why it *is* true." Or maybe they're wondering, "How can they do this? How can they give me a $500 television for $10?" **So you answer that question.** You say, "By now you're probably wondering how in the heck we can offer this $500 television for $10. Let me explain. A whole big bunch of these fell off of a truck and we found them in a ditch, so now we're selling them to you for $10!" Don't ignore the questions in their heads. You don't pretend they're not going to ask — because they will. **What you need to do is come up with a reasonable, credible answer for any question they have.** If you can do that, if you can answer that question, then you've pulled them back into your letter. In some cases you don't have to worry about these big claims, as long as you have a story that makes them reasonable in your reader's mind.

Here's another simple but important point that all of us, as professionals, live by. We get into this state where we write these what I call "National Enquirer" headlines and copy — but we always come back and edit. **Never tell a lie, but don't be afraid to express your opinions. Just be honest.** For example, we have a promotion right now where we're telling our customers that the future's uncertain. We have a solid plan that this is going to bring in a million dollars a month for our company. There are no guarantees or promises, but that's our goal. We believe that this is the million-dollar-a-month plan for us, and you can cash in with us. The promise is out there, the allure that attracts new clients, **but we also make it clear that nothing is guaranteed.** We've been careful to state our claim in a way that's balanced enough so that the customer will understand it, and won't think we're trying to fool them.

SECRET FOURTEEN:

The greatest challenge of Direct-Mail Marketing, and how to overcome it and make huge sums of money.

The greatest challenge of **Direct-Mail is simply the fact that it's an advertising message carrier with no entertainment value.** This can make it harder to get people's attention, and here's an absolute truth: people want to be entertained. They want to see jugglers and dancers, people singing, and all that stuff. Most people in this country are like zombies who are hypnotized by their lives and they're just doing the same thing day after day. They get up and go to work. They have lunch and continue to work. They go home and sit in front of the television for a couple of hours. That's a little bit of entertainment, but they really zone out during television. They go to bed, and then they do it all over again. They're hypnotized.

A lot of people think, "Well, in this situation, it's going to be easy for me to sell, because people like mail. If I send it to them, they're going to read it." But that's not necessarily true. You have to realize, first of all, that **your message really has to stand out because people have other things competing for their attention.** They have television: it's piped into their house 24 hours a day, 365 days a year. They have more channels now than ever before. There's the telephone. There are FAX machines, and now there's the Internet, which is even bigger than cable television or even satellite television — and it's growing all the time. At the same time you're mailing them a sales letter, there are 5 or10 other companies doing that too on that exact same day. So you're saying, "Oh, my gosh. Direct-Mail marketing, I can't do that!

▼▼▼▼▼▼▼▼▼▼▼▼▼▼▼▼▼

If you scare people bad enough, you can get them to do almost anything. They'll follow whoever has the solution.

From the movie "The Mist"

It's an impossible task." **But it's *not* an impossible task — far from it.** What you have to do is ask yourself the right question: "How can I give them some entertainment value in this Direct-Mail piece? How can I separate myself from everything else? What can I do, or what five things can I do, what seven things can I do, what ten powerful things can I do to this Direct-Mail piece that's going to make them stop what they're doing and sit down with this letter and start to read it and get involved?"

There are several other things you can do to get people to read your letter. **First, consider the envelopes you mail it in.** You have to decide if it's going to be sneak-up mail: is it going to look like a Hallmark card that maybe Aunt Mary sent? Is it going to look like an official piece of mail from a lawyer or the IRS? Or is it going to be all junked up with teaser

▼▼▼▼▼▼▼▼▼
MARKETING SECRET

Take-away Se ling: All the things you strive to do to make it seem as if they need you a lot more than you need them!

- It's kind of like the dance of romance... In the dating game, they say: "Run until they catch you!"

copy, giving the benefits that you know that they want because you have that targeted mailing list? **If you know their desires, you can hit them right off the bat on the envelope with that biggest desire and that biggest benefit.**

Another thing you can do is grabbers. If someone gets something in the mail that's kind of lumpy or bumpy, that piques their interest. Hey, maybe there's something of value in it! There can be a lot of different things in an envelope that can stimulate people's curiosity because all the other mail they're getting is Plain Jane ordinary mail. This one has something in it, so they want to open it up.

A third thing has to do with the letter. Once they've opened it up, **you can get their attention with all sorts of different fonts.** You can have Times New Roman, and you can have Courier, and you can have Arial, and any of the hundreds of other different fonts that are available. **You can have bold highlighting or underlining,** and some of the fonts can be larger than others — as long as you break them from their hypnotized state with a little variation. If you have the entire letter — 8, 12, 24 pages or more — all in 10-point Courier with none of it bolded or underlined, you're just putting them right back into the trance state, and they'll go to something more exciting like watching a test pattern on TV.

Another thing you can do is **add pictures.** People love to look at pictures, so add them to your letter. **You can tell them stories.** You can give them **testimonials.** There are tons of different things that you can do, but you have to realize that with all the competition out there, with all the entertainment they have piped into their homes and as hypnotized as these people are, you have to ask yourself the question: *"What can I do to wipe all that other stuff away and put my Direct-Mail piece on the top of the pile and get their full attention?"* If you can answer that question, you've hit the key, and you can have a very successful Direct-Mail campaign that blows everything else away.

While it may go against your grain, **it's important to make that marketing piece as entertaining to the eye as possible.** Use different fonts, different colors, striking graphics. It also makes the mail stand out, and that's very important. This kind of design mixture entertains the eye and gets it excited, just like good copy gets the mind excited. There's one caution you need to take here: if you're selling upscale products to an upscale market, this tactic doesn't work well. Otherwise, it really does make a big difference.

We have a piece out there right now that's working great for us. It's this 17 x 22 poster that's folded down and then mailed in an 8 ½ x 11 format. I swear this piece is terrible looking! It's like a disaster. It has all these weird colors all over it, and the copy is ugly looking and irregular. The whole piece looks like a train wreck — and yet it's pulling. One of the reasons **it's pulling is because it looks different from anything out there in the mail stream.** We knew that people were either going to hate it or respond well to it; there was no middle ground. It was wild, it was crazy, it was loaded with all these odd features... I even included my whole family photograph, with my son-in-law and my daughter-in-law and my grandkids. I blew it up real huge, and put it all on there. Somebody who isn't familiar with our market would go, "What in the hell is this?"

But you see, it's not a train wreck for our market. **It violates a lot of good design rules, but content wise it's absolutely perfect — because it's establishing me as a real person.** The family picture says I'm a family man, and that I've been around awhile. It's all the things that are opposite of the anonymous corporate crap that comes out of New York or Chicago. Visually, it's also exciting, although it violates a lot of rules of visual layout. In marketing terms, it's packed with powerful principles.

What's important, too, is to realize that when people speak to each other, they usually do so informally, but most people make things a lot more formal when they write. It's good to get away from that because **the more we can talk to our prospects one-to-one, informally, the better,**

usually, the sales letter is. Formal grammar and the things you're taught in college don't make a great sales letter. You have to try to talk to people in your communications the same way you'd talk to them if they were sitting just three feet away from you. Write so that your personality comes out on the page — so you sound like you're a real person. **Most people don't really want to do business with companies, they want to do business with other people.** I think that's especially true in Direct-Response Marketing, though maybe not retail so much.

One of the things that we've been doing lately is putting dollar bills in a lot of our mailings. **We get brand new, crisp, uncirculated one-dollar bills and we glue them onto our letters** with a special glue stick that uses the same kind of glue you get on Post-It notes. I even get phone calls — I swear this is true — from people apologizing because they didn't have the money to take us up on the offer but they felt guilty because we sent them a dollar! It's not like our switchboard's always lighting up with calls like these, but we've received them on more than one occasion. Now, we're going to take that idea one step further, and on our more expensive packages we're going to test $2 bills and $5 bills — and we're going to even test $10 bills on our very expensive packages.

Of course, we're going to test these very slowly. Only a fool would test 1,000 letters with $10 bills on them without testing 50 or 100 first — but we're thinking that if you put a $10 bill on a letter to your very best customer for a high-priced item, you're just going to shock them. And that's what you need to do: **you have to find a way to just wake them up and get their attention.** You have to find a way to wake them up and zap them. Jeff Gardner says that when he's writing these pieces, he's thinking of a mental cattle prod. What can he add to his letter that's going to be a cattle prod to zap the readers out of their trance, and get them to pay attention? After all, they have so much other stuff they could pay attention to. **If you don't zap them immediately and put your best offer at the end of the letter, if you make it bland and boring, then you've lost the game.** The game is making money. That's why we're in this business. You can't make that money if you can't get people involved in a letter — and you can't get them involved in a letter if there's not something that shocks them awake, that makes them *want* to become involved in the letter. You absolutely have to cut through the clutter and get their attention.

FOOLPROOF SECRETS of Successful Marketers!

SECTION THREE:

THE RUTHLESS MARKETING ATTACK!

The Golden Key to Destroying All of Your Direct Competitors and Getting All of the Money That Could and Should Be Yours

INTRODUCTION:

"What Ruthless Means to Me"

The system I'm going to teach you in this book is called Ruthless Marketing. I know that sounds somewhat coldblooded, so I thought I'd start off by telling you exactly why I chose that name for both the system and the title of this book.

At first, it doesn't seem like the most charming title, especially given the word with which I started. If you look up its primary definition, "ruthless" isn't a good word at all; it's actually pretty terrible. It describes people who can hurt others without any remorse, or who can inflict pain on somebody else without it bothering them. Sociopaths and psychopaths, in other words.

But that's not what I'm trying to convey here. The English language is constantly evolving, and "ruthless" has more subtle, less-offensive meanings than the one mentioned above. The meaning of "ruthless" I chose for this system is, well, less ruthless than the official meaning. It's closer to "aggressive" or "assertive" than anything else. **With this kind of ruthlessness, you're being proactive by taking your success into your own hands.** You're not just waiting for things to happen; you're out there making things happen. "Ruthless" is a great marketing term because it paints a word picture in your mind. Think of somebody who's "aggressive." Get a word picture? Not so much. "Assertive?" Even weaker. How about "ruthless"? That's it. **If you want to sell something to somebody, you need to engage their mind first.**

I could just as accurately have called this book *Aggressive Marketing Attack* — but it doesn't sound as catchy, does it? It's not as dramatic. **It's not as marketable**. And therein lies the heart of the system: marketing. If you ask a hundred different experts what "marketing" means, you're going to get a hundred different definitions. A college business professor might talk your ear off for 10 or 20 minutes about the definition of marketing, and you won't even understand half of what they're saying. **But my definition of marketing is simple: it's all the things you do in your business to attract and then sell to the right people, the ones who are perfectly**

The 4 laws of self teaching:

1. You are your greatest teacher.

2. You can learn anything you want to learn

3. You must take total responsibility for everything that happens to you.

4. Experience + Reflection = Wisdom!

suited for whatever it is you're selling.

And then there's the third word in the title. What does "attack" mean to you? When I studied that word, I saw plenty of negative definitions. It's a very aggressive word. But whenever I do word studies, I always look at its antonym — that is, the opposite of that particular word. It turns out that the opposite of attack is defend. **There's a certain mindset involved in the act of defending, whether in warfare or in marketing, and there's another involved in the act of attacking.** Again, we encounter words like offensive, proactive, assertive, aggressive.

So think about the whole idea behind the name of this product: *"Ruthless Marketing Attack."* Think of it as something that's offensive, in the best sense of the word, rather than defensive. It's the opposite of passive. That's beneficial to you as a marketer, and do you know why? **Because most business people are unbelievably passive, and you can easily take advantage of their passivity in order to profit.**

I can best define this with a story, which comes from my friend and mentor Russ von Hoelscher. Russ is the man who helped us become millionaires back in the late 1980s; he was the guy who taught us the secrets of effective marketing. Russ used to have (and note that I say used to have) one printer who did all his printing. Russ is a marketing guy, so he was constantly giving his printer all kinds of marketing advice, saying stuff like, "Look, John, you ought to do this and this and this to promote your printing business." But John's answer was always the same: **"Russ, if they want printing, they know where to come."** He had a little sign up in front of his shop and figured that would bring him all the work he needed.

Have you ever seen the movie Field of Dreams, with Kevin Costner? The whole message of that movie was, **"If you build it — they will come."**

Most business owners have adopted that mentality as their own. **It's a passive kind of thing; they're just sitting back, waiting for people to come to them, hoping the market's going to improve, hoping things are going to change**. They're blaming everybody and everything for their circumstances: the economy, the competition, roadwork, maybe the weather. Life gets hard, and the first time they face major adversity they give up. **That mindset is the opposite of the mindset I'm planning to drill into your head with this book**. Think of it as "Passive Marketing Acceptance," as opposed to what you'll be learning here.

Their mindset is good news for you, though, because if you can be ruthless in the right way, you're going to grab their business away from them. You'll be one of those factors they're complaining about, instead of doing something about. **If there's one thing I want you to take away from this book, it's the confidence of knowing that if you choose to use the ideas and methods that I'll be sharing with you, you have a major advantage over most of the business people out there**. And when I say "most," I'm talking about as many as 80-90% of the people selling in your market: the folks who do things in a haphazard, weak, and ineffective way.

Early this morning, I cracked open one of my favorite quote books, and here's the quote that hit me: **"The uncommitted life isn't worth living."** It's a quote from 1963 by a man named Marshall Fishwick. That's a heck of a thing to have hit you at six AM, but I thought it was appropriate. When I think of good marketers — the ones that I respect, the ones from whom I take my cues — I find that they're deeply committed. **There's nothing that's going to stop these guys.** They face all kinds of adversity, they keep getting knocked down, and they keep getting up over and over again. No matter how bad things get, they ain't quitting! And because they refuse to quit, they never lose.

I know that that sounds simplistic, like something you'd get out of some cheesy self-help book, but it's true. These marketers are in it with all their hearts. **They refuse to quit — and because they refuse to quit,**

they can't be beaten. If they keep pushing and keep learning and keep expanding, they eventually develop the knowledge, skills, and experience that take them to the top. And then, of course, everybody says that they got lucky — but that's another story.

The Truth About Talent

There's a show business adage that says, "Talent rises to the top." I believe that's true to some extent, but I also believe something else: **I believe we have it within ourselves to create our own talent.**

A while back, my granddaughter was over at my house. She plays her dad's drums sometimes, and she was telling me that she has absolutely no talent at it. Those were her actual words: an 11-year-old girl told me, "I have absolutely no talent." I told her, "Honey, if you stick with it long enough, you'll develop your talent." **I honestly believe that if you want something bad enough, and you're willing to pay the price and do whatever it takes to get it, eventually you'll develop the necessary ingredients — the knowledge, the skills, and the experience — to take you to the top.**

Take my company, for example. We've worked our tails off and have striven to develop our talent over the course of almost twenty years, and **so far we've earned over $113 million in sales in our first 19 years**. I'm not telling you this to brag, (okay, maybe a little!), but my point is that you really can develop your talent and make loads of money if you just keep trying. That's my definition of talent: not knowing when to quit. In fact, some would say that's my biggest talent, period.

You don't go from $0 to $113 million in 19 years, by doing the opposite of Ruthless Marketing. You have to be aggressive in the marketplace. You have to go out there and do everything within your power — legally, morally, ethically — to get as much of the market share as you can. **It doesn't matter what your business is, what your products or services are, or to whom you're selling**. It's all about being aggressive in your marketplace and attempting to get as many dollars as you can out of that marketplace.

My friend and colleague Chris Lakey defines *Ruthless Marketing*

Attack as "the offensive-minded battle that is waged in the marketplace over who gets the largest share of your market's disposable income." Marketing sissies need not enter the game.

When I was a kid I watched a few of those pro-wrestling survivor matches — you know, where they start with something like 30 wrestlers in the ring, and the goal is to be the last one standing. **Just about anything goes in that kind of match,** and the goal is to get the other guys out of the ring and onto the floor of the arena. They can be hanging on the ropes, or over the side of the ring, and that's okay; but once they hit the floor they're out.

That's what *Ruthless Marketing Attack* is all about: kicking the other guys in your marketplace out of the ring. **Within certain moral, ethical, and legal boundaries, your business is in a fight for survival.** It's do or die. Darwin's theory was survival of the fittest, but in business it's survival of the fattest — fattest bank account, that is! There are hundreds of millions of dollars being spent every year on all kinds of non-essential products and services. **Don't let people tell you they don't have money because they've got it.** We're the richest nation in the world, and people have money. It's just a matter of whether they're spending it with you or with one of your competitors. You've got to learn to attract their attention, to stay in there and take the money that could and should be yours. In large part, that's what talent is, in business or in life: pure tenacity, the will to stick to it and learn to do what needs to be done in order to survive and thrive.

Let me reemphasize that all the money that you want is out there waiting for you right now, in the pockets, purses, bank accounts, and credit card authorizations of millions of people who've been fragmented into smaller and smaller niche markets as our society becomes increasingly technological and complex. It can be hard to get to, sure, because nowadays there are now niches within niches within niches. But this is a good thing! It gives the average entrepreneur like you and me, the person who wasn't born with a silver spoon in his mouth, the chance to use their intelligence and persistence to tease out a fortune from a market that might not have existed yesterday. **The average person has more chances today to make millions of dollars than ever before, just by serving these small niche markets.**

A new twist on the 80/20 rule:

- Focus your attention on the activities that rank in the top 20% in terms of importance — and you'll get an 80% return on your investment!

- Are you all spread out — or are you focused on the few key areas that can bring you the maximum sum of money?

That can require some hard work, but it can often generate obscene profits — the kind of money you'd never make in a regular job, even by working overtime and getting double time on holidays. **You can work when you want, as much as you want, and dress any way you want to**. That's the kind of power that having your own business can give you — and why else would you start your own business? Admittedly, you sometimes have to scramble and reassess your business, especially if the market changes. It's always a challenge because, since the can be so fickle, what works today might not work tomorrow. **But the principles of Ruthless Marketing — whether you're selling information, opportunity, products, or services — are applicable to just about any market, and any business.** And remember: the right idea, just one little idea, can make you a million dollars.

Case in point: my colleague Chris Hollinger was recently talking about a sandwich shop that had opened up near his house. Ironically, the name of the shop was T.J.'s Deli! He'd go in there and see how they were doing, and they always seemed to be hurting for a little business. Once he became a "regular," he started giving them some ideas about how they could advertise. Chris noticed that that they had some very attractive young ladies working there, and suggested something he'd heard Russ von Hoelscher recommend for another sandwich shop in San Diego. Russ told the owner of that place, "Take these young girls you have working here, give them some samples of sandwiches, and have them go to these office complexes and pass out these sandwiches. It will get your business going!"

When Chris made the same suggestion to the folks at his local sandwich shop, the owner said, "Well, I don't know about that," but Chris said, "Trust me; it will work." They may or may not have done what Chris suggested, but a couple days later Chris drove by and saw one of those nice-looking girls out on the street with a sign that said "T.J. needs your business!" **And the parking lot was full at lunchtime**. So maybe Chris gave him an idea that will eventually earn the owner that million bucks.

The Zen of Ruthless Marketing

As you read this book, I want you to keep in mind these basic facts: **the secret to effectively making money in the marketing field is to find a niche, stubbornly develop that niche, and be ruthless in exploiting it in every legal, ethical, and moral way possible**. Can you be a ruthless, nice guy? Sure, as long as you're not nice to the wrong people — that is, your competitors. But you can make even them respect you. While being ruthless can have negative connotations in the business world, it does have a component that's very much admired: a relentlessness that people respect because the ruthless person is firm in their purpose and they never, never stop.

Ruthlessness is a mindset that you have to develop in order to make it and survive and prosper in business. **The reason is this: if you have a ruthless marketing mindset, you understand that the only activity that produces revenue in your business is marketing: communicating with your customers to get them to buy more from you, or to improve your relationship with your customer so that they will continue to buy from you in the future.**

Russ von Hoelscher's former printer is a perfect example of somebody who didn't understand why this is so important. He thought his business was about the printing. But business is not about the making of the thing, the delivering of the thing, or the hiring of the employees to manage the thing. **The only activity in your business that produces revenue is marketing**. As a business owner, marketing is the highest-value task you can do. When you adopt this ruthless marketing mindset, that's the thing that will carry you forward. **If you get caught up in the minutia of the accounting and the customer service and the shipping — things that other people are much better at doing — and you don't do the** marketing, then <u>your business will collapse</u>. Period.

A ruthless marketing mindset orients you to the fact that you've got to be using your time on the only thing that produces revenue in your business, which is marketing. And you have to be ruthless with yourself about that! <u>You have to be relentless with yourself</u>! You have to be aggressive about it on a day-to-day basis. Because if you're not, your revenue is going to dry up and you're going to end up being a passive pushover. That's no good because those guys go broke! So study the steps I've outlined in this book, chapter by chapter, take some notes, and apply what works to your business. **Get sufficiently ruthless, and <u>I guarantee</u> you'll see a difference in your income in less time than you thought possible.**

"My Story; or, a Tale of Two Men"

When I first started in business, I was in a bad place. I was broke, I was homeless, and my first business partner had just gotten out of prison. I've never told anybody this story before, but I want to tell it now because it serves a couple of points I want to make that are very important.

Think back to where you were in the summer of 1985, assuming you're old enough to remember that far back. Here's where I was: bouncing from one sales job to another. I'd been in sales for two years at that point, I didn't have a formal education, and that hurt me. I did want to make a lot of money, and the only way I could figure out how to do that was to sell stuff. So I bounced around from here to there, like so many other salespeople, going from one job to another to another.

There's a proverb from the 16th Century that says, "Little hinges swing big doors." For me, that happened when I answered an ad in a Wichita, Kansas, newspaper — a tiny ad that literally changed my life. It was a "Sales Help Wanted" ad that asked for route drivers. I went to apply and found that the location of the interview was somebody's house, which I thought was kind of strange. It turned out that this young couple had just bought into a carpet cleaning franchise — Rainbow International, out of Waco, Texas.

They were looking for drivers who would go out and work on commission and clean carpets. They'd spent all of their money, but even though they were leveraged to the hilt to buy this franchise, they were excited. They were about my age — in their early- to mid-20's — **and because they were so excited about the business, they got me excited about it, too!** Right away, I wanted to become a carpet cleaner. It was a good deal because I could keep 60% of whatever I booked — and I knew I could sell. That was my one big business talent.

The only problem was, in order to have this tremendous opportunity, I had to invest in a certain type of van on my own; they didn't have the money to provide it, and they wanted to see an act of faith on my part. So I went around and tried to get one, but I was broke, and no banker would loan me money to buy the kind of nice van they required me to get. **That's how bad my credit was**. I couldn't find anything I could afford, no matter what I did. The couple kept telling me, "Look, if you'll just get a vehicle, we'll supply the equipment."

To make a long story short, that deal fell through because I couldn't get a loan to buy that nice van I needed. But I was so sold on the idea of carpet cleaning that I went to the phone book and started calling up all the carpet cleaners in the area. I told them, "Look, I want to go to work for you on straight commission," and they all said no. I called 20 or 30 numbers before I finally found a guy in Canton, Kansas, about 30 miles from where I lived, and he said, "Okay, come out and see me. Let's talk."

> Having thousands of powerful direct mail sales letters (and the follow-up sales material that goes out after you generate the leads) is like having a GIANT ARMY of the very best salespeople who never complain... always deliver their best performance... and never ask for a raise!

So I borrowed a friend's car, because I was so broke that I didn't even have a car of my own. I was riding a bicycle, that's how broke I was. I went over there and basically sold this guy on the idea of me going to work

Think bigger! Focus on hitting the ball over the fence — and you can take your time walking around the bases!

- Sometimes you must keep your eyes to the stars and dream big dreams.

- Other times, you must keep your head down and charge forward like a raging bull!

for him. He had a Rainbow Carpet Cleaning franchise, too, which was good because I was already a little familiar with that. He had one van, and he immediately gave it to me to work with. I was out there right away, booking my own carpet cleaning jobs, getting 60% commission, and I fell in love with the business. I really liked it. He even sent me to carpet cleaning school in Waco, Texas. I was there for a couple of weeks, surrounded by all these guys who had just paid $50,000 for their franchises, and I was the only employee present. I went through all the same training they went through, even though I had to borrow the money to get on the Greyhound bus just to get to Waco. That's how poor I was in 1985. But these guys were all great. They just assumed I was a franchise owner, too, and I didn't tell them otherwise. I made some good friends, and it was a great experience.

On the way home from Waco, I got off the bus at Ark City, Kansas, and went to visit my best friend, who was in prison. His name was Gary Purvis. Gary was just getting ready to get out of prison, but I hadn't seen him for a couple years because I was living in another city when he got into trouble. Now, Gary was a great guy. I want you to know that he wasn't in prison because he was a hardened criminal; he was in prison because he was an idiot. He did the stupidest thing in the world, and it cost him 18 months of his life. I know this is going to sound crazy, but here's how it happened.

It all started because we used to fish in a little creek that runs through Newton, Kansas, called Sand Creek. At the end of that creek there used to be a rubber dam, and we always fished right there at the dam. Well, there was a little hole in the rubber, and every once in a while a fish would pop out. Honest to God! We used to joke, "Hey, what are we doing fishing here? Let's just hold our net down here and we'll catch the fish as they pop out of the hole."

So one day, Gary comes up with this idea: "Well, maybe I'll just make that hole a little bigger. Then more fish will pop out, and we'll just sit here with our net and catch them without even trying." **I'm not making this up!** So he pulls out his knife and widens the hole! Was it criminal? Yes, it was, but it was mostly just stupid. The hole was already there; he just made it a little bigger, and you know what? More fish did start popping out! But the hole weakened the dam, and it collapsed. Thousands of fish died, all because of that idiotic, stupid thing my friend Gary did.

If Gary had gone right to the authorities immediately, they would have slapped him on the wrists and put him on probation — he wouldn't have spent one day behind bars. But he was stupid and tried to hide it...except he told some of his friends about it, and they told some of their friends, and nine months later the police came knocking on his door, and ultimately Gary spent 18 months in prison. It was a valuable lesson for him in the end, and I can tell you this: he'll never go back to prison again.

So there I was, fresh out of carpet cleaning school in Waco, and I stopped by to see best friend Gary, who was just about to be released. I was so excited about the carpet cleaning business, and I told him all about it — and then I hitchhiked home because I was too broke to get back on the bus!

Gary got out of prison in November 1985 and came to see me right away. It was the fall season — one of the best seasons in the carpet cleaning business — and on a good week I was bringing home a thousand a week. Of course, I had to give 40% of it to the guy in Canton, but I was making pretty good money for a guy without any skills or education, a guy who had no family to support. **And so I was waving the cash in front of Gary and, sure enough, Gary gets excited and says, "T.J., let's go into the carpet cleaning business together!"**

I swear that if it hadn't been for Gary I would have never done it because I didn't have any money to buy the equipment. Even though I was making hundreds of dollars a week, I was spending it just as fast. And at the time, I'd just broken up with a woman I'd been living with, so I was basically homeless, crashing on friends' couches, and such. I pointed all that out and Gary told me, "Don't worry, T.J., we can get all the stuff we need." And sure enough, he was right.

Not that it was easy, by any means, because by then it was December (which is the worst time you could start a carpet cleaning business). When I told all my friends and family, "I'm getting ready to start my own carpet cleaning business now," they told me, "T.J., you're a fool! First of all, your partner just got out of prison. Second of all, it's December!" Once the snow comes in Kansas, people don't want you to come in to clean their carpets.

So there were all kinds of reasons why I should have never done it; if I'd been a sane, rational, intelligent human being, there's no way on God's green Earth that I would ever have gotten in the carpet cleaning business with somebody like Gary in December, with no money, with no equipment, with no nothing.

The thing is, I didn't listen to any of those people. Later, I'll talk about how entrepreneurship is tied to the same qualities that make some people into juvenile delinquents — at least according to Harvard business professor Abraham Zaleznik. **Those same qualities can serve us well in the world of entrepreneurialism because entrepreneurs go out there and make things happen.** They don't wait for the perfect circumstances. They take everything that could be against them and just say, **"To hell with it! I'm going to find a way to either go around it, through it, or over it."**

Both Gary and I were the entrepreneurial type, and we were entirely different from Dwayne, the man I was working for at the time. That's why I've subtitled this chapter "The Tale of Two Men," because it's a good way to contrast Dwayne and Gary.

Dwayne, my boss, was a man who grew up with money. His family owned hundreds of acres right here in Kansas, and when his parents died, they left it all to him. He spent $50,000 on this Rainbow Carpet Cleaning franchise six months before I met him. However — and this is not a put down to Dwayne, but it does serve as a good example here — what was he doing with that franchise? Nothing. The day I called him in the late summer of 1985, he was working at a factory in McPherson, Kansas, for $9 an hour, despite the fact that he'd spent $50,000 on this carpet cleaning franchise. **This is because Dwayne, although he was a nice and honest man, was also a very meek and mild man.** He was afraid of his own shadow, and should never have been self-employed — unless he first found a partner who had some of the qualities he lacked.

There are so many people who get into business for themselves who are like Dwayne: they lack what I call "hustle." **It's not a matter of being smart or dumb; it's just something else.** Dwayne was a very good and smart man, but he couldn't sell his way out of a paper bag. He was afraid of his own shadow. He was afraid of rejection. Well, by then I'd already been selling for a couple years, and I'd already had 10,000 phones hung up on me, and doors slammed in my face, I was immune to it all. But some people, like Dwayne, just can't handle that. They're not very aggressive and they don't have it within them to be turned down repeatedly. Dwayne had had the money, and he had invested in this franchise, and his carpet cleaning van was just collecting dust because he didn't know how to go out there and hustle.

That's one man. Then there's my friend, Gary, from Brooklyn. Gary was a hustler. Now, he wasn't a real criminal; he was a good man, or he would have never been my best friend, I can promise you that. **But he was a hustler; he was a guy who just made things happen.** So even though we were broke and he was just out of prison, he wanted it so bad that we went ahead and started the business. **There were a million reasons why we shouldn't have done it; any rational person would have said, "No way," and in fact I had people who cared about me beg me not to do it, telling me I was crazy.** Other people laughed at me. They all said I was being swayed by Gary. We did it anyway, and the truth is, the partnership didn't last very long. We made it less than a year before it broke down. But by that time we had two carpet cleaning trucks and two sets of equipment, and our split was easy — we just cut the business in half, and he went his way and I went mine. We weren't friends anymore, unfortunately. **Business can complicate pre-existing relationships, so be careful about that.**

But the bottom line is: it didn't matter if we were broke. It didn't matter if we didn't have equipment. He went out and found a guy with this beat-up van he wanted $300 for. Well, we didn't have $300! So what did Gary do? He offers the guy a thousand bucks — a hundred dollars a week for 10 weeks. And if we missed even one payment during those 10

▼▼▼▼▼▼▼▼▼
MARKETING SECRET

Henry David Thoreau was way ahead of his time... Here's what he said 150 years before pop psychology:

- "What you think of yourself is what determines your fate!"

- And most people spend their entire lives selling themselves short.

---

weeks, the guy got to keep all the money and we had to give him the van back. That was Gary.

Then he went out there and he found a little janitorial supply house in Wichita, and he hustled the guy and worked out a deal where we got all of our equipment without any money down. **Then he went out there and drummed up the business, just like I'd been drumming up the business.**

Even though it was the middle of winter and nobody wanted their carpets cleaned, we made it work. We got into these senior citizen towers over in Newton (there's two of them) and we just started knocking on doors and cleaning carpets and furniture. **We did great work, and they told their friends about us, and they told their friends.** We spent the winter of 1985-1986 working like crazy. We did almost every single apartment in these two senior citizen towers because we sat down with those older people, we ate food with them, we met them, we befriended them, we loved them, and they loved us. **We ended up surviving that difficult period because we treated our customers well, and we then built on those relationships.**

Even though our partnership ultimately folded, it was still a great partnership. I never would have gotten into business if it hadn't been for Gary. **We both had the right entrepreneurial skills, what I call "the skills of a salesperson," a hustler, somebody who's going to go out there and make it no matter what.** If you lack that, you need to find a partner who has it. The partnership may not last, but at least it'll get you started. That experience eventually led to me meeting my wife and forging a partnership that ended up making us

---

millions of dollars. **When you get it right, success is a little like dominoes**: when one goes down, the next one falls, and the next one, and so on. But like Theodore Roosevelt once said, you have to, "Begin where you are with what you have."

I think if there's anyone who represents what a ruthless marketer is all about, it's Gary, who could sell to anyone and wouldn't take no for an answer. Now, Gary's a very flawed individual. He's a good person — he was raised right, and came from a good, solid family environment — but he's a little bit crazy, which I think is typical of all entrepreneurs. Compare him to Dwayne, another great guy, who was born with a silver spoon in his mouth, and lived in one of the nicest homes in the area. Dwayne had always had money; his life was always pretty much set. And yet, he got involved in this business and didn't know what to do with it.

I'm very proud to be an entrepreneur, and I love other people who share those types of dreams, who want to make things happen. Take my current best friend, who owns Midwest Pest Control in Wichita, Kansas. Although Wichita's a relatively small market, she has over a hundred competitors — yet her company is one of the biggest and most successful in the business. Kerry Thomas, the guy who runs the whole thing for her, has this great quote that I just love because it's a ruthless marketing-type quote. Kerry once told me, "<u>**Look, T.J., you're right. We do have a hundred competitors — but we have no competition**</u>." I wrote that down in my journal that night, and I've been thinking about it ever since. Kerry's just made that way: he's got that swagger, that confident thing going, and his attitude has permeated the entire organization. All their pest control operators carry themselves confidently, their trucks are immaculately clean, their uniforms are crisply pressed, and their attitude is, "We're the best." As a matter of fact, that's part of their slogan: "If you want the best, call Midwest!"

Part of what the ruthless mindset is all about is having that attitude. It's a certain spirit, a way of believing, that can help you succeed no matter the obstacles. Gary had it, Dwayne didn't.

Realize that "The Secret" is Really Hard Work

Most books on business success don't talk about the hard, focused work, the discipline, the sacrifice, and the commitments that characterize all super-successful people. Why? **Because this is not something that most people want to hear**. My best example is the popular book called *The Secret*. Like so many other books out there, *The Secret* tells you that everything will work out fine if you just think positively. That's all there is to *The Secret*. **If you believe in *The Secret*, God bless you — maybe there's some truth to it**. But it sounds like your basic wish fulfillment fantasy to me.

Books full of affirmation and similar New Age claptrap tend to sell a lot; people eat that stuff up. Hey, I do too! I'm not going to be a hypocrite and tell you I haven't spent a lot of money buying into the "three steps to this," "two steps to that," "one step to the other," "the one-minute whatever," or "the instant millionaire." But the bald truth is that while some of this stuff is helpful, most of it's crap.

Probably the best book on business I've ever read is called *McDonald's: Behind the Arches* by John F. Love. It was written in the mid-1980s, so it's outdated a little, but I tell everyone about it. **Why they're not teaching this in business school is beyond me because this is the real, unvarnished truth about one man and his dream**, and what it took to create what's now the world's largest holder of commercial real estate in the world: the McDonald's Corporation. They're really in the real estate business, by the way, even though everybody thinks they're in the fast food business. And there's another book I just finished reading for the third time: it's called *Hard Drive*, and it tells the story of Microsoft. I've got other books about Microsoft, too, and I've got books about Steve Jobs, Michael Dell, and Sam Walton. **You read those books and you'll realize that the real formula for success is hard, focused work**. That's probably why they don't teach them in business schools: because that's not what people want to hear.

The willingness to put in hard, focused work is the common element in all the successful companies and entrepreneurs out there,

▼▼▼▼▼▼▼▼▼▼▼▼▼

S TOP fooling yourself! Nothing is easier than being busy and nothing is more difficult than being effective.

What are you doing (today) to dramatically increase your bottom line sales and profits?

and you'll see it repeated over and over in all personal and company biographies.

Look at people like Ray Kroc, who started with very little at the age of 52, and all the things it took to build McDonald's, a tremendous corporation that's still thriving years after his death.

Look at Bill Gates. The day he officially dropped out of college and told his father, "I'm not going back, Dad," his father said, "Son, you've just thrown your whole life away." Of course, we all know the story didn't turn out that way; he worked his tail off, and now he's reaping the profits.

When you read books about people who have actually turned small sums of money into huge fortunes, you'll find out they didn't use *The Secret* to make themselves the successes they are today. They didn't just sit around and affirm it all, and chant positive things, and get their minds right. All that has its place — attitude definitely plays a big role in success, there's no question about that — but it's hardly the major component in business success. **These people all worked hard, focused constantly on what they wanted, and practiced dramatic self-discipline and sacrifice to get where they are today.**

So look at the facts, and let those facts guide you. Read the stories of other super-successful people, the ones that are mostly told in biographies (not autobiographies — they're too unreliable), and you'll find that it took a lot of work for that success to happen. They serve as models for all of us.

Let's look at Bill Gates again. **Want to talk about ruthless marketing?** Here is your primary model. He's one of the most ruthless marketers in history. Books like *Hard Drive* prove just how ruthless, how relentless, he is. When he got the IBM deal in 1981 — the catalyst for building his whole corporation — he called his Mom up. He used to go to his parents' house for dinner every Sunday, but after the IBM deal he told his mother, "Mom, I'm not going to see you or call you for the next six

Direct-Response marketing takes a day to learn and a lifetime to master!

- There are so many variables — and few absolutes. The master is continually learning, growing, adapting, and taking his or her skills to a higher level.

- It's better to know some of the questions than all of the answers.

months. You're not going to hear from me." **He was so focused, so dedicated, so committed, so passionate about putting that whole thing together that he knew he was going to be sacrificing most of his personal life for a long time.** Whole weeks would go by, and he would barely leave his office. Sometimes he didn't even take time off to take a shower!

Another book of which I'm a big fan is Robert Ringer's *Winning Through Intimidation*. In that book, Ringer presents a view of business reality that I've found really holds up. **When a lot of people get into the business, they've got this idea that maybe they'll do a little bit of work, they'll become successful, and they'll stay that way.** In other words, they don't have a firm grasp of reality — and therefore, they make bad decisions about their business. **Let me reiterate this: the reality of succeeding in business, no matter the field, is to accept that you're going to have to devote a lot of time, energy, and effort to it if you want to succeed**. So you might as well recognize that and embrace it. Once you do, it turns you into a completely different person — and you realize that books like *The Secret* and *The Four Hour Work Week* are so much B.S. That's not to say that they're completely useless; there are some good ideas here and there, and they've got excellent marketing titles. But come on — affirming your way to success without working hard? Succeeding on four hours a week? **A lot of people want to accept the impression that they're going to be able to work four hours a week and spend the rest of the week screwing off, and they're still going to have a successful business**. If you believe that, well, I have this bridge in Brooklyn I can sell ya, cheap! Come on, you know none of that's true; if wishes were horses, beggars really would ride. If you're going to run a successful business — if you're going to make money and keep your money — you'd better spend more than four hours a week working on it.

The point is that if you want to be successful, you do have to devote a lot of time, energy, and effort to what you've chosen. But the other side of that coin is that it has to be something that you really believe is worth doing. There's a point where you have to look at what you're doing and say, "Look, if I don't want to devote everything I need to to this business, then I should quit trying to become successful from a financial point of view, and go off and just have a good time and do something else." Because that's the price that has to be paid for success in any business. That's reality. That's the real secret: you've got to recognize and embrace reality. That doesn't mean you can't enjoy yourself; applying the analogy of business as a game, you can find that playing this game really is a lot of fun. If you get into it, and it's the right thing, what you thought was work really isn't work after all. So you end up devoting a lot of hours to it, and the payoff both in financial terms and in what you become and achieve is well worth the effort that's involved. But, there is effort involved.

For years I've been accused of being a workaholic because I put in a lot of hours every week. But the truth is, a lot of what I do is anything but work. That's not to say that it's easy; that's not to say that I'm not putting in a lot of effort. But it's fun, so putting in long hours doesn't burn me out. I think for a lot of business people, "work" is a nasty four-letter word. The way that they look at their businesses causes working in them to be real drudgery. Whereas to an entrepreneur, work is fun — it's interesting, it's challenging. **You put your passion into it, your excitement, your enthusiasm, and it actually enhances rather than depletes you. It actually builds you up**.

Chris Hollinger told me a story recently about going into a convenience store to get some Gatorade after a stiff game of basketball with his brother. He found a little newspaper called *The Rural Messenger* that included a quote from Henry David Thoreau that went something like this: *"The cost of anything is measured in the amount of life you're willing to exchange for it."* After Chris read it aloud, the lady who was working behind the counter looked at him and said, "What am I doing here?" She was trading those hours that she spent behind the counter for a paycheck at the end of the week. **And Chris got to reflecting about how, given the astronomical number of hours he and his wife were putting into their business, they ought to be total wiped out by the end of the week.** If they'd been putting in that time in a classroom or regular job they sure would have been. But they're not! They're energetic and happy with their work.

Here's a good way to make you understand that: look at a time in your life when you were doing something you were good at, and you really had fun doing it... like a hobby or vocation. **It can even be something hard, like algebra, once that light bulb clicks on in your head — suddenly it makes sense, everything works, and you look forward to doing it.** It's not work. That's how it is with direct-response marketing, once you get in the groove. It's a lot of work putting the systems together, getting the back-end offers all ready, building the lead generation systems, and then building that relationship with customers. Sure, it can be a lot of work. But man, it's a great game to play!

The Real Power of a Positive Attitude

Real success requires a lot of real work — enjoyable work, maybe, but hard work nonetheless. Nothing's just going to come to you unless you're incredibly lucky. But should you throw *The Secret* out the window altogether? Actually, no. The book has a few ideas that are worth listening to. **The most important thing you can learn from it is that an optimistic and positive attitude, is self-fulfilling. Whereas if you think negatively of yourself all the time, you may never take that first step that leads you to the answer you need.** The danger is that some of these books on manifestation and affirmation take advantage of people by making them believe that as long as they think those positive thoughts, everything will come to them automatically. My mentor Dan Kennedy has a real good take on that. He says that all that stuff is fine, but it's a lie of omission, because in addition to having a positive attitude, you have to have a realistic attitude toward work. **They tell you, "If you just do it you'll get the results," but don't mention that you have to take action in conjunction with that positive attitude.**

And I understand that. It's based on an important marketing principle: **sell people what they want, give them what they need.** I could write a sales letter right now that said, "Look, I've got this great business opportunity; it's got the potential to make you a lot of money, but you're going to have to work long hours. You're going to have to bust your butt. You're going to have to put in the time," and guess what? There's no way that I would make any sales.

Frankly, I probably wouldn't be here today if that hadn't happened to me. If people would have told me how difficult some things that I've gone after really would be, and the price that I'd have to pay to achieve some of the things I've achieved in this world, there's no way I would have ever gotten started. I promise you that. **Back in the 1980s, I just wanted to become a millionaire; I didn't want to have to do all the things I've had to do to develop my knowledge and skills and whatever abilities I've managed to acquire so far**. Other people are the same way, and they've helped us build our business. We've got programs where we do everything for the customer. And yet the people who want to make the most money are the ones who take it way beyond all that.

Case in point: the first distributorship we made available was called "Dialing For Dollars." We sold 150,000, and out of those we had maybe five or six hundred people who were really successful. Think about that. That's kind of shocking to some people, but not to those who understand how it worked. When we were just a baby company back in 1989 or 1990, one guy was doing $5 million a year working our "Dialing For Dollars" program, when we were only doing about two million a year. **He was doing more than twice the amount of business we were doing, and he was one of our distributors!** But he was a renegade in every way. **He broke all the rules we outlined in our "Dialing For Dollars" book — everything we told him to do, he did the exact opposite and he was making the most money out of all of them!** He tested a lot of things. He tried a lot of things. <u>He had his own ideas. He was independent. He was a ruthless marketer</u>!

Remember what Henry David Thoreau said: *"The cost of anything is measured by the amount of life you're willing to exchange for it."* If you want to make millions of dollars, there's no easy simple way to do it that I know of. And I would be very suspicious of anybody who came along and told me that there was. In fact, I'd grab my wallet and start backing away toward the door! That was my point in discussing the business biographies earlier. These are the people who have paid the largest price in terms of the sacrifice, the commitment, the dedication, the hours they've put into their enterprises. Those entrepreneurs are people who are willing to do for a short time what most people are not willing to do at all.

Take the example of Bill Gates, when he was just absolutely focused for six months. Sure, he went to the Mercedes dealer and got a new Mercedes. But the first thing he told them before he drove it off the lot was, "I want you to take the radio out of it." When they asked, "Why?" He just said, "Just do it." **The reason he took his radio out of the car was, he didn't want any distractions**. While he was driving to and from work, he just wanted to stay focused on his work. That's an extreme example, but still it represents a man who was totally into his vision. He didn't want anything to get in the way of his thinking through where he was headed. **If you really want to make a lot of money, you'll have to be that focused on your business, too**. As Abraham Lincoln once put it, *"Good things come to those who wait, but only what's left over from those who hustle."*

"Hope for the Best, Prepare for the Worst..."

Every business owner has their dream, or they wouldn't be in business. We all need to be audacious, to take calculated risks to get to where we want to go. We want to be ruthless, aggressive, go-getters. **But part of being properly ruthless is learning how to fail**

successfully. If that sounds like an oxymoron, you don't have your head in the right place quite yet. **What I mean is this: you need to be able to prepare for the worst possible outcome, to set your company up so you can still make money with terrible numbers.** It's possible to do this realistically, in such a way that you can, by other people's definitions, fail — and still make money.

This is a very important point that you'll have to grasp before you can be truly successful in this field. **Some business owners never learn this**. I've met people who think they're going to succeed in Direct Response Marketing because they've got a $29.95 product that the whole world wants, and they're going to go out and sell it to them — and they have no chance, because you can't make money with a single product for $29.95. Your cost of obtaining that sale is too high.

Now, if you have a product that's designed to attract the best type of customer so you can ultimately sell them many more expensive things, then your idea for a $29.95 product is fine. It all comes back to measuring risk. You must set things up so that if you're starting a business, or if you're engaging in a particular marketing campaign, you want to ensure that you make money with bad economics — so you're not saying something like, "Gee, in order for me to at least break even on this, I have to get a 2% response." **The correct way of thinking is, "If I get an eighth of a percent response or even less, how do I still make money with this?"** Don't base your success on the best possible outcome; prepare for the worst possible outcome, and design your marketing campaign so that you still make money based on bad economics. The worst thing you can do is set your business up so that everything has to go exactly right for you to make money. Because nothing ever goes right! **Once again, you want to set it up so that if everything goes wrong, you can still make money.**

One thing that can keep you out of the red ink, so to speak, is something called "self-liquidating lead generation." You can use something like a small $5, $10, or even $50 hand-raiser that lets you attract a qualified lead. However your process is set up, they're actually paying you to mail that nice big package to them, and you're covering your costs. **Another excellent way to protect yourself against the worst case scenarios is to up-sell high-priced products every time you send out an offer** — any offer. In fact, one of the most effective ways to increase the transaction value for a product is by putting your up-sells right on the Order

Form. You can offer, for example, a $297 product, an additional option for another $200, and another option for another $300. John Alanis was recently telling me about one of his products where the base price was $797, but with up-sells he got the average transaction price up to $1,200. In some campaigns, if you just offer the initial product, you might lose money.

We've all had that happen before. But if you consider the worst that can happen, you can add up-sells to the offer, and make it into a winning campaign because you increased the average transaction value.

So the mindset you should maintain when going into any marketing campaign is, "How do I set this up so that even if everything goes wrong — even if the Post Office throws half the mail away — I still make excellent profits?" **You need to consider the worst case scenarios and create plans protecting yourself against them, so if everything does happen to go right, you make a lot of money and you're happy**. But if everything goes wrong (and something almost always is going to go wrong), you're still going to make money and you're going to do okay.

Certainly, you should always be thinking positively about your business, but you need to be realistic too. **No sitting around the office, affirming away, while ignoring the reality of hard work and preparation**; that's just stupid, because eventually that kind of behavior will come back and bite you. Most of us realize that, on a conscious level, but it's easy to fall into the optimism trap.

Even if you're still working away on marketing formulas, or working hard on the numbers and trying to figure out what you need to do to make a profit, or just thinking through marketing scenarios, it's human nature to want to make things a little rosier than they really are. So we have a tendency to skew the numbers high, and so we think, "Yeah, I might get a 5% response," and we look at all those numbers and say, "Wow, that'd be great!"

But that's not necessarily reality. Like this principle says, we need to be thinking the other way — **we need to be thinking worst-case scenario**. What happens if the offer absolutely does horribly? What if only one out of a thousand people you mail this offer to responds? That's a tenth of a percent. Can you make a profit there? Better yet, how can you make a profit there? How can you make that scenario work? Anything that does better than you expect is always great. But plan for the worst-case scenarios, and then, when you do better than the worst case, you're still okay. **You don't want to plan for the best case scenarios, and expect to have all those numbers be exactly what you need, and then have the worst case hit**.

Going into something like this with high expectations and then falling absolutely flat can be devastating. I see this happen a lot, with marketers who fall in love with their product — something I've already cautioned you against. **They make an optimistic offer, and don't even consider that the offer might not be that well received.** The next thing they know it tanks, and they've not only lost a lot of money, they're an emotional basket case because they've been so disappointed.

> **S**elling is the <u>most</u> <u>important</u> profession on earth!
>
> The entire world depends on those of us who bring in the business and who are most responsible for making the cash register ring.

It's so easy to avoid this problem by offering your customers as many up-sells as possible. We've all encountered the principle before in our own lives: it's like when you buy a burger at a fast food joint and they ask you, "Hey, do you want fries with that?" Up-selling your own products follows the same principle.

You can start by up-selling on your Order Form. List your up-sell offer right there on the Order Form as an option. Let's say your initial package is $149; that's your product price point. Yet you know that everybody who buys that is going to receive the offer for your $1,500 package. Well, go ahead and put the $1,500 package as an option right on the initial Order Form. Maybe spend a paragraph or two — but not a whole lot of space — in your sales letter talking about the bigger package you have. **It usually works out that a small percentage of prospects will chose that option, which helps you increase your chances of offsetting your mailing expenses in the worst case scenario.**

Once again, I'm going to use my friend Chris Hollinger as an example. When he and his wife Kim first started out, the highest-level website they were selling went for $1297. Coming from a Midwestern point of view, he said to himself, "Twelve hundred and ninety-seven dollars... I'd never pay that!" Well, guess what? About 99% of the people who purchased from Chris did pay for that top-of-the-line website! **You need to list your different pricing levels — because despite what you think people are going to buy, you'll invariably have some people who will want the highest level product you're offering.** You must make it available for them, or you'll lose a lot of the money you should have made.

I call this type of high-dollar product a "slack adjuster." **Properly defined, a slack adjuster is a product or service that's sufficiently high in price so all you need to do is make one sale to tighten up all your sales' slack and cover all your expenses.** Because, everything always costs more than you think it will. There was theme park entrepreneur near here that was blindsided by expenses that were double what he expected. It should have cost him $15 million; instead, it cost $30 million. You probably won't have that kind of cost overrun, but remember that everything's more expensive than expected. **A high-ticket item in your product mix, one that you regularly offer as an option to your customers, will more than make up for any losses that are incurred along the way, or any extra expenses you didn't factor in.**

Here's another point you should keep in mind. **As long as you're selling these items first and foremost to the customers that you have the best relationships with, you'll never lose money!**

You must segment your list and work with your best customers first. That list segment becomes your testing ground. Every time you come up with some new product, service, or promotion, you go to that smaller group of best people with it first. They know you, they trust you, and there's a relationship built with you. Even if they don't go crazy over what you're offering, at least you know they're going to buy in sufficient numbers that you never have to worry about losing money.

Be Cautious, But Optimistic

One last thing before we move on to the next chapter. Earlier, when I discussed *The Secret*, I told you that affirmation is useless without hard work. I really mean that, but I don't want to imply for one second that attitude doesn't matter. Of course it does. **Part of what being a ruthless marketer is all about is attitude!** Even as you're preparing for the absolute worst that can happen, you don't want to be pessimistic. **Being ruthless is all about envisioning the good things that can happen while planning logically to stave off the bad things.**

My favorite Robert J. Ringer book is called *Million-Dollar Habits*. Ringer talks about developing a positive attitude based on factoring in a negative outcome, and he offers a four-step process for doing so. **The first step is to expect problems.** You're not looking for some false world where everything always works out the way you want it to, where everything always comes together smoothly. You need to know in advance that things are going to go wrong, and have contingencies in place just in case they do. If you have a solid plan drawn up in advance, you're better organized. Then, if things do go wrong, you're in a much more powerful position.

The second step is to find something good within those problems you encounter. Call this the black cloud's silver lining. We can all look back in our past and see terrible things; usually we can see some good that came out of them, even though back when we were going through them, we couldn't see anything good. Ringer suggests that if something unexpected goes wrong with your life or business, you try to find those good outcomes more quickly, right now, instead of waiting for five or ten years down the road.

The third step is simply taking action. Often, people become immobilized by their problems; they get what our friend Ken Pedersen calls "vapor locked:" so caught up in their problems, that all of a sudden they lose their edge. <u>Instead of letting that happen to you, keep moving forward</u>. Even if it's in the wrong direction, at least you're not stuck in the same hole.

The fourth thing is a little bit hard to describe, because it's slightly metaphysical. somewhat in the realm of *The Secret*. **You need to realize that as long as you do those first three things, good things will happen**. Fortune favors the prepared person who continues to take positive action in spite of all the setbacks. <u>Don't expect the world to be perfect; find ways to take advantage of unexpected occurrences that you might normally term failures; take action</u> — <u>and you'll eventually get where you're going</u>.

Good things do happen to people who keep getting back up every time they get their butts kicked. They refuse to give up. They refuse to quit. We all know people like that. I have a friend I call "the young King Midas." Well. all successful entrepreneurs have a little bit of that King Midas in them. <u>They get lucky because they keep moving forward and make their own luck</u>.

Practice Ruthless Lead Generation

One of your biggest goals as a marketer must be lead generation — finding well-qualified people who are willing to raise their hand and say "Yes, your product sounds right for me. I'd like to know more about it." That's how you get people into your business on the front-end. How you keep them and cultivate that relationship so that you sell them more products for more and more money, is part of your back-end strategy, and it's where the real money is; I'll cover that later. **But the front-end is where it all starts, and that's what I'll teach you about in this chapter.**

Any lead generation is good, but if you're really ruthless, you need to make your prospective customers qualify themselves. **Basically, you're sifting the wheat from the chaff, so that you end up with a pool of prospects you're more likely to convert to customers.** The wannabes and merely interested are left by the wayside; the people you end up with

---

are the ones who are burning to have what you've got, and are willing to spend to get it. **The best way to get these people is to spend more money on your leads. You'll reach fewer people, but they're better qualified prospects, and you'll end up making more money in the long run.**

This is something that a lot of beginning business owners really don't get. When they get into business they think, "Well, I want to sell to everybody; the world is my market." **But if you want to sell to everybody, you're going to wind up selling to <u>nobody</u>, because you can't write a sales message that's going to appeal to everyone.** <u>The most effective form of selling will always be one-on-one</u>.

I can sit down with you one-on-one, have a dialogue with you, ask you questions about what's important to you, find out what your values are, and sell you a particular product based on the feedback that you've given me. I can go on to the next person and have a similar sales presentation, but ask different questions, and sell them the same product for a completely different reason than you bought it.

In Direct Response Marketing, though, we don't have the benefit of doing the one-on-one stuff. So we have to write sales letters that appeal to a broad group of people. **The more that you can "niche" your particular group of prospects — the more you can boil it down to people who have the same hopes, dreams, desires, fears, failures and frustrations — the more successful you're going to be**. It makes sense, in your business, to spend more money to reach these better-qualified prospects, because the response you're going to get is going to be much better, and you'll end up with long-term customers willing to give you a lot of money to solve their problems

Let's say you have a product to sell to realtors. That's a kind of niche market where people think and behave the same way, though it's big, broad one. For example, while both may be realtors, there's a vast difference between a realtor who's a buyer's agent or who sells to first time homebuyers, versus a realtor who sells only high-end homes. **Their day-to-day experiences are different, and to a certain extent, their way of thinking.** Think of them as sub-niches within the wider niche market of all realtors. If you take the time and effort, and spend the money, to craft a particular marketing message for each one, you'll sell much more on both the front-end and the back-end because you targeted your sales

Direct-mail can give you tremendous leverage. Every direct-marketing piece is a salesman in an envelope! It's out there working for you — without your direct effort!

• Sending out 1,000 direct-mail letters to your best customers is like sending out a sales force of 1,000 of the best salespeople!

message to get fewer but better qualified prospects. When you're able to do that, you're able to spend your marketing budget on communicating with those people more often, which gets them to give you more money.

Here's a rather extreme example. I had a consultant I was working with a few years ago whose average ticket sale is fifty grand. Every time he gets a job, he knows he'll average $50,000 cash. I was trying to educate him and help him understand how useful this concept could be to him from a marketing perspective. **How much money are you willing to spend if you know you're going to make fifty grand every time you make a new sale?** How much money are you willing to spend to get the sale? I told him, "As long as you're pre-qualifying and screening and you know that you're only working with that top of the pyramid of highly-qualified prospects, then what you must do is get radical! You must go to the bank, get some fresh, crisp, brand-new one hundred dollar bills, and put one on top of every personal letter that goes out to one of those extremely highly-qualified prospects, with the offer being that you'll follow up with a personal phone call in a few days. **The idea is, since their time is valuable, you're going to reward them for listening by giving them that hundred dollar bill so they can take the wife out to dinner or whatever.** And then you send it by Federal Express or another courier service overnight." Well, I never could get him to see that that would be worthy of a test. But don't you see the logic here?

This whole concept of spending more money to get and sell to fewer, better qualified leads gets lost on a lot of people, because the inclination is to think that you need more people to sell to — that if you just had more customers, you'd be better off. And certainly more customers is a good thing, but when you're trying to sell to someone, this concept of narrowing down your market by spending more money to reach fewer people and more qualified is much better.

More Money from Fewer People

We used to joke about how if we could just have a million people give us one dollar, we'd be instant millionaires! Obviously, it's not easy to get a million people to give you a dollar, but you know what? It's comparatively easier to get smaller groups of people to give you more money. **It's actually easier to get 10,000 people to give you a hundred bucks each; in the same way, it's easier to make a few $5,000 sales than thousands and thousands of $50 sales**. So there's a lot of truth in this concept that you can make more money by selling to smaller numbers of people.

It's all about target marketing — serving niche markets, the concept I outlined in the introduction. **The smaller the niche, the more money you can make, within certain limits, of course.** Obviously, if your niche is limited to five people, there's not a lot of marketplace there! But in general, the smaller the group of people you have to work with and the more targeted they are — the more money you can make, because you've singled them out as a group with something in common. **You know what they're looking for, you know what kinds of products and services they want, and you can make a lot of money with that small group**. That means that you do everything you can to qualify your leads. When you're throwing your fishnet out there, you want to attract the right kinds of fish, the ones who are most likely to buy your product from you. <u>You don't want to cast your net too wide, because then you're wasting your money getting leads you can't convert</u>.

So it's all about qualifying: <u>you want the biggest number of the highest-qualified leads you can get</u>. The emphasis here is on the word "qualified." You may end up with smaller, absolute numbers of people in your net, but they're more likely to buy from you. Quantity does not mean quality! Oh, sure, there's no problem generating huge numbers of leads if you want them, but **if you don't make an effort to trim that number down until you're dealing only with the highest quality leads, you're**

shooting yourself in the foot.

Here's an example. Early in his marketing career, my friend Chris Hollinger ran a lead-generated program that got a lot of people to raise their hands and say, "Hey, I'm interested." But, then his conversion rate to actual sales was horrible, because they were poorly qualified for what he was selling, and nothing he could do would make them buy. **That's the bottom line right there. If you can't convert them, you're not making any money!**

So I suggested to Chris that he try to generate a pool of higher-qualified leads — and after experimenting a little, he made that work. He does it by, using what's called a $5 hand-raiser. **Basically, he'll write a lead generation mailing piece, targeting a list of people he feels would be receptive to the type of product he's trying to sell.** This is a very effective way of targeting your marketing. When you do this, you qualify your lead by the list that you buy or rent, or if you're working with a joint venture partner, what you've learned of his list after studying it. **In your piece, hit them with some very bold headlines, which you back up with a very good, logical argument about why these headlines are what they are, and what the prospect can get out of your product.** You're trying to get their attention, and once you've got it, you ask them to send you five or ten dollars so that they can get your next package filled with all kinds of great information and/or a valuable free gift.

Asking for money is an excellent way to get rid of all the people who aren't serious. Now, when someone has raised their hand and said, "I want to know more and, by the way, here's five or ten dollars," is that person a qualified lead? You bet they are. That's a good model that can be directly applied to about any business. **People vote with their wallets, and that's one of the ways they qualify themselves**. You can look at getting qualified leads as making your customer actually have to jump through hoops to do business with you. **If you can get them to jump through a couple of different hoops, they've raised their hand at that point and said, "Okay, I really want to know more."**

From then on, whenever you call them or send them another sales piece, they're receptive to it — as opposed to the life insurance salesman who calls them out of the blue in the middle of dinner. How receptive are you to that guy? You're not. You're hungry, and you're irritated that they've bothered you during time with your family. That's how anyone feels when they're cold-called. But, if they've raised their hand already, it's clear they want to know more about what you're selling, what you have to offer. **Give it to them, make them happy, and they often end up buying.**

As I've mentioned previously, Chris Hollinger used to be a teacher, and he was recently telling me about one of his former students. He's a real go-getter entrepreneur, dominating the decorative concrete business in the Kansas City area. **There are guys out there who have been in the concrete business for years, but he quickly dominated the market because**

▼▼▼▼▼▼▼▼▼▼▼▼▼▼▼▼▼

People are not only irrational, but they are <u>predictably</u> irrational!

In other words, they keep doing the same stupid stuff over and over again.

he used online lead generation and had people from all over that area answering his very specific ads. They were raising their hands and saying, "Hey, I'm interested in decorative concrete work." He perfected his lead generation and is generating tons of really good qualified leads. Ironically, this whole year he hasn't touched a single piece of concrete. You know what he does now? He sells those qualified leads to all his former competitors, and he makes more money now than he ever did pushing mud. **He hasn't gotten his hands dirty in the practical aspects of the business for a long time, all because he understood something that his competitors didn't – and he's getting ready to launch that whole service in 37 cities across the country.** So, as you can see, qualified leads are powerful, and they can really turn your business around.

What Kind of Bait's on Your Hook?

One of my heroes is P.T. Barnum, one of history's greatest marketers. Back in the 1850s he said, "Most people are trying to catch a whale by using a minnow as bait." I love that quote, because think about it — you're out there in the deep sea, fishing for a huge whale, and you're trying to use a little minnow as bait. It isn't going to work, is it? That's even truer now than it was a century and a half ago.

But, that's the way that most people think, in a general sort of way at

A two-step strategy for every marketing system:

- Step One: Generate as many qualified leads as you can.

- Step Two: Bombard these leads with as many follow-up offers as you can possibly think of!

- You must do everything to squeeze every last dollar out of the leads you generate. Bombard them with a ton of sequenced mailings. And keep bombing them — until it's no longer profitable.

least, when it comes to marketing. **They're focused on the obstacles rather than the outcomes. They're looking at their costs, and trying to keep everything as inexpensive as possible. That can backfire on you.** Instead, you need to reverse that and spend more money to reach better qualified people. It's all about conversion. It's all about how much money you spend versus how much money you make. Every sale must be bought. Most people don't realize that. **There's a price that you have to pay for your sales; and paying that price includes all of your advertising and your marketing, and can cover a wide variety of other things too.** For example, as I'm this writing, my company, M.O.R.E., Inc. has a brand new promotion out there that we're testing that could be worth many tens of millions to us. It may take us a couple years of testing and re-testing and re-testing before we finally figure out how to crack the code — but there's a 30-50 million dollar business here, if we can just figure it out. Now, it may take us a while to do it, but we're going to do it! That's part of the price we'll have to pay to get the payoff down the line.

We know we're going to have to re-test and re-test over the years. It's a huge market we're trying to reach, and figuring out the right way to do it may take us a while. So we're starting out relatively small. Notice that term "relatively." With some promotions we ask for $5 to get people to raise their hands, but in this case, we've got a $5,000 product that we're trying to sell — so in order to find qualified prospects, our first test is to try to sell them a $749 product. If that doesn't work, then we'll try to sell them a $495 package. If that doesn't work, we'll take it down to $295, then $195, or even $149 or $99.

But whatever we ask for, the end goal is to sell that $5,000 package. **To take it a little bit further than that, all we're trying to do (and this is really important) is to make $1,000 off of that initial $5,000 sale.**

What does that mean? That means that we're willing to spend $4,000 to get that $5,000 sale! We can do this because there's very little hard cost involved; it's a proprietary, informational-based product where the only real cost is our time. **Plus, that $5,000 sale also has continuity revenue attached to it, and that income can be almost all profit and add up fast! We're trying to build up a nice, steady revenue stream.** There's a monthly hit to it, plus those people will be customers for life (hopefully), and we'll end up making our money that way. So we're willing to spend $4,000 to get a $5,000 sale. But we're even willing to spend a little bit more than that, because we're first making them a $749 sale. That's the first part of our strategy.

Now think about that. That's the reverse of how most people think. They're trying to make that $5,000 sale up front, and they want to keep as much of that money as possible. They're more interested in keeping $4,900 out of that $5,000 rather than figuring out how to build a long-term relationship that will flood them with money over the years. **They're shortsighted; they don't realize that every sale has to be bought, especially if you want to make more money on the back-end**. They don't realize that there's an investment that has to be made in terms of marketing dollars to make sales, and they're not thinking long-term about all of the repeat business that can come to them.

This concept with which I started this chapter, where you spend more money to reach higher qualified prospects, is crucial here. **The reason you want those higher qualified prospects is because they end up doing more business with you over a long period of time — and they end up causing you fewer customer service problems, too**. That's a little secret of our business: the better the customer, the fewer the customer service problems! The more people spend with you, the better qualified they are, because people vote with their pocketbooks. **The only way you can tell anything about a customer is through their actions, and in our business the most important action is how they spend their money**. So, you're looking for the highest qualified prospects possible, and you've got to be willing to spend more money to reach those people. You can be very aggressive with your marketing when you think like that. When you set out to do something bold like that, you end up with a kind of power that most marketers never have.

When you focus on fewer and better qualified prospects, a lot of the money you put in your pocket is going to come from saving on infrastructure. If you're trying to build a business that services 100,000 lower-end customers, you're going to be spending a tremendous amount of money on customer service and updating your database and all that type of stuff. That's why a lot of these information-marketing businesses are really what we call "power small-number businesses," where they may only have 1,000 or 2,000 customers. You can manage 2,000 customers with one employee easily, and still make them feel like they're important — which they are. But, over the lifetimes of such customers, each may be worth $3,000 or more, which brings up an important point.

The really sophisticated information marketer doesn't think in terms of present revenue — i.e., "How much can I get today?" Because when you get a customer in the door, you know that if you do this right — if you have back-end products, and coaching programs, and services and continuity to sell them — then when they come in the door, you know that over "x" number of years they're going to be worth a certain amount of money to you. When you get a customer in the door today, you've just put, say, $3,000 in your bank account in the future. And so you have future money coming in. When you start to think like that, you start making decisions to bring a maximum number of customers in because you know they'll pay off down the road, which will cause you to do vastly different things than if you're just trying to get a customer in, get the money out of them, and that's that.

So think in terms of customers. Sure, you may lose money today; you may tell yourself in the evening, "Well, that was a bad day; revenue wasn't good. But hey, I got 26 new customers! It was really a good day!" **That's because you know that over the long run with the right marketing, those customers are going to pay off.** And so it re-orients your thinking away from the average business owner who thinks in terms of dollars per second to how many new customers you acquire, how much they're worth, and what you can do to make them worth more. It's a very important way to think in this business, and it's what separates the "also rans" from the few who are really successful.

Here's a good example of the concept. My step daughter — who happens to be Chris Lakey's wife — is into scrapbooking. That's a huge niche today, by the way. There's a store in our town owned by a small entrepreneur who serves that niche, and carries other arts and crafts supplies. The lady who opened that store is having trouble competing with Wal-Mart, just as a lot of people are. Wal-Mart buys in massive quantities, so it can sell things cheaper than a regular Mom-and-Pop shop can. There's a certain kit that scrapbookers use that Wal-Mart has for about $60, while the scrapbooking store has it for $89. She just can't buy them cheaper straight from the supplier, so she ought to be buying them from Wal-Mart and selling them for the same price — or even less! She won't make any money off them, but she'll draw people into her store, where there are other items they're going to buy while they're there. Just by thinking things through a little bit, and thinking longer than the short-term, she could survive the Wal-Mart onslaught. **The key is to get customers used to buying from her and to turn them into repeat, long-term customers.** When you do that, they're going to continue buying those products from you, and they'll buy other products while they're in your store.

It's just a matter of changing your thinking a little. **Don't think about making a sale right now; think about the lifetime value of that customer.** If you've got a good business model based on the long-term value of a customer, you can lose money on an initial sale and make it up on the back-end on all the additional business with that client after they become a good customer. **That's a form of practical lead generation; you're getting people to raise their hands and buy more from you by using what we call a loss leader.** You may be losing a little bit on the front end, but you're gaining a good customer. And consider this: even if you spend $4,000 to ultimately make $5,000, that's a heck of a profit. Investment bankers would kill to make a 25 percent return! **You can make these killer profits by continuing to build your customer relationship, and continuing to offer more products and services to the highly-qualified client you spent all that money to acquire.**

Don't Be a Passive Pushover!

If you don't maintain your aggressive, ruthless marketing stance, and go after the best possible clients using the right bait for that whale you want to land, you run the risk of becoming the exact opposite of what you need

▼▼▼▼▼▼▼
MARKETING SECRET

Don't waste your time or money trying to change your prospects' beliefs.

- People believe what they want to believe and see what they want to see.

- Position your message according to their beliefs. Speck their language. Use metaphors, stories, and analogies that are centered around their perceptions.

to be: a passive pushover. Let me give you an example. Twelve miles from my headquarters in Goessel, Kansas, is a little town called Hillsboro. They had a little Ben Franklin store downtown on Main Street that was there forever until a company called Alco decided to move in. Alco's kind of like a mini-Wal-Mart; Hillsboro's a real small town, and Wal-Mart can't go into those small towns anymore, but Alco can. **Well, as soon as Alco made the announcement that they were coming to Hillsboro, the guy who'd owned that Ben Franklin for 30 years put a "Going Out of Business" sign on his window**. I was shocked! I said to him, "Look, they're not even going to open for ten more months. What are you doing?"

And he said, "Well, I can't compete with Alco." And that was it. He just gave up, because he was a passive pushover. **Most business owners are exactly like that.** As soon as their equivalent of Wal-Mart comes to town, they cry and whine like little babies, and put up their "Going Out Of Business" signs. Sorry if that sounds harsh, but it's true. **If you look at the Wal-Mart (or whoever your big competitor is) and let it shake you, you're going to fail.**

Frankly, Sam Walton was a man after my own heart — a true entrepreneur, if ever there was one. He started from nothing, and built the greatest retail empire on Earth. And he knew, if anyone did, how to run a ruthless marketing attack. But at the same time, he was happy to tell his competitors how they could co-exist with him. In fact, he had a whole chapter in his book, *Made in America*, that was devoted to how you could compete against Wal-Mart. Why did he have that chapter in there? Because the way other business owners reacted to Wal-Mart's expansion upset him greatly; not the resentment or even the lawsuits — he could handle that. **What bothered him were the passive pushovers, the business owners who just gave up whenever Wal-Mart came to town, rather than trying to compete.**

You see, Sam was a warrior — a competitor! He was an aggressive marketer. In that chapter, he said basically, **"What do you mean, you can't compete with Wal-Mart? There are only two real things Wal-Mart can beat you on: we offer great selection and great prices. But that's it!"** He went on to point out that there are all kinds of other things that people want, like customer service, and the best that Wal-Mart can do there are those greeters who meet you when you come in, and check your purchases on the way out.

That's as good as it gets at Wal-Mart. Try finding somebody to help you — it's not an easy task. And even then, a lot of them don't know what's in their own store. **There's no personal service. There's none of those things that people really want.** So if you really want to compete with a Wal-Mart, you should do what we recommended earlier for the scrapbook store — if you have to, go and get your initial widget (whatever it is) from Wal-Mart, sell it for less money than Wal-Mart is selling it for, and bring in a whole bunch of customers and then treat them like Kings and Queens. **That's ruthless lead generation: being willing to lose money at first to bring in quality customers. Once those customers are in the store, you can up-sell them on specialized niche items that Wal-Mart doesn't carry, and you can wow them with the personalized service they'll never get from Wal-Mart.** There are a million things you can do with your business that Wal-Mart could never do, because they don't specialize in the niche that you do.

I've got proof that this approach works. There was a recent article in the Wichita Eagle on just this subject — about how Wal-Mart is losing market share these days. **Slowly, people are realizing that they can get some really good deals from niche marketers for stuff that's just not available at Wal-Mart.** Once upon a time, everybody shopped at Wal-Mart, because that's where the lowest price was, and for a while that was most important to a lot of people. It's starting to shift now, as people are starting to remember what good service is and how much they miss it. Now, they're starting to go back and do more and more business with these smaller shops and the independent retailers. That doesn't mean Wal-Mart is going to go out of business; they're probably still going to be one of the world's largest retailers. **What it means is that small businesses and local entrepreneurs are starting to realize that they can compete, <u>if they do things ruthlessly enough</u>.**

If I ran that local store with the scrapbooking supplies, I'd run ads telling people that if you're a scrapbooker, we've got this widget you need for less than Wal-Mart, and show both Wal-Mart's price and our price. If you lose a few dollars on that, so what? **The chances are that when they come into the store they're going to spend enough to make up that couple of bucks on other things while they're there.** If not the first time they visit, then maybe next week, or over the next six months. You've got to look to the future! I can't stress that enough. **Too many entrepreneurs are just lazy. They're not real marketers, they're just business owners; they don't think about strategies that can help them gain long-time, lifetime customers.** They think that you just show up, and business just happens — like the printer I talked about in the introduction. Do you think he's still in business? Heck no. You can't just sit there and wait for the world to come to you. You have to be proactive, to go out and get the customer to come to you. **Just because you're in love with your business doesn't mean anyone else is. That's actually a pretty arrogant mindset. Don't think that arrogant is the same as aggressive and ruthless; in this case, it's synonymous with "stupid."**

There's a great barbeque joint in Wichita that's been there for 10 or 15 years — but the owners recently announced that they're going out of business. Their reason? Too much competition! Too many other barbeque joints have popped up since they went into business. In other words, when they were the only gig, they felt okay. But now that they have to compete with other barbeque joints, they've decided it's not worth the effort. How sad is that? Obviously, where there's one barbeque joint is, there should be more! People want a range of choices in restaurants.

The fact that there are a lot of barbecue joints in Wichita proves that it's a good barbeque town, and that there's plenty of business to go around. **If the barbecue joint that's closing had been performing their marketing right, they would have had no problem filling their restaurant with barbeque-lovers.** And yet, here they are, going out of business, just because there are too many other barbeque places in town now — which is basically the easy thing to say. **They don't want to** admit, maybe even to themselves, that they're just passive pushovers who were too lazy to rigorously and ruthlessly market their business. What they should have done was asked questions like, "What makes our barbeque place unique? What can we do to make ourselves look different or unique, or seem different from all the other barbeque joints? What advantages can we put into the minds of the marketplace that separates us from the herd?"

What you need is a good way to bring those new customers in and absolutely embrace them with the fact that this is the kind of service, these are the kinds of ideas, these are the kinds of things you're getting from our store. **And what you're actually saying to them is, "You're not going to get this at our competition. You're not going to get this at Wal-Mart. You're only going to get it here."** You have to have the forethought to have already said to yourself, "Okay, if I'm going to sell this as a loss leader to bring people in the door, then I'm going to have a system in place that's going to embrace these new customers and make them mine." **Whatever you decide to do, you need to get really creative when it comes to getting customers. That's what ruthless lead generation — ruthless marketing in general — is all about.**

You see, from a marketing standpoint, being ruthless is the opposite of being a victim — in this case, a victim of your own unwillingness to do what needs to be done. This type of victim is somebody who is just making excuses; they've got all kinds of reasons for their failures. **More aggressive marketers don't make excuses. They're out there to make it happen.**

Nobody gets paid until something gets <u>sold</u>!

Therefore, those who are most directly responsible for being in the sales deserve to make the most money.

I read in *Forbes* about a company that does nothing but buy bankrupt businesses, and then turns them around and resells them. They've got a whole process that they use to turn them around within 18 months, and they sell them for a lot more money than they bought them for — because when they turn a business around, they really turn it around. **They're looking for a certain size of business, and the first thing they do after buying those companies for pennies on the** dollar is to go in and meet with the management staff — and then fire every last one of them.** Their thinking goes like this: "Those are the guys who led the company into bankruptcy! We need a whole new style of thinking, so we need to get rid of them all." And they do, and then they bring in their managers, who train new people to think differently. **And that's really what we're talking about here with the whole subject of ruthless marketing. It's about thinking differently.**

How Thinking Differently Can Make You Rich

Here's a personal example of how thinking differently about lead generation can pull in the big bucks. As I've mentioned several times already, our first lead generation was for a little book we called "Dialing For Dollars." Our mailing list — a subject that we're going to get back to in detail, incidentally — was initially generated through space advertising by running a one-sixth page ad in a national business opportunity magazine. It would probably cost you $600 now. Because it went out to people interested in business opportunities, it specifically targeted the type of people we wanted to reach. People raised their hand by listening to a recorded message, and then we sent them a sales letter which tried to make a $12.95 sale. We can't do that today very well, but remember, this was back in the late 1980s. That was the little spark that started the mighty fire for us. Only later did we start using Direct Mail and more expensive marketing methods to expand on it. **But almost from the beginning, we started doing things to do more business**

with our customers. Our first initial product was a distributorship, so we could get them involved with us. They became distributors, and as we helped them succeed they did more business with us, and that was the beginning of our relationship with them.

That's one way you can build your mailing list. **You can either run ads to get leads, or you can rent mailing lists that are already on the marketplace** — lists of people who've bought products and services similar to yours from other companies.

Obviously, we've been doing this for a long time, so we've got it down to a science now, and we have a huge list of our own. But we still rent new mailing lists. Every week we test new lists, depending on our offer, and we get leads from those lists. **Sometimes the leads are free — they just have to raise their hand and say they're interested. We add a free report or a free audio program, and they send away for that**. Other times we ask for $5, $10, $15, and even as much as $20, sometimes, to get a better qualified lead, the kind we prefer. We do this on a weekly basis.

We're building two lists. All the people who request the information from us become a part of our lead list. Those on the lead list who make purchases become a part of our buyers list. **The buyers list is the most important to us, of course**. Occasionally we test to our lead list, but generally if they didn't buy what we were selling at that time, we don't go back to them with new offers, unless we've got a really hot offer.

This has worked very well for us. People have called our rise phenomenal; within four years of placing that first ad, we did ten million dollars worth of business. The reason is simply this: hindsight being 20/20, **we had a hot item that was very timely**. **Without going into the specific details, we found the right product at the right time.** We had a lot of help along the way, initially from Russ von Hoelscher and then Dan Kennedy — and then we started just selling more and building relationships with our customers. Believe or not, I learned this from the carpet cleaning business I first started in 1985... That business taught me how to develop relationships with customers; the whole idea was to gain their repeats business, to keep cleaning their carpets over and over, and then to tell all their friends and relatives and neighbors.

That was the only kind of marketing I knew. What we did in the

Direct Response Marketing business was a natural extension of that. **I knew that even though we'd never meet most of these people, would never even talk to them, the real money was in the relationships we built with them — so I did things to get more business from the people who initially did business with us.** Ultimately, it's not a numbers game; it's a relationship game. Once we got into Direct Mail our income just shot straight up, because it allowed us to reach more people in a much more effective way. **It's a fact that a customer generated through Direct Mail tends to be a much more loyal and better customer than you could attract in any other way**

My colleague John Alanis took a different approach, one that was predicated partially on the technology available to him at the time. He developed a model, and set up his business as a kind of a test of his skill. His product is a method that men can use to get attractive women to approach them no matter their looks, income or education. He wanted to see if he really knew and understood the model he'd developed, his vision of where his business would go, and what it was going to look like. He started with a digital eBook product and bought Google Pay-Per-Click traffic, driving people to an opt-in page to build an email list. That $29.95 eBook allowed him to test his copy, and let folks respond to him in a risk-free manner. Because Google charges your credit card two weeks after you buy the Pay-Per-Clicks, John was profitable the first day! In a sense, he was playing with house money, which is good.

After John knew that the copy worked, he started to raise his prices, and add in basic and deluxe versions, along with upsells. Then he took the copy that worked and transferred it to other media. Later, a guy contacted him who had a list of people who were similar to John's buyers, so they did a Joint Venture. John created a postcard based on the copy that worked on his website and put his name on it, sent it out, and the response was phenomenal. Now he had a postcard that he knew worked, so he decided to test it on rented names. That worked too, so he took the same copy and tested it as a full-page ad in magazines like *Grappling* and *Black Belt*.

At this stage, on the front-end, it's all about lead generation. As John's example shows, once you have copy that you know works, it's just a matter of expanding it into different media that allow you to get bigger and bigger, and then re-investing those profits. **This will generate more leads and**

feedback into the system.

Creative Borrowing

One last little point before we go on to the next chapter: when you're putting together lead generation copy, don't hesitate to practice "creative borrowing." There are other words for it — some people would call it swiping, or stealing, but maybe "modeling" is a better word. I'm not advocating plagiarism by any means, but you can easily and legally use other copy as a model for your own. You're stealing ideas, which is ruthless. Call it "market research," if you like. **You're doing market research and applying it to your own copy. If nothing else, you can look at each piece and try to identify what makes that a good piece, and then figure out how you can make use of those elements.** You can use the same concept, the same ideas, the same use of headlines... even to the point of copying how each page is put together. **So, if you're unsure, but you know you need a lead generation piece, borrow liberally from the sales materials others are using to generate leads for their own product, service or company.**

"Do Less Work – Make More Money"

Do you want to make more money by working less? Well, hey, who doesn't?

The most effective way to do it is no secret: <u>you have to focus on reselling to your best customers</u>. Sounds easy, doesn't it? Well, while it can be a challenge just like any other aspect of marketing, in most cases it really is that easy, as long as you already have customers with whom you've built a good relationship. (That's the hard part.) If you handle it right, it's a perfect way to generate immediate cash whenever your business needs it, and all you have to do is keep making your customers good, solid offers.

The reason I bring this up is too many businesses don't even bother

MARKETING SECRET

A two-step marketing principle:

- Make BIG promises in the front-end sales letter...

- Then scramble to fill these BIG promises in the back-end package!

with reselling. However, this practice is absolutely essential to the back-end portion of your business, which is where you'll make most of your money if you do things right. I've seen so many retailers who always focus on making that one sale, and totally discount the lifetime value of the customer. That's just dumb. **You need to go back to your customers on a regular basis and make them new offers. It's a simple concept that so many business people forget**. They're hurting themselves by not going back to their customers and making them good offers on a regular basis, and worse, they're doing their customers a disservice.

Now, think about this. Say you have a new product or service you want to launch. **Where's the best place you could possibly test a new offer? To your existing customer base, of course!** Because I'm telling you, if you put together a brand new product, service, or opportunity and you make that offer to your best customers and they don't buy it, well, you're probably not going to be able to sell it profitably to your target market. **Because of this, your existing customer base is an excellent place to test.** If you make that offer to your best customers and it flops, that'll save you a ton of money that you don't have spend trying to sell it to brand new customers in your market. <u>The bottom line: the best pre-qualified prospects you'll ever have are the people in your customer base</u>.

Smart marketers understand this, and have a system in place to take advantage of it. A perfect example of this kind of back-end marketing would be a restaurant. Chris Hollinger was telling me recently about his morning routine. He takes his daughter to school every morning, and after he drops her off, he usually goes to this restaurant, a little greasy spoon right around the corner from his neighborhood, and has some coffee. He's a regular, they know him by name, and they know his habits. When he comes in they set him up with his coffee and his water and everything else, because they know him. **The owner of this particular restaurant does a really good job of knowing his regulars' names. He takes care of them, gives them special little deals, and lets them try stuff for free.** This keeps Chris and the other customers coming back. **The owner does this because he knows he's not going to make it without his regular customers.**

So, get in the mindset, that as you build your business, you need to focus heavily on existing customers. As you launch any new offer, test it with your best customers. Always have a set strategy in mind, and plan on what you're going to do with a brand new customer, and how you'll keep them coming back again and again. It's a simple concept that gets overlooked, and not enough marketers do it. They end being up the ones with the "Going Out of Business" signs in their front windows, or going the way of pushover... which is basically the same thing.

Constant Communication is the Key!

Probably the biggest reason you should keep reselling to your best customers, especially in this business, is one that most marketers never learn. **It's simply this: that the end-game of being in this business is the acquisition of a proprietary house list of customers who like you and who give you money whenever you ask them.** But that can't happen in a vacuum. For that asset to maintain its value, you have to constantly and consistently communicate with your customers with new offers, new products, newsletters, and new services. Here's a principle that I learned from Dan Kennedy: **for each month you don't contact them, the customer list loses one-tenth of its value, until after ten months it's basically as valuable as cold leads from the White Pages.**

And so, in addition to reselling to the customers on your list in order to get the immediate cash out of them, there's a more compelling reason to continue to make offers: it upholds the value of your list. Even those who don't buy into a particular offer still know that you're around. You're still contacting them, and the next time you mail them the promotion they may go ahead and buy. We mail to our customer lists relentlessly, and it makes them more valuable, because the more they buy the more likely they are to buy in the future.

When you've gotten your list fine-tuned properly, and when you keep communicating on a regular basis, **the fastest way to make money when you need it is to create an offer and mail it to your house list — to your list of existing customers**. It's as simple as that, and it can be insanely profitable, assuming you've kept those relationships current. **With almost no question and almost a full guarantee, I can tell you that if you have a list of customers with whom you already have a relationship, not customers that you did business with several years ago, you could mail just about any offer that fits their needs and wants and it will make you a profit.** Now I'll admit that sometimes, it doesn't happen — but that's a rare fluke. If you have your own list of existing customers who like and trust you, there's almost a 100% guarantee that if you give them a good offer for a good product or service, you'll make a profit.

That's the power of focusing on reselling to your existing customers. **It's much easier to make the second, third, and fourth sale to an existing customer than it is to make the first sale to a customer who doesn't know you, doesn't like you, doesn't trust you, and has no reason to choose to buy from you over somebody else**. So building that list of customers — of people who have done business with you, know you, and trust you — is the ultimate resource to long-term profitability, because you've got that established group of people who have no problem doing business with you, since they've already done business with you in the past and have had a positive experience.

By now you might be thinking, "But what if I'm new at this, and don't have a list of existing customers I can sell to?" It's true you can't start in a vacuum, but let me say that you can apply these aggressive marketing techniques to your business from the very beginning. Earlier, I mentioned how my company got started out with a little product called "Dialing for Dollars," and how we built our stake up from just $300 to more than $10,000,000 in just four years. That sounds exciting, right — to go from broke and struggling to happily profitable? Well, it's only through hindsight that I can tell you exactly how it happened, because at the time I was too inexperienced and too caught up in the whole thing.

Basically, we had something that was very timely — it was the right product at the right time, and we rolled it out and got very aggressive. Because I'm an extremely ambitious person, once we started making millions of

▼▼▼▼▼▼▼▼▼▼▼▼▼▼▼▼▼▼▼▼

You must separate the message from the messenger!

"The worst men often give the best advice."

P.J. Bailey

dollars, all I wanted to do was make millions more! It was just like throwing gasoline on a fire — the money just made me want to make more money! Which got us into more media like Direct Mail and made us more aggressive. However, I do want to say this: we got lucky, but we sort of created our own luck, too. We're the ones who spent that $300, and we had to sell one of our beat-up carpet cleaning vans to get that money. We took a risk. But we got lucky; we stumbled onto the right offer at the right time. **In large part, that, and our knowledge of superior customer service, was responsible for our tremendous early growth.**

So do you need to get lucky to be successful? Not necessarily. **What I'm trying to say here is that you need to get to know your customers, and one way to do that is by communicating with them regularly.** Most business people make the mistake, again and again, of trying to sell stuff that they're crazy about, when nobody else is. How do you avoid that? **Let your customers tell you what they want.** Research your market constantly, and communicate with your customer list by testing offers with them, and going by what works. Don't guess; don't assume you know what they want. Make an offer to a test audience, and if nobody takes you up on it, abandon it like a hot potato — even if you think it's the best thing since buttered pancakes.

I've got a good friend who's wasting his time with a stupid little product that he's all crazy about. I won't name him, because he might read this someday! But the point is, he drools whenever he talks about this product. His eyes dilate and it's like he's high, like he's intoxicated, when he's talking about his stupid little product. But nobody else cares about it — he's the only one in love with it!

I say forget all that: find out what's hot. You only want to spend your time marketing things that you know are red hot — things that people really

▼▼▼▼▼▼▼▼▼
MARKETING
SECRET

Product knowledge is highly overrated.

- Every salesperson is trained in extensive product knowledge. FORGET THAT! Prospect knowledge is more important than product knowledge. Prospects buy perceived benefits and results. They do not buy product information.

want. Well, how do you find those items? Maybe we got lucky back in 1988, but now we find them because we go to our best customers and communicate with them to see what works. **Every time we get an idea for a new product, service or promotion, if our best customers don't go crazy over it, we blow it off.** We gauge this stuff. We watch the numbers. We let the market tell us what to do. We don't fall in love with our products; we let our customers tell us what they want. And the market is constantly changing, so you have to constantly test new things.

Because we segment our list, we know who our best customers are. If our best customers go crazy about something we throw out there, we'll test below that top segment, to the customers who haven't done as much business with us as the top guys. And if they go crazy about it, if the numbers are good... well, we have still other people at the bottom of the pyramid. This is a larger group we'd love to be our best customers, but so far they're not. And if they go crazy about it, then we start testing to lists of people in our target market who have never done business with us. That's how we find our best secrets. **If nobody likes the idea, or there's limited response, then we table it**. It's as simple as that.

So, constantly communicating with your customers, testing offers and seeing how they respond, is an almost no-risk way to make money. Did I say "almost?" No, that's wrong — it's a no-risk way to make money, period, because even if our best customers don't go crazy over something we offer, they'll always buy enough that we'll never lose money. So we never ever, ever have to worry about losing money when we go to our smaller group of best

---

262   FOOLPROOF SECRETS of Successful Marketers!

customers at the top of the pyramid, and then we just filter down. Once we get to the bottom of our customer base, which is the larger group of people who've spent less money on our offers, if those numbers still look good, then we know we can go out to people in our market with whom we have no relationship and test it further.

We're fortunate to live in this day and age, the Age of the Internet, because when you're first starting out, it's very easy to find out what people want. That's why a lot of us do a great deal of online marketing, too, and build an email list from that.

Take my friend and colleague John Alanis: whenever he comes up with an idea for a new product, he'll just send an email out to his customers and say, "Okay, fellas, I'm thinking about coming up with this product here."

He just finished doing one called "Secrets of Supreme Confidence." He told his client base, "Alright, I'm thinking about putting this product together, fellas. But I'm not a guy to waste time — so if you're not going to buy, I'm not going to waste my time creating it. Here's what I want you to do: I want you to tell me, what do you want covered in this thing? What do you want to know? I'll give you a free report about something really good if you respond to me."

So basically he gave them a bribe to get their interest — and it worked remarkable well. He got 150 or 200 responses saying, "I want this in... I want this in... I want this in... I want this in...," and there he had it right there — the outline for the product, and also what went into the sales letter. **And so when he gets around to launching this thing, which he'll do via email first, there's almost zero risk involved, because he knows that people are going to buy it.** If he'd gotten little or no response to his communication, then he wouldn't have bothered doing it. That's an excellent example of how, in this day and age, you can communicate with your customers quickly and effectively via e-mail, do some market research on the fly, and come up with products that are almost guaranteed to be winners before you even start developing them. <u>Spend some time finding out what your best customers want, and you'll find that the marriage between your offer and your market is seamless, and your profits will go up because of it</u>.

Finding the Right Product from the Get-Go

John Alanis' example is a good illustration of how effective customer communication and careful marketing research go hand in hand — in fact, sometimes they're the same things, though not always.

In our case, we couldn't do any preliminary communication with our first product, so on one hand, I suppose we did get lucky. **But on the other hand, although we didn't realize it at the time, we understood our market in a very intimate way**. You see, for years, I was that person who was sending away for every single money-making plan and program I could get my hands on, joining every Multi-Level Marketing company possible, and getting crazy about all these ideas; **so when it came time for us to enter into that marketplace after we had found a moneymaking program that really worked, we were ready**.

That's what our first "Dialing For Dollars" program was all about — it was a program that we had actually tested and tried and proven. We knew the market. We knew who the competitors were. We knew the people we were selling to, because they were just like we were. Sure, you can sell to markets that you have no real affinity with, but I think you're doing yourself a disservice, especially in the beginning, if you don't choose a market that you really understand well to begin with.

Once you've got that level of understanding, you need the right kind of product to go with it. Not just a product you love, but one you think will be very profitable. Remember my friend who's in love with his stupid product? He's got a bright, shiny object he's going to try to sell, and it's not going to work. <u>Too many people end up infatuated with products they love and others don't</u> — <u>and the hardest thing to do is to try to sell a product that people don't want</u>. That's the value of doing your market research and finding out what people want. Even before you start out, you can start communicating with your prospective client base — even if you don't have a product to sell.

This is one of the secrets that makes information marketing such a dynamic field, and here's how it works. **These days, when a lot of us start our information marketing businesses, we don't create or find the product first.** John Alanis is a good example: he wrote a sales letter first.

He created the sales letter, he tested it, and when it was a hit he quickly created the product. Then John reworked his original product into a high-income professional product — a $3,700 product for busy professionals who just didn't have the time to look for the women of their dreams.

That thing was a monster product! The sales letter alone came to 44 pages. Let me re-emphasize — John didn't create that product first. First he sat down, wrote the lead generation piece, wrote the sales letter, and then he went and tested it with a pre-publication offer, saying, "It's going to be ready in 60 days, fellas. If you put your order in now, you'll get it in 60 days and I won't charge your credit card or cash your check before then." It ended up taking more than 60 days to put together, but that's beside the point: he was able to test it without investing in the creation first. The actual creation came after he got some orders; if he hadn't gotten those orders, he wouldn't have created it. **The point is, even if you don't have a product in hand, you can still kick your business into profitability very fast.** You may find it hard to fathom, but in many ways the product is the least relevant part of your business. The market is so much more important.

Sometimes it can actually be good not to have a product in hand — that keeps you from doing what writers call "working on spec." The word "spec" is short for speculation. That's where you write something and toss it into the marketplace, hoping someone will publish it. Well, maybe they won't, no matter how good it is — sometimes the market doesn't need want you've got. The smart writer starts out with a kind of sales letter called a query, where they approach a publisher and say, "Hey, I've got this idea for an article. Here's what it's about, and here's how long it'll be." That's not quite a sales letter like you and I would write, because it's a one-on-one thing, but it accomplishes the same purpose. If no one is interested, the topic goes back into the idea folder and the writer moves on to something else. **So the best thing to do if you want to create a product is go get some orders.** Do a pre-publication sales letter for now, and then create the product if there's enough interest in it. But be aware that you actually have to deliver the product at some point. They put you in jail if you don't.

But even before you sit down to write your pre-publication sales letter, the first thing you want to do is find a marketplace. In some ways that can be simple, or it can be overwhelming. Have you ever heard the story of the donkey between the two mangers? They both looked so tasty that he couldn't choose one to eat from, and so he starved to death. Well, if you suffer from entrepreneurial disease as I do — this affliction for which there's no cure — you might have a similar problem. **I see product opportunities all over the place, everywhere I look. I read an article in the paper, and I see a product. I'm watching TV and the news is talking about something, and I'm thinking, "Wow, there's a product opportunity!"** When you're an information marketer, like most of my friends are, all you have to do is find a group of people who have a need, or who have something wrong that they need to fix, and you've got a product opportunity. The problem is focusing on just one! If you're an information marketer, you could have 30 different information products reaching 30 different niches, all bringing you revenue despite the fact that none of them are related.

The customers who buy one might not buy any of the others, but collectively, you're making good money from all those niche markets. So being an information marketer just means being in tune with certain groups of people, and then finding products and services that those people want. **So if you don't having a specific product, you could still start right now by looking for niche markets and then finding products to satisfy them.** If you find a great market and create a sales message that communicates with that market, then eventually creating a product is not a problem.

While you need to have some of your own products eventually, an easy way to get

started is by affiliating yourself with someone else and selling their product. Affiliate programs are great places to cut your marketing teeth. If you know of a niche market out there, chances are somebody on the Internet has an affiliate program you can join that would allow you to sell to that marketplace without having to create a product. Here are two good options: **Commission Junction (http://www.cj.com) is a great place to start, and so is Click Bank (http://www.clickbank.com).** Both let you sign up for one account, and then sell thousands of different products.

So find a niche and marketplace, and find an affiliate program with a good product that you feel comfortable selling — and then all you have to do is run ads, write sales letters, and use Pay-Per-Click advertising. A lot of people have businesses on the Internet where they're making money with niche markets without ever having products that they created themselves, because all they do is become affiliates for other people. That's a great way to get your feet wet without having to create an information product yourself.

Now, if you're going to go that route, do everything with the idea that you really do want to create a customer list. **Every time someone buys something from you, capture all the customer information you can**, because, even though you're just an affiliate for another company, you fronted the money to get them a customer, which is the most expensive part of the operation. And keep in mind the one point that I've really hammered home: <u>the lifetime value of the customer</u>. At some point, you may be able to make them your own customer; so even if you're someone else's affiliate, strive to build a valuable relationship with that customer, so you can come back later and make them another offer that they'll like. After all, that's the basis of making more money with less work!

"Practice Smart Marketing"

In this chapter, I'm going to discuss a big, broad topic that I call "Smart Marketing." It consists of ten steps that you absolutely have to master if you want to make the big bucks.

I think of Smart Marketing as a blueprint for creating a successful sales organization regardless of your product, your service,

or your opportunity. I've seen many, many people come in, start a business, and then flounder and say to themselves, "Well, what is it that I need to do?" They get so caught up they get vapor locked — they don't know what to do next. This framework gives you areas on which to focus in your business in order to maximize your chance of success.

I'm going to talk about each topic in detail, but here they are in an easy-to-swallow form:

1. Give people what they want.

2. Develop products and services that appeal to a specific market.

3. Make sure those items have the highest profit margin possible.

4. Develop marketing systems that identify the right prospects and communicate the right message to them.

5. Reach and sell to those prospects fast and make the largest profit.

6. Resell to your customers constantly.

7. Create sales messages that build strong bonds with your customers.

8. Position yourself so you seem unique.

9. Create offensive marketing strategies that let you control the selling process.

10. Make specific offers to your customers on an ongoing basis.

NUMBER ONE is giving people what they want. This seems pretty straightforward, but it's not always easy. I have a friend who's in love with his product and has put hours and hours of time into it, though hasn't really done the market research that it takes to really know if his market is going to like it. But he loves this product, so he thinks everyone else should love it. It's like having a puppy that you love — but it's the ugliest puppy in the world and no one else loves that puppy but you. You can't understand how nobody else wants that puppy, and it can be crushing.

The point is, you need to give your customers what excites them, not necessarily what excites you; that may be two different things. Aside from performing in-depth marketing research, one of the easiest ways to find out exactly what your customers want is to just ask them. That's what John Alanis did. He tailor-made a product based on what his customers told him they wanted. So are they going to buy it? Sure; they already did. In doing what he did, John took a page out of the playbook of the great Ray Kroc, the man who built McDonald's into the powerhouse it is today.

Ray Kroc once said, "Selling is the gentle art of letting the customer have it your way."

▼▼▼▼▼▼▼▼▼

Pain is part of the process.

Embrace it...

Deal with it...

Even learn to enjoy it!

I think that's brilliant, because on one hand it says to give people what they want; and on the other, it says to give it to them your way. I think that's a testament to the concept that when you have a targeted marketplace, you can let customers have it your way because you're in control of everything. You control the selling process. You give people what you want them to have, but in that process, you're giving them what they want.

NUMBER TWO on our list is developing marketing products and services that are appealing to a specific market. Again, it comes back to knowing and having an intimate understanding of your marketplace. Most companies are doing "me too" kinds of things — they're just following the follower. The more you're aware of that, the more you'll see it. **There are exceptions, but those are the exceptions that we model after; those are the guys who look beyond the "follow-the-leader" mentality to see what their clients really want.** You need to become one of them to make the biggest profits.

NUMBER THREE is making sure those items have the largest profit margin possible. Most businesses just set their prices the way everybody else does; and since they're all selling pretty much the same kinds of things and following the follower, they don't really focus enough on creating products with high profit margins. **You need to have slack adjusters in the mix, (a high-ticket, high-profit margin product or**

▼▼▼▼▼▼▼▼
MARKETING SECRET

How do you become a powerful result-getting copywriter (or anything else you most want to be)? The answer lies in this quote from *Stephen King:*

- "When I talk about my craft, I emphasize one point over and over again: You don't have to be great to do a thing, you just have to not get tired of trying to be good at it."

service that gives you a **BIG PAYDAY!**) because you have to make money to keep the doors open.

NUMBER FOUR is to develop marketing systems that identify the right prospect and communicate the right message to them. Again, I've covered some of this. But most business people don't even know what a marketing system is! A marketing system is simply a process that automatically attracts and resells customers again and again for you. Build it right, and it can work just like a machine.

NUMBER FIVE is that you've got strive to reach, and sell, to those people fast enough to make the largest profit you possibly can. Again, most businesses don't have any real strategy for that.

It is the same way with **NUMBER SIX,** which is reselling. **Most business owners don't have a strategy for reselling at all; they're just sitting back waiting for it all to come to them**. They're not aggressive enough. They're not going after it. They're not trying to build strong bonds with their customers. They're not trying to position themselves to be unique, and they're certainly not making their prospects special offers on a regular basis. Again, let's go back to the barbeque joint in Wichita that's going out of business because they can't compete. I'll bet you they don't even have a mailing list of their customers. I know that Chris Lakey loves going to this place, and there are probably hundreds of people in the Wichita area who feel the same. Yet, are the owners of the barbecue place doing anything to try to identify the people who come to the restaurant again and again? **Do they maintain a mailing list, or anything like that?**

Do they make specific offers to their customers, or work on their positioning strategy? I doubt it. And that's one of the main reasons they're going out of business.

NUMBER SEVEN involves creating sales messages that build strong bonds with your customers. One of the underlying themes of this book so far has been what we go through as marketers to develop a relationship with our customers, and the thought process that goes into developing those relationships. It's not unlike dating, in that you're building a long-term relationship. **However, as a marketer, you want to control that business relationship much more than you would a dating relationship.** This is an important concept, because when you're writing a sales letter or making an offer to your customers, you don't just want to make the sale in the moment. You want to do things that set the customer up for the future sale. One of the questions you should ask yourself is, "What's next?" **When you write a sales piece, be sure that it's not just to sell that product. It should also be to set them up for sales of future products, and services.**

NUMBER EIGHT is to position yourself so that you seem unique. When the barbecue place I spoke of earlier decided to go out of business, they said it was because there was just too much competition in their marketplace. Well, instead of bemoaning the fact that you're up against all these other recipes and all these other locations, why not take some steps to make yourself unique? **Find something that sets you apart from your competitors. What could you do to make yourself seem unique? What steps can you take to do that, and in doing so, enhance your business?**

A lot of information-marketing businesses are built on the concept of an attractive character with which people bond. People tell me mine is: I'm the face of the business. It involves being the almost-over-the-top guy that everybody can identify with, the guy who has a likeable sense of authority. Heck, I'm just being me, but people bond with a character like that and enjoy doing business with them because it transcends the sales. They're doing business with you because they like you as a character.

John Alanis is the same way. From the very beginning, he positioned himself as the king of "Let Them Come to You." His business is to teach men how to get women to hit on them, and that makes him memorable. It's an effective way to do business. If you look at the top entrepreneurs on the block, they're all larger-than-life characters. P.T. Barnum was; Bill Gates is, and to a lesser extent, so are Michael Dell and Lee Iacocca. They all have these outrageous over-the-top personality traits. **When you add all that into your marketing, it really increases the relationship that you have with your customers, and it positions your business so that nobody else can knock it off**.

Going back to the barbeque place one of the easiest things they could do is insert an attractive character into their marketing, and make it something like "Big Bob's Barbeque." Big Bob has an interesting story, and different put on different events, and stuff like that. You may be able to knock off everything else, but you can't knock off the character. So when customers begin to bond with this character, the relationship you have with your list really increases — and so do the sales.

One of their biggest competitors does just that. They're called Famous Dave's Barbeque. In their commercials, which they run all the time, they say stuff like "Famous Dave traveled the world for 25 years looking for the best barbeque..." to build up the character and his legend. Basically, what you find in Famous Dave's is the best-of-the-best of the seasonings and sauces he found when he toured the world looking for great barbeque. **That's how you build a story behind the brand and the people in it.** It's kind of a knock-off of the late Dave Thomas, the founder of Wendy's — and the principle worked really well with him. **He hated doing those commercials when he was doing them, but they were the most effective commercials Wendy's ever did, because it put a human face on the business.** He wasn't quite the lovable public character that he appeared to be in the commercials; in fact, he was a ruthless marketer. But, part of being a ruthless marketer was making those commercials. They really made that company.

NUMBER NINE in the Smart Marketing list is creating offensive marketing strategies that allow you to control the selling process. I'm using "offensive" in the military or sports sense, not to mean repugnant. **Taking the offensive is part of being a ruthless marketer. You don't just sit there and take what comes; you take the fight to the competitors.** It's all part of controlling that relationship, from lead generation to customer acquisition to the initial sale to reselling to that customer again and again. It all ties back into the concept of, what have you done to develop that relationship so that your customers will be receptive to that next sale?

And finally, NUMBER TEN is making specific offers to your customers on an ongoing basis. In other words, you have to take them by the hand and compel them to come to you instead of waiting for them to somehow gravitate to you on their own.

One of the things that I like best about the Smart Marketing concept is that it encompasses many of the points in this entire book. It includes a lot of what I've talked about so far, and what I'm going to include in later chapters. In the end, you have ten steps here that you can consistently go back to as your business grows and develops, and you can say things like, "Okay, I need to do a better job of having a slack adjustor that increases my profit margin." Then you can get to work and ask yourself, "How am I going to correct that?" Oftentimes, as I mentioned at the beginning of the chapter, marketers just look at things and say, "Well, I don't know exactly what to do," and so they do nothing. Frankly — and I know this isn't the first time I've said this, and it won't be the last — most business people are pretty stupid when it comes to marketing. I didn't say they're stupid as people, but they are stupid as marketers. **If you want to separate the behavior from the person, say their behavior is stupid, and look no further than these ten things to understand why.** You'll find there are at least a few that they're violating or doing wrong.

This Smart Marketing list is a good guidepost to sit down with and examine your business. If something isn't going right or you want to do it better, come back to the fundamentals and take a look at what you need to fix.

"Challenge Yourself"

One of my favorite ruthless marketing tips is: **"Strive to increase your selling skills. Look for bigger challenges. And remember, you only become stronger by continually pushing yourself beyond your current abilities."** That's one of the tips on which I often focus in my seminars.

What this tip boils down to is the fact that the concepts you'll find in this book, or in any business seminar, aren't just going to develop themselves on their own. The people trying to teach you can speak or write until they're blue in the face, and nothing's going to happen unless you do something with the concepts they're trying to impart. **You have to pick concepts from the pile you're confronted with, and adapt them and put them into your own business — or they're useless**. And even when they're in place, you're going to have to make them work better for you. The only way that happens is if you practice them.

I guarantee you, when your own money is on the line, you're going to be sharp — or else. You're going to look at this and you're going to say, "Okay, here's what I need to do if I want to make my money back and then some." **Going back to those 10 Smart Marketing steps in the last chapter, if you want to succeed in the marketplace to which you're going to be applying those principles, and you're going to be practicing them constantly.** Do that, and pretty soon, those principles — these strategies — are going to be a part of you; they're just going to be applied routinely to everything you do. I can assure you that's the case with me and with all the marketers I interact with on a regular basis, like the three men who spoke at the seminar on which this book is based — John Alanis, Chris Lakey, and Chris Hollinger. All four of us are confident that you can squeeze us on any aspect of marketing, so to speak, and the relevant knowledge is going to ooze out of us like water from a sponge. **We're thinking about our marketing every single day. We practice what we preach; we've thought through all the contingencies, so we always have an explanation and response for whatever's thrown at us.** We've spent many years working on and in our business, and developing all of the ways to put these methods into action.

If you look at the most successful people in any business — you'll find that many of them have a direct selling background. At some point when they were going through their formal schooling (if they did), they had a summer job selling vacuum cleaners or brushes door-to-door, or tele-marketing. **They did something that involved face-to-face, nose-to-nose, toes-to-toes selling. They took that knowledge with them and translated it into their business, so that they understood how to get customers, how to sell people, how to get patients, how to get clients. That's one difference between them and the people that are barely chugging along.** Similarly, in Direct Response Marketing, what we're doing is taking the sales process and putting it into leveraged media. But in order to do that you have to understand the sales process. Therefore, the more you strive to increase your selling skills and work toward bigger challenges, the more successful your business is going to be. What all this means, ultimately, is you have to keep learning and practicing what you've learned.

John Alanis recently attended a huge sales seminar in Washington, D. C. hosted by Dan Kennedy and Sydney Biddle Barrows. It was about crafting powerful sales messages. Now, if you know anything at all about marketing, you'll recognize that first name as someone who's huge in the field. The second name, Sydney Biddle Barrows, is probably a little familiar, but less so than Dan's. Well, let me help you out here: she's better known as "the Mayflower Madame." She used to run a famous brothel. John went to the event because, though it was free, he knew they were going to be selling something involving Ms. Barrows. It turned out to be a 10-week tele-seminar coaching program.

What interested John most was the offer they were going to make, and the crowd's response. He took many notes. **The biggest thing he took out of that event wasn't the coaching program. It was the structure of the selling process: how they set it up, the offer they made, and all the details they used to get people to buy.** John went just to observe, so that if he's ever in a similar environment, selling something big from the front of the room, he wants to do things as much like they did as he can.

Dan Kennedy and Ms. Barrows effectively used techniques like a price drop, a bonus session the next day for everybody who signed up, a free bonus for the first 50 people who purchased — there was a lot of good salesmanship that went into that presentation, and it was very successful. Not only does it come in handy if John ever does that big presentation, but you can also take all those notes and translate them into print copy, web copy, tele-seminars, and every other sales format to make more money.

What's at the heart of this or any business is your ability to sell something to somebody else — whether face-to-face, or through leveraged media. The more you understand, the more you study and the more you put the selling process into practice, the more financially successful you're going to be. That's why John went to the big event. This particular event was free, unlike a lot of similar events, because they wanted to get everybody in the room so they had a chance to sell them the ten-week coaching program. What they sold John was their sales process that he could duplicate.

Whether it's a paid event or not, most people go to events to listen to a speaker give a presentation, to take notes on the presentation, or the content of the speech. If there's an info product being sold, they listen to the presentation, they hear the benefits about the product or service, they decide if they want to buy it or not, and then they go back home.

But John went to this event not looking for that kind of information; instead, he was studying what they were doing from the front of the room. He was studying how they performed their presentation, how they closed the sales, what their payment structure was and how they asked people to go to the back of the room and place their order. **He was breaking down what they were doing to make money selling the product, so that he could incorporate some of those ideas into his mail campaigns, his web campaigns, any platform selling, and any situation where he's going to be able to sell using some of those powerful techniques.**

At M.O.R.E., Inc., we do the same thing. We buy a lot of products from the top marketers because we sincerely want to know what they're selling. We buy a lot more stuff because we want to see what they're doing. We get on mailing lists so we can see how they follow-up, how they sell people on their product. So there's a lot of educating that takes place, outside of just buying the information and absorbing the knowledge you're being taught. You can learn a great deal just by observing the processes, seeing how other people go about selling their products and services. It's good to attend events just to see how marketers do what they do best.

Keep Pushing

In the business world, it makes good sense to continually push yourself beyond your current abilities. Things happen in the heat of the battle, when you're pushing yourself to go, go, go, and you'll end up learning something about yourself, about your market, or about the technology that you use that you didn't before — and you'll be able to apply it in different venues. For example, when Chris Hollinger first started his business, he knew hardly anything about HTML code. That is ironic, because he sells web sites, which are based on HTML — Hypertext Markup Language. He says everything he really knows he learned just from messing around with it and playing with the code and pushing it (and himself) to see what it would do to web sites. And then, boom! He had an opportunity to say, "Okay, I can manipulate code here and actually sell a product to people because I can do this now,"and it became a matter of copying and pasting code — and he made money. **In the heat of pushing himself and his abilities with web sites and web design, a whole new offer popped out of that, and it still gives him a nice profit margin.**

That's a good example of the kind of thing that can pop into view when you're pushing yourself. Many times you end up with more ideas than you have time with which to work. **Even if you don't, the goal isn't all that important; what's really important is who you become in the process of achieving your goal.** Generally, what you become is a better marketer.

This goes all the way back to the Introduction of this book, when I pointed out that a lot of what we call talent is the result of constant, unrelenting practicing of skills. Selling is a skill, and a skill is something that almost anybody can learn. There's a process, a recipe, you have to go through that most people can follow. Are some people more naturally inclined toward selling? You bet. But that doesn't have to be an excuse. Now, I'm proud of being a salesperson — although a lot of salespeople aren't. Selling has a bad

> ▼▼▼▼▼▼▼▼▼▼▼▼▼▼▼
> Don't be scammed! Nobody has all the answers... no matter how good they may be at fooling people into believing so.

connotation; hardly anyone wants to admit they're a salesperson. They'd rather call themselves marketers, simply because a few bad people have given the whole industry a bad name. But you have to get past that embarrassment! **The bottom line is, at some level, we're all salespeople: we're selling our ideas to those around us, those we want to persuade and influence**. We're all salespeople. Some people will admit it, some won't. Some are better at it than others. But marketing is really selling — and that's all it is. This is especially true with Direct Response Marketing. **It's not advertising, it's not marketing, it's salesmanship that's applied through the leverage of the media you use.** It is what the late Gary Halbert used to call "salesmanship multiplied."

The point is, we're all salespeople. We're all trying to sell something, and some of us are just more proud of it than others, and some of us will admit it more than others. How much you admit it to yourself can affect how hard you're willing to push yourself — and that's the way you really make money.

"Learn to Juggle"

Two of the things you need to learn to be an effective marketer are interrelated at a very basic level, even though, on the surface, they may appear to be contradictory. Two principles I often share with would-be entrepreneurs are, first, **"It's always good to have more projects than you can comfortably handle,"** and, second, **"One of the secrets to a great promotion is to**

allow yourself enough time to work on it." You must live with it for a long enough period of time to discover the best ideas. The longer you rework it, the stronger the ideas. <u>Sometimes the best ideas come in the beginning, but most of the time they come as the deadline approaches</u>. You must set tight deadlines. But if they're set too tight, you'll never discover some of the most powerful selling ideas.

Now, you may be thinking, "If I give myself too many projects, how am I going to be able to give the quality time to the project on which I want to work?" Here's what I'm trying to say: you want to have a bunch of things going at the same time, both in terms of how you rank them and prioritize them for completion. But you also have to be on the lookout for new opportunities that can bump one of those things out of there into the forefront, because you see that the new opportunity is worth pursuing. **The key is to have a little bit more going on than you can comfortably handle. It may be stressful and take up a lot of your time, but it's the key to success in this business, because frankly, most of the things you're going to do simply aren't going to work, though some will**. So when the three or four things that you're working on go bust, but the fifth thing pays off, you're able to continue to profit.

That's why you must always have a bunch of things going on at once. At the same time, you need to prioritize the things you work on; you want to block out enough time to effectively accomplish something on each product. Let's say you choose to work on something for two hours a day, then you're done with it. Then you start the next thing, and you work on that until you're done with it. Then you come back to them the next day. **In other words, always work on multiple projects, but give each project a reasonable amount of development time within the context of your daily schedule.** The trick is to make sure you set deadlines, because otherwise you'll just juggle projects for an endless amount of time and nothing will ever get done. But if you know that by Friday of this week you need these three projects to get done, you'll focus on them, even though you may have five or six or more that are in various stages of completion.

For example, I might have a letter where really all I've written is the headline and maybe the first few paragraphs, and it sits there and I think about it for a few days, and play with it a little bit. But I've also got these other projects, so I might spend 75% of my day working on other items. I've got a certain block of time available to spend on this project, and then

I've got to put my head into this other project. **Sometimes it works that way, and sometimes it doesn't.** If you get knee-deep into a project and you're in the zone, and it comes to the end of the hour or whenever you're supposed to stop…well, don't stop. **If you're in the zone, you stay in the zone and you spill over. So there are certain freedoms within those basic restrictions.**

All in all, though, I think the trick is to be working on a bunch of projects, all at the same time. Be slightly overwhelmed with the quantity of everything you're working on, but also set deadlines to make sure that you're consistently moving projects off your desk. Otherwise, you just end up sitting there working on things you never get done. It's all about putting more on your plate than you can comfortably handle. A little discomfort is good because it forces you to stay active. What you don't want to do, ever, is get too lazy. For those who point out that it's possible to have so much stuff going that nothing gets done — in computer terms, this is called "thrashing" — I would point out that you have to learn to prioritize and to be ruthless about chopping away unprofitable (or even less profitable) items and putting them aside for a while — or even getting rid of them altogether.

You have to be constantly willing to evaluate new opportunities even if you're so busy you can't think, because an opportunity may come along that's better than the one on which you're working — even if you have time invested in the existing opportunity. **You have to be careful about that, though**: I know several marketers who like to chase bright, shiny objects, and they often think that another opportunity is better than the one they're working on because they don't evaluate it correctly. **The key skill is to correctly evaluate opportunities and prioritize them based on their Return on Investment (ROI)**. Don't get married to a project, because it just may happen that another opportunity may come up that fits into the context of your business, and you'll have to chop off the original idea and put it aside for a while. Being able to identify those new opportunities, to say no or yes to them and prioritize the ones you do accept, is a key entrepreneurial skill.

One of the aspects of being an entrepreneur that's both a blessing and a curse is that you don't have a time clock. You don't have a boss telling you when you have to be somewhere, or what you have to do. It's especially difficult when you're one of those people who just operate better under that type of regimen. **If that's the case, you absolutely need to put**

deadlines on certain things. If you don't say, "Okay, I want to get this all together and have it out there by this date," the damn thing may just sit there and not get done. So at the very least, arbitrarily pick a date as your drop-dead deadline. Otherwise, your existing schedule may dictate when you actually have time to do a project. **Whatever the case, you absolutely must set deadlines so you'll be sure to put yourself to work on that project regularly.** And you know what? You'll probably get it done more quickly than you expect. The simple act of being engaged — especially in something that's rewarding and exciting — makes the time really fly by. When you come up for air, look back and say, "Okay, what did I get done on my list?" Look at the checkmarks there, and decide how productive you were. <u>And be honest with yourself about the direction that you're heading and the deadlines that you're meeting, and keep yourself on task — or you can flounder.</u>

There's self-discipline, and there's self-imposed discipline. The latter is where the idea of the deadline comes in. Let's say there's a monthly meeting you're involved in where you commit to something. You don't want to look like a schmoe at the next meeting and say, "Well, um, I didn't get all this stuff done," so you work hard and get done what you've committed to. That's self-imposed discipline. You say to yourself, "Okay, I've got this deadline, and I'm going to look like a fool if I don't finish this, so I'd better get on the ball." **Instead of just setting your deadlines, which you can't enforce, you create a self-imposed, disciplined work environment that gets you to do things.** You tell yourself, "I've gotta write this number of words by this time in the morning for this person, or I'm going to get fired." **That's self-imposed discipline. If you look for ways to impose discipline on yourself, you get a heck of a lot more done.**

Here's an example from John Alanis. His business is basically run off his laptop. But during the day, when he sits down to write copy or do just about anything productive, he disconnects the damn thing from the Internet and moves it to another room where he can't access the Internet at all. This is an example of self-imposed discipline. **You often get more done when you create this environment of self-imposed discipline, rather than trying to force yourself through willpower and self-discipline** — which are very hard concepts even for the best of the best to wrap their brains around. If you're able to create this self-imposed disciplined environment, you'll find your productivity increases dramatically.

▼▼▼▼▼▼▼▼
MARKETING SECRET

The P.A.S. Advertising Formula:

- **Pain** — Bring up the pain your best prospects feel.

- **Agitate** — Make it real! Let them identify with a personal, emotional, dramatic story.

- **Solution** — Sell the solution to the pain!

Keep finding many ways to weave this little advertising formula into your ads/sales letters.

It is based on this solid theory: People will do MORE to avoid pain — than to gain pleasure.

This is very, very important, because entrepreneurs have the freedom to sluff off all day. **If you work for yourself, you can decide when you work or when you don't work**. If it occurs to you, you could decide to hang out by the beach every day and do nothing. Or you can decide that you're going to spend twelve hours a day working your business and making sure you get things done and meet your goals. With the freedom to be able to do all those things and choose how you spend your time comes the responsibility to yourself to be productive, and to do things that will further your business.

The best thing about being self-employed is the fact that you are your own boss — and the worst thing about being self-employed is the fact that you are your own boss!

It's similar to what they say about defending yourself in court — that you've got a fool for a lawyer, because you're the worst lawyer in the world for yourself. It can be the same way when it comes to working for yourself. **When it comes to human motivation, the best advice I can give you after almost 30 years of studying all this is, find a hundred ways to motivate yourself.** Try a bunch of different things, and you'll find that different things work at different times.

Getting back to the quotes with which I started this chapter, I recognize that they're slightly contradictory in a way. But only slightly. I think the synergy between them is much more important than the slight differences. **It all comes down to the fact that if you don't want to lose any money, then you build a customer list and always, always focus on your best customers first**, so every project you're involved in follows a logical sequence of actions. I've talked about this principle repeatedly throughout this book. **As long as you're constantly developing new things for your best customers first, you never have to worry about losing money** — because they trust you, they like you, there's a relationship with you, and they will always buy. Maybe they won't go crazy over what you're offering, but they'll at least buy in sufficient numbers so that you're trading dollars for dollars. You're not losing money. And they'll be willing to see what you come up with next, which they may very well be crazy about.

The creative process is a little different for everybody, and we all have to find what works for us and what doesn't. The only way to do that is by experimenting with lots of things. One of the things I like to do is always have a variety of projects I'm juggling. Sometimes I don't want to do them; sometimes I don't like to do them. But I have to. And you know what's interesting? **Sometimes I come up with my greatest ideas when I'm in terrible pain because I've got to do something, and all of a sudden my brain starts going in 40 million other directions that turn out to be profitable.** I start a lot of new projects just because I'm going through this terrible mental pain of forcing myself to work on a project, where it's like pulling teeth to get anything done. My brain automatically gives me good ideas as a result — maybe as compensation. **That's why I like to always have a bunch of projects in my head constantly, to put that pressure on me — because that pressure can be very, very good.**

I remember when I was a member of Dan Kennedy's Platinum Group. Out of respect for all the other members in that group (there were 15 or 18 or us), you have to sit there and listen to them one at a time as they do their presentations. Well, I found some of those presentations to be tremendously boring — which some of them would no doubt say about my presentations. Now, I don't like to sit still; I can't sit still. But part of being a member of Dan Kennedy's Platinum Group was that you had to put your butt in the seat for two days. Well, that drove me crazy! So for two days I was sitting there and I was working on all kinds of creative projects, because I was going nuts. I couldn't stand just sitting there, so I would come up with some really creative, breakthrough ideas while undergoing that that terrible "pain" of having to keep my butt in that seat.

Despite what some of us might think, we're all creative; or at least, we all start out being creative as kids. Somewhere along the line, though, that creativity is stifled. We lose that edge, or maybe society beats it out of us. Part of this whole multi-project thing I'm telling you about in this chapter is supposed to be fun; it's not supposed to be a bunch of projects that are nothing but work. The idea's not to make you groan, "Oh man, I've got too much work." **You need to focus on stuff that excites you, stuff that interests you, stuff that makes you feel alive.** I think that's what happens to a lot of business owners who end up working in their business instead of on their business. They get wrapped up in so many of the details, and then it gets to a point to where they just don't like it. It's painful, they're bored, and they've lost any creative spark. **Why are they still doing it? Because it pays the bills, and that's what they do.**

But let that creativity flow, and it can be amazing how 12, 14, or 16 hours can just fly by some days. Chris Hollinger tells me that if he doesn't totally lay it out there 100% and go nuts every day, he won't sleep at night. It'll bug him, or he'll have too much energy to sleep well. I can understand that. It's the kind of thing where if you want to get a good night's sleep and be any good the next day, you've got to expend that energy — whether it's physical energy or mental energy. (I can assure you that mental energy will also wear you out quickly.) **It's important to realize, too, that when you're in the zone, whatever it is you're doing, you shouldn't leave it until it goes by on its own.** Because sometimes you'll get to working and everything will just mesh and click and come together, and it will just flow right out of you. Though, of course, often you don't get in the zone right away. I walk on the treadmill a lot. Most often it's like this: the first 10 minutes I'm forcing myself to do it. But then after about 10 minutes, I start getting into it; and by the time an hour has gone by I'm way into it, and it feels totally different. But still, those first 10 minutes I have to force myself!

The same thing can happen with work. **You may find yourself facing something late in the day, and you're tired and don't want to deal with it.** But it's a project you have to do, so you force yourself to sit down and work on it — and maybe for the first ten minutes you hate every second of it. But, more often than not, you start getting into it after a while, and the rest of that block of time goes smoothly. This is especially the case when you're working on focused activities, which all of your projects should be. As I've mentioned before, **that focus comes from having a list of customers, segmenting it into your best customers and everyone** else, and focusing on creating more and more products and services that are designed to give them more of what they want.

As far as self-discipline goes, one of our greatest secrets at M.O.R.E., Incorporated is this: we create all kinds of lead generation offers where we send out the mailing pieces first. Then the leads come in. **Well, every single day you let those leads sit there, they lose value. Because when people want something, they want it now. <u>Not tomorrow, but now</u>!** There's a tremendous sense of urgency when you've got hundreds of leads piling up and you don't yet have all the lead fulfillment put together for it.

Now, all of a sudden, talk about flogging yourself! You're motivated now! We play that game with ourselves constantly, where we throw out all the lead generating stuff first, then people start requesting the information. **It ain't ready yet, but it will be in a matter of a week or so, because we could never let a lead sit for more than a week — ever.**

Think of it this way: you've got to be aware of your own mental processes. If you don't understand the fact that you have to get to Minute 11 on the days you don't start off in the zone, then you never get there. John

---

▼▼▼▼▼▼▼▼▼▼▼▼

Become a marketing pitbull!

Most marketers give up on their prospective buyers way too soon. Don't do this! Be more relentless in all of your marketing efforts. Go after them in the most aggressive way — <u>and stay after them</u>.

Alanis tells me that every time he sits down to write a new sales letter, he thinks, "There's no way I can write a 20-page sales letter. It's just impossible!" I know how he feels: you're thinking that, for whatever reason, you've lost it — you'll never be able to do that again. But you can write a headline and a first sentence. If you can do that, you know that it's going to start going from there. That's John's mental process. Maybe he can't sit down to write a sales letter, but he can sit down to write that. What does he do to get past that? Sometimes he has to sit down and handwrite some old sales letters. **Or he'll read through some old copy, he'll just start writing something, and then it will catch fire.**

Awareness of that mental process is very important, very powerful. Figuring out the things that motivate you and get you to work, helps you

MARKETING SECRET

All of us are in the exact same business:

- The business of giving our customers more of what they want.

- The business of customer acquisition and development.

Every person who is truly an entrepreneur knows this. That's why these people can move from business to business — and make money in all of them.

keep going on those days when you feel less than perfect — the days you're not in the zone, which, quite frankly, is more often than not — so you're still able to be productive. If you're not aware of that mental process and start something and say, "Oh, I don't feel like doing it; I'm going to quit," then you never get it done.

Many people bypass their reluctance to get started with a "To Do" list; this may work well for you. Before you leave the office Thursday night, do your list, and then when you come into the office Friday morning, you're launched. People who use "To Do" lists this way tell me that on the days they don't do that, they go into the office and bounce from one thing to another and never really get anything done. That "To Do" list works for them, and they need to stick with it. I do something similar: I set up all my work for the morning the night before, so it's staring me right in the face when I come in. Now, I don't always feel like getting up in the morning, but I do, because I know that those first few hours are my most productive time. I have to get up at five o'clock in the morning or I lose that most creative period. So on the mornings when I'd just rather just lay there right next to my wife and not get up, I always tell myself "To thine own self be true," and that quote from Shakespeare gets me out of bed, because I know that's what it's all about. **Just because you can get away with a lot when you're your own boss doesn't mean you're not hurting yourself when you treat yourself too easily.** You have to have a mechanism in place to help you hold yourself accountable.

Forcing yourself to do what you need to do is what self-discipline is all about. You've got the intellectual side and the emotional side to self-discipline. Sometimes those two sides battle each other. **We all know what we should be doing intellectually, but our emotions oftentimes don't allow us to do those things — so you've got to try to mesh those two**. Self-imposed discipline is what bridges the gap.

Maybe you don't work best by starting out at five in the morning like I do, but whenever you work best, you've got to set up a mechanism to force that. For example, John Alanis usually sets up his "To Do" list a week in advance, because he knows he's not going to be as productive if he doesn't. Of course, now that he's no longer in the military, he's not getting up at 5:00 AM for anything! What works best for him is to get up, go to the gym to work out physically, and then move on to the work day. His work day doesn't start, sometimes, until around noon. But he's most productive after that, and he can work late into the night — maybe to 1:00 AM or 2:00 AM — and be fantastically productive. That's because he knows himself, and he knows that if he gets up at 5:00 AM, his day is worthless — especially if he doesn't go to the gym.

This may sound like a cliché, but that's only because it's so true: everybody is different. **You have to know yourself, and mesh your work environment and schedule to your personal reality. And, you have to demand more from yourself!**

Every time I see the Forbes 400 list or read the story of a super-successful entrepreneur, and notice how they always seem to be back on the lists year after year, I think to myself, "Man, I'd love to see their goal sheets." Because I know that somewhere, these people have what they want to accomplish written down. Oh, maybe not 100 percent of them do, but more often than not, when someone is making a ton of money, they've got goals written down somewhere. My business plan, for example, is right there in my bathroom. That may fall into the "too much information" category for you, but I think it's a good example of how you can keep your goals where you can see them.

You have to reward yourself, too, because if no one else pats you on the back, you have to pat yourself on the back. So when you accomplish a task, you have to give yourself a little reward, even if it's just to go get a cup of coffee or do something. At the very least, allow yourself that feeling of completion, that brief feeling of accomplishment.

Too much reward can be a bad thing, of course. For example, as Chris Hollinger told me once, on a beautiful fall day he might want to be out on the lake fishing, but if he were, he'd know there were a whole bunch of things that he really needed to get done at the office — and it just wouldn't feel right. He'd feel like he was cheating himself and cheating his wife and cheating their business.

The reason he knows that feeling is because he's said, "Oh, the heck with it," and loaded the boat up in the truck and gone over to the lake and put the boat in and gone fishing, and the whole time he was catching fish, something was gnawing on him. **To really enjoy something, then, you have to make sure that the "i's" are dotted and the "t's" are crossed, and that you've taken care of your business before you go and reward yourself.** If you work very, very hard and you know you've really done your best, then when you go out there to enjoy yourself, you're completely relaxed and in the moment. You work hard, you play hard, and it feels so good! But if you haven't taken care of business, then it's worthless.

"Take It Step By Step"

Never, never ignore the potential for multi-step marketing in your business. It's an important aspect of building long-term customer relationships and setting up additional sales on the back-end — and it's those things that guarantee long-term success. **Whenever you sell a product, whether it's to someone on your customer list or somebody else's, that prospect should immediately become a lead to buy the next product you have to offer.** So if somebody gives you $300 for something, immediately start them on a multi-step sequence to buy more — because someone who's just spent $300 is a perfect prospect for something similar. If you start them on a new marketing sequence as soon as they buy something, it can be very profitable in the end.

Now, conversion rates between the steps in your system will vary all over the place, depend on what you're selling, how well your marketing copy is working, how hot the market is, the lists you're using, where the lead was generated, the source, and so on. There are no real norms, because there are too many variables. **The only thing you should really care about is Return on Investment — ROI. How much did you spend, versus how**

much you made? A corollary to this is that you don't want to get caught up too much in response rates, because those vary widely according to the media used and all the other variables I've already mentioned.

What it comes down to, once again, is how much money you can spend to get the customer. I talked about this at length earlier, but I think it's worth re-emphasizing here, because it's a significant aspect of multi-step marketing. The guy who can spend a hundred bucks to get a customer can't do as much as the guy who can spend a thousand dollars to get the customer; that's just reality. What you want to do is engineer your business so you can afford to spend more to get the customer.

So what do you do when the customer comes in? How do you increase their lifetime value? On the initial sale, what kind of up-sells can you add to get the transaction value higher? Can you put telemarketing to work? Do you have a bounce-back offer in the initial package that gets them excited? Do you have a "thank you, send more money" letter that shows up a week later to get that transaction value up? **How can you get that money out of them faster, so that you can overcome the initial cost to get the customer, so you can go out in more places and spend more money to get more customers?** The more places you can go, the more you can spend to get a customer, the faster you can grow your business. We call this "closing the gap." There's always that gap between how much money you spend and when you actually make that money back. We're always looking for ways to make money faster so that we can be more aggressive, and more ruthless in our marketing.

Even if you've got a multi-step marketing plan in place, it's well worth the effort to sit down and analyze how effectively it helps you maximize the lifetime value of each customer. Look at ways to tweak that, by category, so you can get in the position to begin to expand your business a lot faster. **The better you can position yourself so you're profitable on the front-end or can shorten the return time of the money that you spend, the faster you can ramp your business up and roll out new products and new services that appeal to your clients.** If you do that right, you get a snowball effect, because you can get that money back faster, you can get more customers in faster, you can create the customer list faster, and you have more resources and time to spend on building those relationships and developing the back-end, which is where the real money is. So that's the way to think about it: How do I increase the lifetime

A great salesperson cannot make anyone buy something they don't want... That's why we must get prospects to "raise their hand" and show us that they are interested.

- Let the prospects qualify themselves by jumping through the hoops we hold in front of them!

- This is the secret to making easy sales!

value of my customer and shorten the time it takes me to get my initial investment back?

Let's say you move out of the normal marketing channels into radio. There are a lot of places you can try on radio: FM and AM radio all over the country, XM and Sirius satellite radio, you name it. If you can figure out how to get the economics to work in this kind of marketing venture, you can build your list so fast it's not even funny. **It's a matter of testing. It's a matter of adding up-sells. It's a matter of adding in things like telemarketing, if you need to**. If you can make your marketing plan work in that medium, you can ramp your business up just as fast as you want to go.

Then there's the Internet, of course. I've been hurt by the Internet, but I've been helped, too. You just have to know how to approach it correctly. You see, the Internet doesn't care where you are; if you've got Internet access and a cabin up in Montana, you can still do business using the multi-step model. **In fact, the Internet offers several ways to have prospects raise their hands so you can build a list, which is where the gold is in any marketing system.**

Whatever opportunity you're in right now or want to get started in, the Internet is definitely one of the most cost-effective ways to proceed. You can inexpensively run banner ads or pay-per-click ads and drive your customers to an opt-in page, where you can squeeze more information out of them. In the process of doing that, they qualify themselves. They've raised their hand. **They've put down their name and their email address, so they want to hear more — and you've hooked them. Now that they're on your list, you don't run nearly as high a risk of them**

deleting your email than if you were sending your stuff out blind. These days more than ever, people don't want stuff to show up unasked-for in their inboxes. For people to actually give you their real contact information means you've got a much better chance of converting the prospect, because they're interested in what you've got. **By forcing them to go through that opt-in page, you're qualifying them.** You may not get as many leads as you might like, but they're by far more valuable than most of the worthless internet leads that many people are trying to sell to.

Now, the trick on that opt-in page is that you want to make some pretty bold promises. You want them to say to themselves, "Okay, this looks like something I have to know more about. I'll go ahead and give them my email address and move forward." By doing that, they've qualified themselves. **So learning how opt-in pages work and getting that system set up can be insanely profitable. It's not that hard, either — trust me, you can go online and find a number of systems that will allow you to build your own opt-in pages.** And Heaven knows that there are plenty of existing opt-in pages, no matter what your market, that you can use as models. They're all over the place — and if they've been up for any length of time, you know they're working, and so you come up with one like that and you test it, tweak it, and it works.

With that in mind, the Internet is the greatest way to spy on people or get ideas. Some of the software programs you can buy, for example, just let you strip all the text out of an existing page and re-write it, leaving all the background coding intact.

There's another program called Spyfu (spyfu.com) that lets you spy on your online competitors; it'll show you all their organic search terms, the keywords, the ads they're running, how much they're paying, you name it. It's a dumb name, but it's a hell of a piece of software.

The competitive intelligence stuff out there is amazing, and it can be massively useful if you chose to work the Internet. Now, I don't know how long some of these will last, so my advice is to use them while you can. Eventually there might be laws written against them , but it's more likely that Google and the other big Internet portal sites will find a way to just block them off.

That's a simple model that works great for folks like my colleagues

Chris Hollinger and John Alanis, but it may not work for everyone — especially if your business is primarily offline, like mine. Our model is equally as simple: primarily we use all Direct Mail. We've used other marketing methods over the years, but these days what works the best for us is to send out a Direct Mail offer that just gets people to raise their hand. Then we send a package that offers a product in the range of $649-749. That range can change, because we're constantly testing new things, but that's our current "sweet spot," as I call it. The next step is to follow up with a monthly continuity program. That's the model that we're using right now to bring in millions of dollars.

There's nothing complicated about our model; really, it's so simple a school kid could understand it. **We mail Direct Mail offers that just ask people to raise their hand; that's it. Our initial offer doesn't ask for any money. We just want people to raise their hand**. They send for a free Report or information that we sell to them, and then we send them our big sales letter that sells them our first package for that basic price range of under a thousand dollars, plus a monthly continuity. And then we have a Direct Mail sequence that goes out to them; right now our sequence is ten steps, so they get up to ten different pieces of mail that continue to knock on their door, sort of like a salesperson. It's all very simple — there's nothing to it. That little model has worked for us for the last three or four years; before that we used other models. We've done all different kinds of things.

John Alanis uses a different model, and it's one that's used by thousands of people. It all goes back to the old Jeff Paul model that drives people to 24-hour recorded phone messages, although John gives them the option to go to a website and get on his email list. The Jeff Paul model was basically the one we started with back in the late 1980s. That was what "Dialing For Dollars" was all about, by the way — driving people to a simple recorded message, only we were using answering machines back then. Nowadays John is using voice mail, and he's getting people to go to his website, too. **However you go about it, you need a multi-step model that helps you draw in prospects and make them customers for life. Maybe it's a two-step system — maybe it's three or more**. Whatever system you set up, whatever model you choose to use, you have to <u>aggressively go after those leads and attempt to close the largest number of sales and then re-sell them the largest number of related products and services for the longest period of time</u>.

Learn to Write
Long-Form Sales Letters

Long form sales letters are an important part of most Direct Mail marketing efforts, but most people do not realize that these letters are not designed to be read word-for-word, they're designed to be skimmed. **You want your reader to be able to passively skim through your sales letter and absorb enough of your message to be sold.**

Writing these letters is very formulaic: the purpose of the headline is to get them into it. The first sentence is there to get them to read the second sentence, and so on and so forth. People tend to skip around. There's a certain set of people who are going to sit down and read everything, just as there's a certain set of people who are going to read nothing. **In between,**

▼▼▼▼▼▼▼▼▼▼▼▼▼

The best direct response marketing copywriters are <u>not</u> freelancers!

The best are the men and women whose businesses *live or die* by the words they write.

though, there's this huge crowd of people who are going to read portions of the letter here and there. And so with your sub-heads and pictures, (particularly on the Internet) what you want to do, is have something that stops them if they're skimming through the sales letter. For example, John Alanis might have a picture of a woman with a caption under it that gets them back into the copy. **You need to sprinkle teasers throughout your sales letters that are intended to get people back into the copy they might be skimming.** <u>The more you can get them to stop and read, the more committed they are, and the more likely they are to buy</u>.

Follow the Double Readership Path

Dan Kennedy taught me that when writing marketing copy, I needed to develop what he calls a double readership path. Here's how that works. As I've mentioned already, a few of the people who get your sales letter are going to sit down and read the whole thing; that's one readership path, so the letter has to be coherent for the people who choose to do that. But

The #1 common denominator all really successful people have is this:

They are hungry!

And they stay hungry!

- This hunger drives them forward — it gives them an intense desire to be their best — to see how far they can go — to push themselves even further.

you've got to assume that they're only a small portion of your audience; by far the biggest readership path is comprised of the skimmers. They're busy, they're harried, they have a lot of distractions. **You want to be able to stop them and get them back into the text on a regular basis, so they can be sold by the time they get to the Order Form.** If you're writing copy in big block with no sub-heads, it's very intimidating to read, like a textbook. They won't be sold on that, because it doesn't get them involved in the sales process. You have to assume from the beginning that they're going to get distracted by something while they're reading, so you'd better do everything you can to get them back into the copy.

What it boils down to is this: <u>you have to fight for their attention and interest</u>. You have to overcome all the everyday headaches they face, and you have to get past all your competitors. Now, I want to emphasize that having competitors is good for your business, especially if you're in a lucrative market with lots of good prospects — but you still have to be aware of your competition, and do everything you can to get people to ignore their messages in favor of yours. **The sad reality is that people have a limited amount of attention to give. They've got all kinds of other things vying for their attention constantly, and they've most likely developed some sales resistance because they're tired, overwhelmed, and apathetic.** You're competing with all that, so you must engage them emotionally. Building these psychological messages into your sales letters can be powerful; but having said that, you have to realize that it's not always easy. I've discussed the fact that certain words provoke better imagery than others, like "ruthless" as opposed to "assertive." So when you're sitting there debating on a word to use in a headline, ask yourself, "What emotion does it invoke in my reader?" Fear and love and greed are some pretty big emotions with which you can pack your sales letters that can really increase your performance and conversion.

That's one of the reasons, by the way, that big, fat sales letters can be effective. The best example is our current Platinum Membership sales letter — it's 64 pages long. Why 64 pages? One reason is that it's selling a $5,000 package. While five grand is no big deal in other markets, for our market, that's a high price. So there's a psychological, emotional thing happening: the more money you're trying to ask people to give, in return, you'd better show them some meat. People see a 64-page sales letter and emotionally they think, "Man, there must really be some substance here." In addition to just doing what we call "killing trees" by writing a lengthy sales letter, for your higher-priced items you can add colorful inserts, CDs, even DVDs — these are especially effective for people who aren't readers. **But whatever you do, it's all designed to loop them back into the copy, and lead them to the Order Form** — which ultimately is a snapshot of the sales letter all over again, although it needs to stand on its own and be a sales piece in and of itself.

Speaking of the Order Form, here's something John Alanis tried for his. During one discussion a while back, he and I talked about the importance of confidence, and that sparked an idea in him. So he sent out an email, asking all the ladies on his list to write back and say why it's important for a man to have confidence in himself. He got a lot of responses — some of them were pretty brutal — and he put some of them on the back of the Order Form along with a nice picture of a sexy woman. This is real, true stuff, and any guy who reads that is going to pay attention to it — he's going to get involved. He'll say to himself, "Oh my God, these women... what the heck is this?" **It's an involvement device to move them back into your copy, which will help sell them on what you're asking them to buy.**

Experiment with Structure

Various structural elements of the text can also make good involvement devices, and they're often amazingly easy to use: really, regaining a person's attention may be as simple as changing the color or size of the text. **Bullets are another good example of a simple structural involvement device. They often do most of the selling in long sales letters, so you should spend a lot of time writing bullets and learning how to do it well**. Because if somebody is skimming through and they see one bullet that's really interesting to them, and they say, "I really want that one thing," then that's what closes the sale.

At my company, M.O.R.E., Incorporated, we're very cognizant of the importance of text bullets, so we use them a lot, and vary their use significantly. One thing we do is make our bullets different sizes. If our sales letter is 10-point Courier, our bullets might mostly be 10-point Courier — but we increase the size of the ones we want our readers to focus on and pay attention to. Instead of them being 10-point, we might make them 16-point. Instead of Courier, they might be Tahoma, or another font that contrasts with Courier. Doing this makes those bullets really jump out on the page. **If you've got a page, a page and a half, or two pages worth of bullets, you can really emphasize the ones that you want them to pay the most attention to by changing their size or font type; you can even put a box around an important bullet point.** Doing things like this grabs the skimmer's attention and draw them back to what you want them to read. They're naturally going to be drawn to those things that look different from the rest of the sales letter.

You also need to take the general physical structure of your text into consideration. I've read sales letters that were written in a blocky form, without even spaces between paragraphs — the writers just treat it as a normal text, like this book, and simply drop down a line whenever they start a new paragraph. They don't even indent anything. **It's all blah, like they threw up on a piece of paper.** It's just there, one page after another. So maybe they end up with an eight-page sales letter of boring text that, if they're lucky, the read-it-all folks will take a look at — whereas if they'd taken the time to format it properly for the double path of readership, that eight pages of dense, boring text might have turned into 16, 20, or 24 exciting pages.

One of the things I like to do when writing copy is keep my paragraphs short. My fellow ruthless marketer Jeff Gardner is a master at doing this. Sometimes he'll reel off several paragraphs with just one sentence each. They may be short, they may not say much all at once, but they're easy to read as you're scanning the page.

This tactic makes the page look like there's less copy on it; it makes it look like it's going to take less time to read, which in fact it does, because you have fewer words on each page. Do it right, and you can string enough of these easy-to-read pages together to form long-form sales letters that people don't mind reading. **A good rule of thumb is that if you have a paragraph that's seven lines long, break it up, otherwise most people are going to get lost in it — especially if it's drab and boring, and the font is all the same, with no subheads or bullets to read**.

I'm not trying to say your readers are stupid; they're not. But they don't have the time or the attention span to read a bunch of fine print. So if you've got a big, thick paragraph, do something to break it up, because it's going to be a lot easier for those apathetic readers to grasp. Otherwise, all the information in that big paragraph is probably going to be lost.

Repeat, Repeat, Repeat Your Message

Another thing you should keep in mind while working with the long-form sales letter is this: <u>don't be afraid to repeat the main benefits and features of your product, your service, or your opportunity over and over again, because the skimmers might not see it the first time</u>. They might not hit those benefits and features until two pages later, when they get to the next easy-to-read bulleted list.

You can't just repeat it all word-for-word — the people who follow the read-it-all readership path will catch that and get bored — so you need to work at it to make the same thing sound a little different. Ultimately, your job is to convince them that the money they're going to give you for whatever it is you're offering pales in comparison to what they're going to receive.

I've been accused of beating people over the head with my message — in fact, I've told a lot of my clients that it's a good idea repeat your message least ten times in your copy, if that's possible. **I took Dan Kennedy's double readership path, and I turned the volume up on it full blast!**

Part of the reason I do it is out of laziness. **The running joke**

MARKETING SECRET

Good marketing is a process of:

1. Seeking and finding the people who desire what we sell...

2. Convincing them that we can give them what they desire...

3. And then continuing to give them a wide range of products and services that somehow satisfies their desires.

amongst my peers is that with any of my sales letters, if you really want to figure out what I'm selling, you just read the first five out of the first 36 pages and you've got it — because I spend the rest of the pages repeating what I said in the first five. That's true to some extent, because often I just copy, paste, copy, paste, and re-write a little bit. But then, magalogs — those catalog/magazine hybrids you see sometimes — are written in a similar way.

If you take a close look at one of those you may think, "Hey, this isn't a sales letter that flows. This is a bunch of small ads that are basically repeated over and over again." A magalog is a patchwork quilt kind of marketing copy — but they're effective, simply because most people are going to skip around rather than read the whole thing. The reader may miss all the stuff that's repeated on the first 16 pages, but he hits page 17, something jumps out at him, and he's sold. That's the way a good magalog works, and it's how a good sales letter works, too.

It's a matter of sitting down in the beginning and trying to spell out your best benefits, and then just trying to play off that as much as you can, covering them in different ways as you go. You never know what's going to hit somebody a certain way, which is why you look for different ways to say the same things over and over. We don't just do it in marketing. Politicians do it, and religious leaders do it. Any communicators do it — they're constantly beating people over the head with the same messages over and over again, but they repeat them in different ways.

That's why I love putting stories in a good

sales letter. Even if you've said something a bunch of times already, well, you can say it again in a different way with a story about somebody. **People love to read stories, so then may resonate, whereas your point might not have in previous repetitions.** Different repetitions, in fact, will resonate with different individuals, which is why we sometimes beat our customers over the head with our messages.

Of course, this method just irritates some people — especially the people who like to read every single word. Remember, though, your copy isn't just for them. While they may gripe that you repeat yourself four or five times — which irritates them because you make them read more copy than they need to — keep this important principle in mind: **It doesn't matter who you upset, it only matters who you sell.** One of Russ von Hoelscher's favorite stories he likes to tell about me is along those lines. Apparently, there was a doctor who was sitting next to Russ at one of our $5,000 seminars, and he said to Russ, "You know, I've been getting T.J.'s sales letters for years, and it just drives me crazy the way he keeps repeating himself over and over and over again. Russ, you should talk to him about that." And Russ said, "Look, how much money did you pay to attend this event?" And the guys says, "Well, um, five thousand dollars." End of story. **If he was willing to spend that much money after being irritated by my repetitiveness, then my message must have been getting through!**

You're going to offend people; accept that. You have to willingly set out with the understanding that some people are going to be upset. You can't let that bother you. **You have to continue to realize that the basic selling principle is this: The more you tell, the more you sell**. As marketers, we cannot concern ourselves with the people in our market who don't like us, who don't trust us, who don't appreciate us, who aren't going to re-buy from us again and again. **We only focus on serving the people who are our best prospects.** History has shown, through repeated testing, that the way to do that is through repetitive long-form sales letters, which will always out-pull short-form sales letters. And keep in mind that in Direct Response Marketing, when you're selling by mail, you're getting a response that's a small fraction of the entire list to which you mailed. **So you might make 80% of the people mad because you wrote the way you did — and yet you got a 20% response, and <u>it was a raving success among those folks</u>.**

We've had promotions where we've done phenomenally well when only three people out of a thousand responded! That's 0.3 percent. Now, think about that. Those other 997 people could have used our sales letters as toilet paper, or burned it, or stomped on it, or cursed it, or whatever. But even if they were absolutely, positively mad as hell about the whole thing and hated our guts, we still made millions of dollars on that promotion, because we were focused on those three out of a thousand — not the other 997. Now, obviously not all those 997 out of 1,000 were mad at us. While maybe a few of them were upset and think we did something they didn't like — like repeated ourselves seven times — that's a tiny percentage of the whole. The rest didn't really care. Maybe they just ignored our offer, or it didn't hit them at the right time, or they just weren't interested, or whatever. **You're not making everybody mad who didn't buy; they had their own reasons for not responding.** You're writing to the ones that are going to respond, not writing to the ones that won't. The problem is, you don't know exactly which three among that thousand are the ones who will buy, so you have to send to everybody on your list.

That's why you've got to repeat yourself, even if some people don't like it. It's all about salesmanship. **I like to say, "I can explain the product in two pages, but I can't sell it in two pages," and that's a truism in all forms of marketing.** That's why, when I'm writing copy, I take my time and explain repeatedly what the benefits are. If you have a sales rep working for you, you don't tell them, "Only talk for five minutes and that's it, guys. And don't repeat anything." No way! You tell them, "Do whatever it takes to make the sale!"

As long as your customers know that you're not lying to them, and that they can get their money back if they're not happy, you're fine. **That's what trust is all about, and it's the absolute bedrock upon which your customer relationships — and all the money that comes with them — are built.**

Sure, if we ever find out our sales reps are misleading people or outright lying to people, they're fired. They don't get a second chance; they're out the door no matter how good they are. But, I tell them, "As long as you're not lying to the prospects, as long as you're not misleading them and making promises that aren't true, do whatever you have to do to make the sale! If you have to keep the prospect on the phone for 90 minutes, repeating everything over and over, then keep them on the phone for 90 minutes — assuming it's a big enough sale."

Subconscious Selling

One thing to keep in mind about using long-form letters is that in large part, <u>the selling takes place on a subconscious level</u>. If you ask even the most ardent of Mail Order customers, "Would you ever buy anything from a 20-page sales letter after you've read it all the way through?", they'll all tell you no. But even so, they've all got a pile of crap that they've bought because they did just that. So it's clear that a lot of this kind of selling takes place on a very subconscious level, using tested, proven strategies. **You have to focus on what actually works to get the customer to buy, not what the customer tells you will work**. If you look at what they say versus what they actually do, you'll find you're looking at totally different things.

That's why focus groups are so worthless: the participants want to please you, so at some level — and maybe it's not even conscious — they'll lie to you about what you're testing. Consciously they think one thing, but subconsciously the selling process guides them to do another thing. **You can't base your marketing and sales messages or processes on what people say**. <u>You have to look at their behavior</u>. Like the doctor who was complaining to Russ about my redundant nature, a lot of times the people who act the most offended and gripe the most also buy the most.

> ▼▼▼▼▼▼▼▼▼▼▼▼▼▼▼▼
>
> You must put yourself in the right position where the best prospective buyers can find you.
>
> *This way you are selling to people <u>who</u> <u>don't</u> <u>need</u> <u>to</u> <u>be</u> <u>sold</u>!*

"P.T. Barnumize Every Offer"

▼▼▼▼▼▼▼▼
MARKETING SECRET

Customers vote with their checkbooks. This is true marketing research:

1. Try many new things.

2. Track the results carefully.

3. "Listen" to the message behind the numbers.

• Slowly — through extensive testing — you develop a solid knowledge of what your market wants the most.

There's no doubt about it: hype sells, whether you're a heavy-metal band like KISS or you've got some pieces of miracle plastic you're convinced will change American life as we know it.

Hype makes people sit up and take notice; it's bigger than life and lots more interesting.

The consummate marketer P.T. Barnum knew it, and marketers ever since have made it a part of their repertoire. **Take a look at any of my sales letters, and you'll notice that it's big, it's bold, it's blown up, it's explosive!** Lead generation pieces must be that way, because you absolutely, positively have to wow 'em. You have to have the whiz-bang in there to get their attention. You see this every single day.

Take a lot of TV commercials: "You must act now, because if you don't, you're going to miss out on the greatest ever super-duper cooker, slicer, manipulator you've ever seen in your life!" What they're selling is not a fancy potato peeler — but the greatest revolution in kitchen technology ever!

You absolutely have to hype your products, just like my hero P. T. Barnum would. **You don't want to lie and cheat or do anything illegal, but within that framework you must hype it up!** This works like magic. That's the reason you see it used over and over again; it helps get people to raise their hands and say, "Yeah, I want to know more," and it helps to convert those leads into sales. The marketer side of me absolutely knows that this principle works, when the other side of me doesn't like to do it sometimes — even though I know I have to. A headline in 72-point type may seem to scream at people, but that's because it needs to in order to be heard over everything else. **Every little sales letter is a salesman who's going out there into the world, and it's got to be a good salesman if you want to make any money.** To do that, it needs to get, and keep, the prospect's attention; it's got to tell them a story and engage their imagination. It does that by hyping it up. And it works.

One of the sales letters that's doing really well for us right now is headlined in 100-point type, which frankly is pretty big. There's one three-letter word in that headline, and that word is "NEW." Underneath it is the sub-head, and then underneath that is another sub-head. But it all starts out with that one word in 100-point type: "NEW." Why? **Because that's what people want!** We've tested it, and it works better that anything else we've tried so far for that offer. As you may recall, giving people what they want is point number one on the ten-step Smart Marketing process I outlined in earlier. **People want something new. When you haven't seen somebody for a long time, the first thing they ask you is, "What's new?"** We all want something new. The only problem is, there's nothing new under the sun. And that's a quote from an ancient philosopher from 600 B.C. So we must make it seem as if it is new.

Because we all want something new, our job as marketers — like it, hate it, accept it, don't accept it, it doesn't matter — is to offer them that next new thing. **If you want to make the most money, you've got to P. T. Barnumize things. You've got to blow them up bigger than life.** Our tests have proven that's where the money is. Oh, maybe you don't want to show it to your mother — maybe you don't want to show it to your grandmother or your friends or neighbors — but that where the money is, like it or not.

I was reading John Alanis' headline this morning: *"The Amazing Secret of a Former Loser from Texas that Can Get You All the Girls You Want, No Matter Your Looks, Age, or Income..."* **Now, that headline is a great one, and it's as full of hype as anything you can imagine (John will back me up on this). It has to be hyped, because more and more, people have short attention spans.** That's not a reflection on their intelligence or anything — it's societal. These days, especially with the

Internet and cell phones, everybody's day is nothing but one big interruption. This molds their perceptions and their entire lifestyles. Let me give you an example.

I have a friend of mine who loves old movies, and he's given me a bunch of them over the years to watch. I'm amazed at how slow those movies are compared to movies today. Oftentimes, the camera stayed on one person for quite a while. Nowadays, if you turn the sound down on your TV on a popular show, you'll see that that picture is changing constantly — in most cases, you can't even count to three before the scene changes. **Modern people are bombarded with so much information overload and so many things coming at them, and they're so used to change and instant gratification, that it's like they've all got ADD.**

So to make an impression, you've got to be their biggest interruption — because the first part of the sales process is attention. If you don't get their attention, you can't create interest and the desire to take action.

You've got to capture their attention first, and then immediately hook them in. The more outrageous, the better. I like when people see a headline and say, "What the heck is that?" Because when they do, they've just got to read more. That's really your goal. The more you can put this outrageousness, this bold, explosive stuff in your copywriting, the better. You have to cut through the cloud of everything else, because if you don't get their attention, your message is going in the garbage can or the delete file — and it's gone.

Even if this kind of hype doesn't appeal to you, keep in mind that this is what has always worked, and it's what always will work. P.T. Barnum knew it 150 years ago, and it's still true. I believe it was Dan Kennedy who said, "All business is, is applied psychology and measurement." **Well, in order to succeed you've got to understand the applied psychology and the big, bold P. T. Barnum stuff that gets people's attention**. It's simply what works.

"Never Compare Apples to Apples!"

When you're in the marketing game and you're trying to sell something, always compare apples to oranges. It's a simple idea, and yet it's one of those ideas about which most people don't know. We discovered it by accident.

Back in 1994, my company made more money during a 2½ month period than we'd ever made before. That was back when we first got involved with computer bulletin boards. **We made millions of dollars, by taking the apples of the mail order world and comparing them to the oranges of the electronic marketing world**. In our marketing copy, we spent four or five pages using examples that made it very clear how a person could make money with traditional mail order; we showed people what it would cost to run an ad, and all the problems and challenges they would incur if they did it in a traditional way.

We laid the whole thing out, then showed them that with the technology of computer bulletin boards — and later with the Internet — they could basically wipe out all those hard costs if they started selling electronically. **And because people saw the difference — the contrast — between the two ways to handle their marketing, it helped them to realize, at an emotional level, just how great this new electronic marketing world really was!** Without that apples-and-oranges contrast, people wouldn't have gotten nearly as excited as they did.

With one of our current offers, we go through a long process of showing people what they'd have to go through if they did something on their own. **We make everything very, very clear, and spell it all out. Then we offer our solution, which is, "Oh, just let us take care of everything for you."** And because we spent page after page showing them what they'd have to do if they did it all themselves, when we offer our solution, they're much more excited and happy. They understand better the value we have to offer.

Therefore, whatever it is you're selling, do as much as you can to compare it to other types of things they understand. You always want to

---

Advertising formula:

Problem = Make them feel it

Agitate = Bring up the pain

Solution = Sell the solution

People will do more to avoid pain — than to gain pleasure.

shine the light on what you're doing, so in general, you must compare it to as many other examples as you can. **You only know how good something is when you have something else with which to compare it.** That could be anything from John Alanis' world of dating, to selling information products, or new cars. Comparisons are a good way to make your products and services look better, and to rise above everybody else's.

Let's look closer at John Alanis' marketing. One place where he likes to use the apples-and-oranges comparison is in price justification. **When you have something that's somewhat unfamiliar to somebody, one way to help them decide to buy is to compare it to something in real life that's very cheap**. So John compares one of his higher-priced products to a McDonald's burger and fries, and says (and I paraphrase loosely), "If you sit down and break it out over a year's time, this product is going to cost you $2.18 cents a day — which is half what you'll pay for a Big Mac and fries, which will only make you fat anyway. So what kind of person are you? Are you the person who's going to take action and create the life you want, or are you a Big Mac-and-fries kind of guy?" **That gives the prospect a decision to make right there, and puts a definite image in his head.** Yes, it's comparing the familiar to the unfamiliar, but it's very effective in a price justification and sales-closing way.

My company's doing exactly the same thing with our Platinum Membership in our coaching program, which is designed to help business owners make more money. **Our basic USP (Unique Selling Position) is that you can**

attend up to 40 different marketing workshops for about the same amount of money as many marketing experts charge for one. Then you can get our continual, ongoing help for about the same price you pay, normally, for a daily fast-food meal. It's a way to make our price seem smaller, by comparing it to other things.

You can also make them feel a little bit guilty at the same time, because they all know they're wasting money. **One thing you can say is, "Look, any man can afford this. I can look at your expenses and see you're spending money on beer, burgers, and video games, all of which are only going to make you fat, drunk, and dumb. So you can afford this. You just have to decide what you want to spend the money on."** The idea is to make them say, "Hey, I'm not one of those beer and video games guys. I want to be a guy who's going to be successful in life."

That appeal works well in nudging prospects over the line when they're uncertain about the price. Here are the apples, sure — but how about those oranges? You're doing the thinking for them, in some ways, and helping to make your case. But that's okay — you're also helping them to see things a little more clearly. Do that properly, and some will nod and say, "Hey, that's right! I am spending all my money on beer, burgers, and video games. What the heck am I thinking?"

Chris Lakey recently wrote a sales letter where he broke out the cost by the day. It's a one-year program, and the total ends up being about eight bucks a day. It's not cheap, but you can make it seem more reasonable if you use the apples-and-oranges approach, as Chris did. You can tell someone that something costs $3,000, and that sounds like a lot of money; but when you break it down and say, "Well, this is a one-year program, so this is how much it's going to cost you per day," that can be pretty effective. After all, what's eight bucks? A couple of venti lattes at Starbucks, or the price of a first-run movie.

In Chris Lakey's letter, he compares the cost of the program to hiring someone to take care of the work for you. **The wording he uses is, "A gum-chewing, text-messaging teenager would cost you six bucks an hour, minimum, to do this work for you."** Again, he's comparing apples to oranges here. Assuming that gum-chewing, text-messaging teenager worked for you full time and had insurance and other benefits, he'd cost you maybe $20,000 a year. Or, you can hire some of the most successful entrepreneurs in the business to help you with coaching and other high-end tasks, and it's only going to cost you eight bucks a day.

So what's more attractive, $6 an hour, or $8 a day? What's going to make you more money, that minimum-wage employee or what we have to offer? You could make it even more attractive by bringing it down to the hourly level: what's better, a dollar an hour, or six? **Break it down to the lowest possible number, and that number is what sticks in people's minds instead of the $3,000 price that you're really asking**. Only when they really dig in do you ever actually tell them how much to write the check. The rest of it's all about talking up that minimum price point and convincing them that they're getting tremendous value for their money.

Outwitting the Confused Mind

One of the truisms of marketing is that a confused mind will always say no. Therefore, if you have a complicated offer and you need to get your prospects from where you believe they're at to understanding the features, benefits, and concepts of your offer, you need to make some analogies. **That's what analogies are all about — bridging the gap from where they're at to where you want them to be; from confused mind to confirmed seller.**

My colleague Chris Hollinger tells me that all teachers do this in the classroom; they look at where the majority of the class is, and build on those concepts by using things to which the kids can relate. Those analogies may vary widely from inner-city schools to rural schools, just as they do from market to market in business.

The analogies you choose depend on where you want to take them. You absolutely have to fill that gap in their mind to where they can at least see themselves profiting from the product you're offering them. It's up to you to help people understand why what you have is valuable to them, and the apples-to-oranges analogy is a great way to accomplish it.

"Always, Always Follow Up!"

As I've said repeatedly in this book, effective, long-term profitability in any business boils down to developing good relationships with your customers and reselling to them repeatedly.

If you're not following up on every sale, this isn't going to happen. And once you've made a sale, you must send them additional marketing material about your next product or service.

Plain and simply, you're losing money without a strong follow-up marketing campaign. **The secret to maximizing your sales and profits is to put a ton of pressure on your prospects by raining mail, email, phone calls and faxes on their heads, because the resulting pressure stimulates sales.** Most marketers simply aren't aggressive enough on their follow-up marketing campaigns. They're giving up on their leads far too soon, and they aren't putting enough pressure on their prospective buyers. Because of this, they're losing a ton of money that should and could be theirs. **One thing that keeps marketers from applying that pressure is that they get worried about upsetting people; I've talked about that before. But you can't worry about who you're going to offend, or you're limiting your potential profits.**

A lot of marketers have the sales process down only partially. They get high-qualified leads, and then what do they do with those leads? **They send them their offer, get the response back, and that's it.** Let's say they get a response where 5-10% of the people who requested the information from them bought, and that's it. They either decide at that point whether the campaign lost or made money, and then they move on. Some marketers, though, have it a little more correct: they have

> ▼▼▼▼▼▼▼▼▼▼▼▼▼▼▼
>
> Get on the other side of the cash register!
>
> Part of the secret to becoming a great marketer is to change your entire thought process. How? Easy. Just STOP thinking like a consumer and start thinking like a marketer thinks!

Only 3 ways to build
a business:

a. Get more
   customers.

b. Sell more stuff —
   for bigger profits
   to your customers.

c. Sell more stuff
   more often to your
   customers!

a limited follow-up campaign. Maybe they get leads, they make sales, and then they send out a follow-up letter or two to try to get more of those sales. But then that's it.

Our principle is that you should keep calling, faxing, e-mailing and mailing follow-up offers until it becomes unprofitable to do so. How long that takes is dependent upon your offer, how strong your prospects are, and how highly-qualified your leads are. About a year ago as of this writing, we were running a campaign that had over 20 follow-up sales letters that went out after the initial package.

This was a test of a sort, and we found out that it only took six or seven follow-ups before we started seeing a loss on our investment. So we stopped sending out the subsequent sales letters. Now, keep in mind that this was the number of letters that worked for this particular campaign; it may be the right number for similar campaigns that we run, but the number for other types of campaigns we run may be different, and they may have no resemblance at all to what's necessary for your campaigns.

When running your own, you definitely must test and measure to determine the point where you stop getting a return on your advertising dollars by doing more follow-up marketing. The question becomes, at what point does it cost you more money than you make from the orders you get? But most people never bother to learn that, so essentially they're leaving money on the table.

In addition to testing, determining the right amount of pressure is somewhat subjective. Here's an example of what it means for us. **Let's**

say we have a campaign that we're mailing, where we've got leads coming in and we're responding to them. Let's say they're requesting a free report and a CD. They had to raise their hand and request it, and maybe send five bucks to get it. So we've got thousands of leads that have come in. What we do immediately — within 24 hours if we can — is get the material out to them. **Obviously, a certain percentage are going to respond; so within a week to 10 days after we send that initial package out, we begin our follow-up marketing**. Let's say seven days after that first package goes out, we send a second mailing package out. And then we try to send something out twice a week.

It might just be a postcard, or it might be a full Direct Mail package with a long-form sales letter and Order Form; but whatever the case, <u>we try to touch base with them twice a week until they buy</u>. Again, how long you keep at it with a particular campaign has to do with how profitable it is for you to do so.

As a strategy, raining marketing messages on your prospects' heads, as we like to call it, just means continuously staying on top of them, reminding them about our offer. There are smart ways to do it, and there are dumb ways to do it. **Doing it smartly means being creative with your follow-ups; it means not doing the same thing every time.** If you've got their email address, maybe it means that every couple days, you send them an email; or even every day. But then you also drop a package in the mail to them, or maybe it's a postcard. Sometimes it's a lumpy mail offer with something in the envelope to make it stand out so they're more likely to open it. **It's all about continuously reminding them that they still haven't purchased from you, and bringing up the main reasons why they must do it now; giving them a way to contact you or multiple ways to contact you; keeping your offer on the top of their mind**. The longer you go without communicating with them in follow-ups, the less likely they are to buy.

Ideally, the pressure's coming from them, not us. If we made them an offer and they raised their hand, then they've indicated they're at least mildly interested in our product or service. It's not so much that we're putting pressure on them to buy (although we are, by mailing to them frequently), it's mostly internal pressure that they're feeling. Every time we mail to them, they know they're interested in what we have, and the pressure can be internalized with them as in, "I've got this offer; I need to act. I'm being reminded I need to act. I need to do something about this. I either need to decide I'm not going to buy, or I need to decide to buy."

Our follow-up marketing campaigns usually last about six to eight weeks, and again that's based on how profitable it is to continue. <u>The key is to keep mailing often enough that you're reminding them consistently that they still need to do business with you</u>. **Don't think, "Well, I just sent them the offer a week ago, so I'm going to wait a couple more weeks to follow-up with them."** By that time, they're on to something else. You need to hit them with a follow-up offer quickly enough that they don't lose sight of the fact that they did request this information from you, and that they still haven't made a decision to buy. **What's more likely to get acted upon: the one mailing that gets put on the bottom of the pile and forgotten, or the multiple mailings that keep hitting you?**

Sometimes it takes a handful of contacts, or more, before the average prospect buys. Some marketers get high numbers the third time they contact the prospect; for others it's the seventh contact, (especially with email), that gets the biggest response and more conversions. But it varies for each market and offer and you learn that through testing.

Here's an example. There's a guy named Dean Cipriano who does niche marketing to the insurance field. If you get on his list, you're going to get three faxes a day from Dean — he's the King of Faxing. If you get on his list and give him all your contact info, you're going to get on his Direct Mail sequence, his email sequence, his fax sequence, and he's got all kinds of stuff that he'll send you. You'll still be getting it six months later, even if you don't buy anything. The reason Dean is doing this is because it works. It's tremendously effective. This "rain" of marketing messages cuts through all the clutter and gets them to respond.

The other thing about the multi-step, multi-media stuff is the fact that, again, it's a moving parade of interest. **In other words, you never know when something is going to happen that triggers someone's interest**. There's a percentage of the people who request information because they're interested and they're ready to buy right now, but there's a bigger percentage who are just kind of curious. So, when they get your copy they take a look, then set it aside — and then something happens and they're ready to buy. **Well, if you're not in front of them when they're ready to buy, they're going to buy from somebody else.**

Then again, there's a certain percentage of people who just won't buy the first time they get something. They won't buy the second or third time, either. It might take them seven or eight times to buy, for whatever reason. **But finally they call and say, said, "Okay, you got me! I've been thinking about it, and I read it, and you got me!"** That's just their buying mechanism; different people have different buying mechanisms. There are those people who see something and buy it immediately. There are those who see something and have to study everything about it before they buy. There are people who have to be exposed to something 18 times before the light finally comes on. **That's why you've got to keep following up with these multi-step, multi-media approaches if you want to be a truly effective marketer**.

It's a good idea to re-mail to your old leads, too, because that all loops around to the concept of lifetime value. Old leads — the people you've already established contact with who didn't buy — are another whole universe to tap in order to get more customers. Maybe you couldn't interest them on that original campaign, but they might respond the next one. So don't give up on them too soon. **You may not be profitable on the first transaction, but you know that if you do things carefully, the money you spend is going to be made up on the back-end**.

Here's a case in point. When we first started working with Dan Kennedy in 1993, he produced an infomercial for us. It was a great infomercial, a lead-generation type where interested people could send in for a free video and report. At that time, we ran into a problem that we often encounter. **We rarely have any trouble generating leads; quite the opposite, in fact. We can generate all the leads in the world, but so what?** The important thing is converting those leads profitably. We ran this infomercial, tested it in 14 different cities, and it generated a lot of leads — as usual. I tried everything I could to convert those leads, but I was having some severe problems doing so.

One day, we met with Dan and took him out to lunch. I kept showing him all these things I was doing to try to convert the leads we'd gotten from this infomercial, and no matter what I said, Dan always said the same thing: "You're giving up on them too soon." Dan's always been blunt and straightforward that way. Well, I told him, "But Dan, I'm doing this and this and this." And he kept saying, "So? You're giving up on them too soon."

Man, was I ticked off! **I was so angry and frustrated, and I didn't want to believe what he told me.** But ultimately, the experience taught me a valuable lesson — and that's when I started becoming a firm believer in the principal of following up with prospects. I saw through that anger, and started really thinking it through — and realized he was right. I was giving up on those leads too soon. I give the same advice now to other marketers.

Patience is a Marketing Virtue

When you're working with a highly-qualified prospect who has shown an interest in what you are offering, then <u>you're doing them a disservice if you don't do everything possible to follow up as often as possible</u>. Obviously you're offering something that can help them and add value to their life and is real and solid, or you shouldn't be pushing it in the first place. **Now, there may be some lag time before you see results; you can't expect instant gratification, especially if you're working through print ads.**

Let me give you a perfect example of that, courtesy of my colleague John Alanis. He has a pretty good, long follow-up sequence in both Direct Mail and email. He ran an ad in Iron Man Magazine, and the cost was steep: $2,200. Well, it did okay, but just okay, so he was a little disappointed in it. **Eight months later, John went back and looked at the whole marketing campaign and realized, "This thing finally turned out to be profitable."** In fact, it turned out to be <u>really profitable</u> — but it took eight months of follow-up for it to get there.

Let's say you're able to run in a hundred

Marketing is simply a 3-Step process:

1. Attracting qualified leads

2. Converting the highest percentage possible into sales

3. And then re-selling the largest number of these customers

That's it! There are only 3 steps!

- However, each one is distinct. And it must be done right.

magazines a month, and all you made on each magazine was a thousand dollars worth of lifetime customer value. Well, that's a hundred thousand dollars a month, net. With the right follow up, it may still take a long time for it to pay off, but it will eventually pay off. **And so when evaluating some of these methods, especially the offline methods, just recall that success won't happen overnight**.

Remember, it took John eight long months for that ad to become super-profitable. But those eight months are going to pass eventually. <u>So never give up on your leads too early, because they've got a lot of residual value</u>. Yes, it takes a while, and part of the game is trying to shorten so that you can manage your cash flow and expand faster. But the money is really made in the relentless way you keep trying to re-sell to your prospects and customers.

"Demand Their Money!"

A marketing principle I try to live by is this: don't ask the people reading your sales material for their order. **Demand that they give you their money!** Make them feel bad if they don't. <u>This is what separates the big dogs from the whimpering puppies in the marketing field</u>.

In your Call to Action, whatever that may be — whether you're asking for $5,000 or $50,000 — you can't be passive-aggressive about it. **You've got to take them by the hand, you've got to lead them right where you want them to go, you've got to pick up the pen, you've got to put it in their hand, and you've got to get them to write that check or to sign that credit card authorization.** That's the bottom line, and you can't be passive about it. By that point, you need to have already built a good, strong case with the features and the benefits and the reasons why they should buy.

Going back to the PAS example I mentioned, you've peeled that scab back, you've poured salt in it, you've made them feel the pain, and now the only solution is that they must buy whatever it is you're selling. At that point you can't be wimpy about it. **You're asking them for money, and you must be very bold.** As I like to say, **"<u>Timid salespeople raise skinny kids</u>."**

Which bring us to your Order Form. This is a very important part of the sales piece, because it's where you're reiterating those main features and benefits and reasons why they need your product or service. Boom — here it is, fill it out, mail it in, FAX it in, let's do it! Let's act now! It also helps to have a little bit of urgency built in. **Whether it's contrived urgency or not, there's got to be a deadline to act now because it will increase your conversions**. You have to demand that they act immediately.

This is a secret I got from Ted Thomas, one of the top five platform speakers in the world. **Every salesperson knows they're supposed to ask for the order; that's in every marketing book there is**. But Ted Thomas says that one of the secrets of his success is that he doesn't just ask for the order, he demands the order — after he's done a thorough job of delivering his presentation, of course. And does he make enemies? Yes. Do a bunch of people not like him? Yes. **But does he get results? <u>Hell yes</u>.**

Robert Cialdini covers this very important concept, which is something that a lot of people really don't talk about, in his book *Influence: The Psychology of Persuasion*. He talks about all the different forms of persuasion: reciprocity and commitment, consistency, liking and others. **One that he includes is authority**. I don't think people talk about authority enough, at least from a business perspective.

In my business, one thing that I've made sure to do is build my business around an attractive character who has a strong sense of authority, because people gravitate towards people in authority. **When it comes to asking for the order, whether it's in a platform selling environment or whether it's in a sales letter, you have to ask for it with authority — <u>because if you do it from a meek, mild, wimpy point of view, people feel uncomfortable</u>.** They feel nervous. They feel like maybe you're pulling something, and so they don't buy.

When you ask for their order with a firm sense of conviction and a firm sense of authority — what I would call likeable authority — people feel very comfortable and very good about giving you their money. They think, "Okay, here's a person who's going to stand up, act like a leader, take responsibility, and make it acceptable for me to order."

If somebody is looking to you for a solution, they're conferring authority on you. If you're selling something to somebody, they perceive

> ▼▼▼▼▼▼▼▼▼▼▼▼▼▼▼▼
>
> The richest and/or most successful people you know have the same 168 hours a week that you have.
>
> What are they doing that you're not?

you as an expert, and they expect you to act in a particular way — with a sense of authority. **If you don't act like an authority, as they expect you to, they're not going to order, because they feel nervous.** So it's very important that you act the way they expect you to act. If you don't, that will kill the sale. **No matter the sales venue, if you ask for that item in a meek, mild, wimpy manner, <u>you're not going to get it</u>.**

Consider this. Did you guys know that you can tell your doctor "no" when they try to write you a prescription? **But how often does that happen?** <u>Rarely, because they have the authority to make you believe that's what you need (and usually, or course, it is)</u>. Most of us just take the paper right to the pharmacist and have them fill the order. It's because doctors just tell you how it's going to be. They demand you submit to their authority. **When a doctor tells you that you need to do something, you generally do it. That comes from their position as authority in the field of medicine.**

Well, it's the same way with your product or service. **You're the authority, the expert, on that product**. You understand it better than any client could; you know it inside out and know it works. That's what they want to hear: your confidence, your sense of authority. **If you believe in your product, if you believe it's going to provide the promised benefits to your client, then with all your being you should be trying to convince them to place their order now.** If you're shy about asking for the order, then that shows them you don't have any confidence in your product — so why should they? I think that's the key to being authoritative in a way that sells products; it's in having the belief that your product really is worth the money you're asking them to give you... and that you really do believe that they'd be foolish not to get out their wallet right now and order. **If you have that belief, then you can convey that belief to them with confidence.** If you seem reserved or shy, they're going to instantly believe something is up. They're thinking, "Why are you being timid in

THE HAND: Every offer or promotion must meet these five crucial steps:

1. Is it the right offer?

2. Is it going to the right person?

3. Through the right media?

4. With the right hook? (The thumb)

5. And does it fit together with some kind of long-term plan?

There's only a handful — but they're vital. This lets you focus on the essentials.

asking for my money? What's wrong with your product, that you don't even believe in it enough to be confident in telling me I need it?" **Jay Abraham, arguably one of the best marketing experts around, says that <u>people are silently begging to be led</u>.** And I know that you'll probably agree with that, except for when it comes to you!

So once you've made your case, confidently (but politely) demand that they buy. Don't overdo it — just speak your piece, make your argument, and ask them to okay the order. Specific language can be very important: for example, instead of saying "How do you want to pay for this?" it may be more effective to say, "Would you prefer to take care of your investment via Visa or MasterCard?" These are two different approaches that can make a huge difference in selling. **This doesn't just work well in face-to-face selling situations; it translates over to ads, sales letters, web sites, etc; it translates over to how you present yourself; it translates over to everything**. <u>Precision of language and an attitude of total authority is a very powerful thing</u>. You've got to use it to lead your prospects right to the sale. When you come right down to it, leadership is all about persuasion and salesmanship.

"The Benefit is What's Really Important"

I'm going to let you in on a big secret that should underlie everything you do as a marketer: the customer does not want your products and services. That's not why they buy them. **They only want what they perceive as the end result, the benefit they think they'll get when they give you their money**. Most business people never figure this out. This makes life so much easier for those of us who have.

What I've just said may seem counterintuitive. You may be thinking, **"What do you mean my customers don't want my products and services? Why else are they buying?"** Well, that's a good question, isn't it? But think about it. **Whatever people buy, they buy for the perceived benefit it will bring them — whether that's warmth, speed, money, or social prestige.** So really, making any money through marketing ultimately goes back to building a case in their minds that lets them fully perceive the benefits they'll receive from buying a product, service, or opportunity from you. This is directly applicable to many different businesses: people buy perceived value. **You're not necessarily selling that product, service, or opportunity.** You're trying to build a case in their mind of what they're going to get. The picture you're ultimately trying to paint is that if they buy this, their problem will be solved.

Most business people don't really see that. They think they're selling cheeseburgers, but maybe they should be selling fun. Look at Subway sandwiches; to continue the food analogy, that's a perfect example. Subway revolutionized their entire business when they started selling not sandwiches, but a healthy alternative to cheeseburgers. **People don't necessarily want sandwiches; they want their hunger to be fulfilled in a healthy yet tasty way.** In marketing, they teach us that people don't want quarter-inch drill bits; what they want is quarter-inch holes. They go out and buy the quarter-inch bit so they can get their quarter-inch holes — but what if there was an alternative to getting quarter-inch holes? What if you could shine a laser at the wood and drill those holes in a split-second, or dribble a liquid on the wood that drilled that hole? Would those sell? Of course they would, as long as they were reasonably safe. **Many people would completely forgo buying the drill bits, because the drill bits were**

only a means to an end. What they really wanted were the holes.

Years ago, the marketing guru Ted Nicholas invented a copywriting strategy he called "The Hidden Benefit." Basically, what he said was, "If I had God-like super powers and could bestow upon my prospects anything that they wanted, what would it be?" That really forces you to think. His example was a book of corporate forms, and there's nothing more boring than that. But the headline he wrote about that was, *"What will you do when the I.R.S. seizes your personal assets to satisfy a judgment against your corporation?"* **Now, if you're a business owner and you read that, and you have the idea of the I.R.S. coming in, seizing your assets, and putting you in jail — well, you're going to read that thing!** The hidden benefit of it was that it taught you an important lesson: if you're ever taken to tax court about something, you have to keep proper corporate records, or you could pierce the corporate veil and they can come seize your personal assets. Ted's book of corporate forms keeps you from getting in trouble with the I.R.S.; **he scared the holy hell out of everybody with that, and sold $70 million worth.**

To understand the dichotomy between actual products and benefits, you need look no further than what most information marketers sell — for example, this is true of myself, Chris Lakey, John Alanis and, to a lesser extent, Chris Hollinger. If an outsider were to say to me, "Hey, T.J., let's see the product that you sell," I'd have to show them a bunch of CDs and manuals, wouldn't I? Is that what people want? No. **I'll tell you what people want: <u>they want the answers to their problems</u>**.

In John Alanis' case, they want to know how to instantly and automatically attract all the women they want without facing rejection: they want those women to just line up outside the door so that they can say, "You, you, and you." Even more than that, they want to show these women off to their friends and make them jealous. They want to be envied and admired. They want relief from feelings of inadequacy. **It's a matter of tapping into those basic human emotions**. And John can bestow that upon them, if they're willing to take action. Instead of letting them think, "I've been rejected. There must be something wrong with me as a man," John tells them, "No, you just don't have the right skills to get women." And he can pass on those skills, for a price. **John's not just selling some discs and manuals; he's selling a solution to a problem**. When you really tap into these emotions and realize that's really what your product does, that's when you get into some very, very powerful sales copy.

John used to run an art business. He was in the business of selling steel art, and one of the most successful headlines he ever used was a knock-off from an old John Caples headline: *"How to get your cooking bragged about."* John surveyed his customers and asked them, "What's the biggest benefit of this art?" and they'd all talk about they'd get the thing, then hang it in their home. All their friends would come over, cluster around it, and "ooh" and "aah." So John's headline there was, *"Here's how to get your home bragged about."* **That's a good example of tapping into what people really want — in this case, that social admiration from putting a rusty piece of metal on the wall.** That's the hidden benefit: again, the relief of inadequacy. They felt that their home wasn't adequate, and this was a way for them to make their home more than adequate and to show off to people. **It's the same reason why a guy goes and buys a Corvette.** When you get right down to it, he could drive a bicycle to get him from Point A to Point B, and probably end up in better physical shape than anyone out there. **The truth is, if we all bought what we needed, we'd all be driving Yugos and living in trailers.** But some men want to put a 25-year-old hot blonde in the car and drive in front of his old balding buddies and show off what a successful guy he is. That's why he's buying a Corvette! It's the same reason a lot of guys get into the information marketing business — so they can make lots of money they can show off to their buddies and the women in their lives.

If you ignore these basic human emotions and don't link them to your product, you'll never be nearly as effective as you might be. So use the old Ted Nicholas method: **What's the hidden want? What's the hidden benefit? If you were omnipotent, what's the one thing that your product could do, the biggest benefit it could give your customers?** Consider that, and you'll come up with all kinds of amazing ideas that you couldn't think of before!

In a related vein, one of the more enlightened principles sometimes taught to marketers is that you should try to make the object transparent when writing copy. **What that means is, no matter what you're selling, describe it in such a way that the customer can see through it to look at the benefits**. For example, somebody who buys a Bentley isn't buying the car for driving. They can do that in a Ford Focus or a Chevy Nova. Look past the car, and what you're getting is the benefit of prestige. People

▼▼▼▼▼▼▼▼
MARKETING SECRET

It's all about the prospect — not the product! The world is littered with great products that never made it in the marketplace.

- Great products often fail because they were not properly marketed.

look at your car and say, "Wow, you can afford a Bentley." **So the more transparent the object, the better you can see the benefit through it**. Say you've got a big box of tapes, CDs, and manuals that make up, for example, the recorded version of the seminar upon which this book is based. You're not going to say, "Look here! This is a nice box, and it's got some of the best-looking CDs in it you'll ever have!" No, you're selling the "dream" or the "image" that the information here is going to give your customers. **You have to paint that rosy picture of what their life is going to be like once the customer has your product**. The salesman who sold that guy the Corvette I mentioned above probably painted a great picture: "You're really going to be able to pick up babes with this!"

The unspoken part of that is that he probably also painted the negative picture of what would happen if the bald guy didn't buy that little red Corvette. It all goes back to ratcheting up the pain, the practice of opening that scab and pouring in the salt. To go back to John Alanis again, what he does is say, "Look, you're at a crossroads in your life right now. You can either take action and get all these benefits, or you can be forever lonely. You can die alone and unloved and forgotten. So which do you want?" You've got twin forces, positive and negative, working for you. **Remember, in many cases people are more likely to act to avoid pain than to move toward pleasure.** So give them something to move towards, and something to move away from; make them feel bad about not buying and also feel good about buying. In other words, don't be afraid to use both the carrot and the stick to urge people to buy.

"Deal Aggressively with Competition"

The opportunity market, the one in which I've been working since 1988, is loaded with competition. But I've developed an attitude where I don't worry unduly about the competition, and I think most true entrepreneurs are the same way. **How often do we really focus on our competitors?** Well, we take their sales material and put it in our swipe files, and we adapt their ideas sometimes, and sometimes use them as templates to come up with our own products. That's all part of ruthless marketing. But how much time do we really sit around worrying about them and all that nonsense? Not much. **For one thing, they're helping bring more people into our market, which means, in absolute numbers, there's more for us. For another, most of them aren't willing to use the ruthless strategies I discuss in this book, <u>so I'm eventually going to capture some of their market share anyway</u>.**

I actually like having successful competitors in my market space, because it gives me the opportunity to do profitable Joint Ventures with them. Besides, think of it this way: even if you're selling the same type of thing, a buyer is a buyer is a buyer. **A buyer is unlikely to purchase one product of a specific type; they're more likely to purchase them all, so even if he's buying from your competitor, it's quite likely he'll give you a try also.** There's a great old-time mail order marketer named Jim Straw, a fantastically smart guy, who is adamant about the fact there's no competition in this business; there are only contemporaries. All of the other great marketers in the Direct Response Marketing business are investing huge sums of money to get customers, and if they're smart and don't have the scarcity mentality, then it's an opportunity for you to do endorsed Joint Ventures with them, because they've already spent the time and energy and effort and money to build the relationship. **So when you come along and do an endorsed mailing or something to their list, the response is phenomenal!** <u>If you think of other people in your business as cooperation, there's always an opportunity to make more money</u>. It's an environment full of cooperation, not competition.

Having said that, I have to point out that how well you can handle

---

competition depends on the size of your market. For example, my best friend's pest control business is located in a mid-sized city, Wichita, where there's a lot of demand. As for us, we're working with people all over the nation; some of my colleagues, especially those who are Internet-based, have clients all over the world. But, if you're in a small market you may be in trouble. A friend of mine, Keith Banman, owns the local grocery store in Goessel. If another grocery store comes to town, one or the other will probably be going out of business within the year. This market, as it exists, isn't big enough to support two grocery stores. But the key term here is "as it exists." If Keith were able to change his mindset and retool his business, he might still survive. **One way to do this is to remember that the Internet is out there, and that changes your marketplace from local to global, if you want it to be. Look at the Harry & David Company, or Omaha Steaks**. They're selling grocery store commodities to the entire world; they have lists that they market to vigorously, and they're making tons of money.

On the other hand, if you're selling the same thing to the same group of people, the first thing you have to do is differentiate yourself with a Unique Selling Position, or USP. Tell them exactly why they should do business with you as opposed to doing business with anybody else or as opposed to doing nothing. **Then get that USP out there in the marketplace; tell them your story, build a relationship with your customers, send out a monthly newsletter or emails or something similar — and in so doing, put an iron cage around the customers, <u>moving the relationship away from the product that you're selling, to the personality behind the product</u>.** Get that story out there and bond with the customers. If you get that set up right, no one's going to be able to come in and easily take over what you've built, not even something like Wal-Mart or Alco, because people are doing business with people and the story — which transcends the product. <u>The fact is, the product is actually the least important part of the business</u>. You can get products anywhere.

What's really important is the relationship with your customers, and the personality behind it; that's the driving force that gets people to bond with you. **You develop a close relationship with the customer, so that when it comes time for them to buy a specific product, they'll give their money to you rather than one of your competitors.** You see, there's a big dose of politics in business, in addition to that combination of art, science, war, and sports. You have to get people to know you and trust you. As I was writing this book, I saw a news show on TV in which, every night, they interviewed a new politician running for president. One night, they interviewed a candidate whom I'd never heard of before. He had a great story to tell, and I thought. "Why don't more people know about this guy? Why don't I see him in the polls?" **As far as I was concerned, he was an unknown. You can't let that happen to you in business or politics.** In large part, both are about personality, and positioning. Now, that candidate has no shot of winning, but maybe he should; he's got a great story to tell, and yet hardly anyone knows it.

Even in a small town like Goessel, Kansas, you'd better believe that there's a lot of politics that go on here, for a variety of reasons. That would be one of the resources that an entrepreneur like our local grocer, Keith, would be able to tap into. In a situation in which someone new comes and tries to take over the business, my suggestion would be to go back to the 10 key Smart Marketing steps I discussed previously, study them closely, and learn how to leverage them the best you can.

POWER OF LOSING.

All of us want to win and win BIG! We all want things to go our way, but thank goodness they don't. You could never see clearly if everything always worked out in your favor.

Realize that you're in a fight for the life of your business, and you need out-hustle them to survive. **Really address those Smart Marketing steps, and then make up your mind and be realistic with yourself.** Okay, so you've got some serious competition in your marketplace now; it's going to force you to either fail, or to improve — to change, to make yourself seem more unique, to find a niche where you can serve your customer better than any competition. Go that route and you're going to win that battle, but it's not going to come easy. You're going to have to do some serious thinking about your marketing, your positioning in your market, and how you're going to serve those customers better than the competition.

Serving your customers is crucial — because ultimately, competition is good for the consumer. As an example, let's take another look at Keith's

I read a book on survival. It said that the #1 trait of successful survivalists is flexibility. And so it is in business. The flexible person bends and adapts. The rest break.

• Being flexible is all about changing, growing, adapting, and moving forward.

Foods, the local grocery store. Thirty years ago it probably would have been an accurate statement to say that the Co-Op that preceded Keith's Foods had no competition. They were the only gig in town, and very few people who lived here went anywhere else. But today it's easy to drive 10 miles down the road to Wal-Mart or Dillon's in Newton, Kansas, the next closest community, to get your groceries, so at some level he's competing with them.

So Keith has to be smart about what he does, or else he's losing market share. **His ultimate goal would be to have every single person in this town of four or five hundred people buying all their groceries from him and nowhere else.** That's not going to happen, but that would be his ideal. If he does everything right, gains the maximum market share, ideally he'd even have people from other smaller communities around coming here to buy their stuff. **Right now that's not happening; he doesn't have that entire market share, so he's not doing everything he could be doing.** He's got competition, though not in this town directly — he's got people who choose to drive away to the next closest town where they can shop at Wal-Mart or Dillon's.

Of course we all feel a little guilty when we do that, those of us who know Keith... But here's a cool, true story. There I was at Wal-Mart doing my grocery shopping, and who do I run into? Keith from the local grocery store! He'd just had knee surgery so he's driving around in one of those little electric carts, and I started feeling really guilty — I know I should be doing more business with him, because he's a great man. And then all of a sudden I'm thinking, "Well, what the hell is Keith doing here?" **It turns out he buys all of his produce at Wal-Mart, because he can get local produce fresher and cheaper at Wal-Mart than he can from his own produce wholesaler!** That's kind of like what I talked about earlier with the scrapbook store — only Keith is actually doing it. Here he is, shopping at Wal-Mart, so he can resell to his own customers.

But here's another thing he's doing: he has a catering business on the side that represents significant profits for him. He's involved in every single event possible within a 20-mile radius, and he serves up lunch at a lot of our events. **It's a sideline business, and he's doing all kinds of other stuff on the side, too; things he offers that nobody else does.** For example, on Friday afternoons — and sometimes twice a week — Keith grills hamburgers outside his store, and all the local people come. He's put in a fast-food pizza place in his store. He sells videos. He's got an old-fashioned deli that's like stepping back into the fifties, and he's got some really good deli sandwiches — his deli makes better sandwiches than those franchise joints. And his Lebanon bologna…well, he could sell that all across the country. All in all, he's got a nice little quaint small-town American store that comes with a lot of specialty items.

So Keith is competing, and he's doing so effectively. He's gotten beyond the boogeyman or thinking he has to compete with the next guy, instead he's being a good entrepreneur, looking at all the different things available, and creating the business he needs.

Keith has really increased the lifetime value of his customers, and he has all these different products and services. **It's not a product business he's got; it's a customer-driven business.** The way he thinks is, "I've got this customer, and I can sell them videos, and Lebanon bologna, and all this other stuff that other guys won't." So he's got a fantastic opportunity here. But at the same time, he could be doing so much more, and he does have the opportunity to do so.

He may be happy and doing really well with what he's got now, but if he really wanted, he could get in the information business and teach other people how to aggressively compete in their own small towns all across America. **He could go to all kinds of businesses in his related area — the struggling grocery stores who are struggling with the same problems that he is overcoming — and show them how to increase**

their profits. He could do all kinds of workshops, tele-seminars, or offer them a big $30,000 a year coaching program — and in so doing, make ten times more money than he makes working in his own store.

The Real Competition

Here's something about competition that a lot of people don't think about: the competition is real, but it's not really product-versus-product competition. What it's competition for is attention. There's competition for your mailbox space, your e-mail space, your television and radio airwaves. That's why you've got to P.T. Barnumize everything you do. **You've got to make things big, bold, outrageous and audacious, because you're competing for people's attention.** It's not so much competition of one businessperson against another, because there's so much opportunity and so much money out there. **Because the amount of media has just absolutely exploded in the past 30 or so years, people have things coming at them from all directions, so they're going to be able to pay attention to only a portion of it** — and usually that's the part that's bright and flashy, that reaches out and grabs their attention. Everything else fades into the background.

At my company, M.O.R.E., Incorporated, we're not as Internet-based as some people out there, but folks like John Alanis and Chris Hollinger tell me that their big competition is spam email. For example, John does two emails a day, so he's got to find a way to get that email delivered, opened, and read in the face of a deluge of unwanted mail. **His competition is everything else that's happening on the Internet**. Plus, when his prospects check their email, is the dog barking, the kid screaming, the sexy girl they've been waiting to come online finally sending them an instant message? John — and anyone working on the Internet — has to compete for attention on more than a product-versus-product basis.

That's one of the reasons why good marketers constantly follow-up with people, constantly stay in touch with them — because you never know for sure when one of your communications is just going to fail to get through for a wide variety of reasons. We've all had days when we're so busy that all we do is go through all of our emails as fast as we can, just to see how many we can delete in the quickest period of time. You don't want to read any of them, because you're so overwhelmed and you're under all this pressure. So you might miss something you would ordinarily have taken the time to read and act upon, on any other day. **The point is, you never know when you're going to catch a prospect at just the right time.** And face it, even if the prospect looks at every one of your emails (or direct mailings, or magazine ads, or however you're marketing), it might be a long time before they decide to buy.

This is especially the case with John Alanis, who sells products that teach you how to attract women. **He has guys who got on his email list <u>a year</u> before they bought.** They were curious when they got on; they just wanted to see what this crazy guy John had to say, then all of a sudden something happens — their new buddy meets a girl they're showing off, or their wife leaves them, or something else unexpected occurs. John had one guy who'd been on his list for 18 months, when he met this 26-year-old woman on the train to Moscow. They were going to spend two weeks together, but he didn't know what to do. So as soon as he got back, he bought everything John had to offer!

In the opportunity market I serve, around New Year's is often a great time, because the brother-in-law shows up and he's doing real well, and the guy who's going to buy feels bad. So he says to himself, "I'm going to make money this year," and he goes out and buys an opportunity product. **Since you never know when something's going to happen and you're going to be able to break through this constant barrage of attention-grabbing clutter and various life-events, <u>if you're not in front of them constantly, you're not going to get through to them</u>.** That's why this multi-step, multi-media method is more important than ever, and why you have to leverage the power of hype to get their attention.

Let me read you one of John Alanis' ads, which is featured in a great book by some friends of mine called the *Official Get Rich Guide To Information Marketing* (ISBN-10-159918140-1). There's a feature story about John Alanis, and they've got his full-page advertisement on page 77. I want to include it here, because this is what I would call using the power of hype in your market. I'm going to describe it rather than print it, because for my purposes the message, I think, is more important than his graphics.

He starts out with, "Do you hate rejection by women?" (This is the pre-head.) "Imagine no more heartbreak, no more rejection, ever..." He's got a picture of a beautiful young lady right there on the side, which is a nice attention-grabber for people flipping through the pages. And then here's the headline in rather big type. It says, "The amazing natural attraction secrets of a 5' 7" former loser from Texas that literally compels beautiful, desirable women to approach you first, begging you for a date no matter what your looks are, or your age or your income." **That's just brilliant!**

And then he's got another sub-head that says, "WARNING: When you put these women-approach-you secrets to work, you must be careful not to attract too many women too fast. Why would any sane man reveal these secrets in a FREE Report if they were true? Read my amazing message to find out." **This is brilliant stuff. I can't imagine any guy who's struggling with this issue who wouldn't read this full-page advertisement.**

Hype is different for every market, but that's the best example in John's market. **This is what gets people's attention.** It cuts through the clutter. That's where you really have to focus on competition. **You have to realize how apathetic people are these days, how inundated they are with other advertising and marketing messages, how immune they've become.** If there's one good justification for hype, it's that you can break free of the clutter and jump off that radar screen and grab their attention.

By the way, the warning about being careful not to attract too many women may seem a little familiar — it's been used by other markets in a similar ways. John tells me he got it from a weight-loss ad that had a disclaimer that said, "WARNING: When you take this product, you must be careful not to lose too much weight too fast." Certain male enhancement ads do something similar when they warn you about the possibility of the drug working too well — we've all heard the warning about seeing a doctor if an erection lasts for more than four hours, right?

And John got the "Why would any sane man reveal this..." from an old Jeff Paul ad. **In other words, he swiped some good ideas and modified them for his own use, and they worked**. It's that whole psychology of, "if they're warning me against that huge benefit that I'm looking for, then even if I don't get that result, if I get close to that result, I'm doing good!

If it's possible to lose too much weight too fast, then maybe even if I lose just a little bit of weight, I'll still be happy with the results." By the way, there's a warning on that weight loss ad that says something like, "This is not for people who just want to lose a little weight; this is for people who want to lose 30 pounds, 40 pounds, or a hundred pounds!" **Of course, the thought process is, "Wow, if it works for them, what's it going to do for me?"** That's what John Alanis' ad does. Notice the imagery the ad generates in your head. Imagine some guy who wants to meet women. You need to try to crawl into his head and determine what's going to get this guy's attention. Well, John's headline is a "stop-it" for any guy in that market. When he sees it, he's going to think, "Heck yeah, what's this all about?" **It's going to grab his attention because it has that emotional appeal to it — and it works because John knows his market, and those words speak to them.** I'll tell you something very interesting about that ad, too. The "imagine no more heartbreak, no more rejection ever" line came from a series of dating emails that John tested, and for whatever reason, that subject line always got a much better response. It resonated. So when he went back to writing full-page ads, he took all the appeals that had worked via email and put them in there. **That's actually where his marketing copy came from: scientific testing, not just from being a good copywriter.** Every appeal in that ad is something that was tested beforehand via email, which cut down on the risk when John ran that particular advertisement. That's especially important, because if something is catchy enough to stand above the crowd in email, where normally people will hit delete if it doesn't grab them in the first few sentences, then it's likely to work in just about any medium.

Speaking of the Crowd...

I've spoken about how competition is good in many ways, as long as you don't let it scare you. In fact, the last thing you want to do is get involved in a market where there's not a lot of thriving competitors. **You must look for marketplaces where lots of people are already thriving, because that tells you that there is, in fact, a market for what you're selling**. A lot of people make the biggest mistake in their business when they select the wrong market in which to work. If you try to sell something to people who aren't buying, well, of course you're going to have a difficult time. **So when you're doing your initial marketing research, you need to find a market with a lot of competition. But note this — it doesn't have to be good competition!**

The one thing that you have to do in order to be a ruthless marketer is to find a way to stand out. Just like a good politician on the campaign trail who really wants that public office, you've got to find a way to stand head and shoulders above all of the other competitors, to show that you're the best, that you're the one to whom they should give their money. John Alanis tells me that when he did his initial market research, he went to Google and typed in "dating" and similar items to see what would come up. He found a lot of stuff, and he knew it had to be working, since it was based on pay-per-click ads they were paying for every single day. **If it didn't work, people wouldn't have paid for it, and some of these sites were up constantly for weeks, so it was obvious they had to be making money**.

But the plain truth was, their marketing was terrible! That's when John knew he could kick butt in that marketplace. You see, the market was so hungry that even bad marketing could make money. **When you introduce good marketing to those starving people, they respond in droves, and you're going to clean up.** So that's what you want to look for. Is there a marketplace where people are prospering with bad marketing? Because if there is, it's a tremendous opportunity.

Now remember, let's take that one step backwards to what I've talked about earlier in this book. This is not intended as a judgment call; this just happens to be an observation. **Most business people — especially in the local brick-and-mortar sector — are lousy marketers.** That should serve as a great confidence booster for anybody who wants to rise above that and

▼▼▼▼▼▼▼▼▼▼▼▼▼▼▼▼▼

Give away a small piece of the LARGER THING you want to ultimately sell to them.

Give away your <u>BEST</u> <u>STUFF</u> — then upsell the hell out of them!

accomplish something. In the land of the blind, the one-eyed man is king. **You don't have to be that much better that everyone else to kick butt in the marketplace — which should be obvious, since so many people are doing such a lousy job, and they're still making their businesses work.** You know that you can come along and just tweak what they're doing and add some ideas from some of these other sharp marketers — even in other fields — and you'll have an almost unfair advantage over all of your competitors.

"Win Your Battles"

According to the classic book *The Art of War*, which is often as applicable to business as it is to warfare, **"Every battle is won before you go to war."** In a sense, this is similar to that great quote from Abraham Lincoln, who once said, "If I had six hours to chop down a tree, I'd spend the first four sharpening the axe." **In other words, it's all about preparation.**

In war, the generals strategize beforehand and plot out exactly what they're going to do, and where they're going to employ their advanced weaponry. The same thing is true in business; if you plan in advance what you're going to do and, ideally, what you're prepared for, the battle will go more smoothly. If you've prepared properly, you'll be the one who wins.

So you need to win the battle of marketing before you actually do the marketing. It's all about preparation. **It's all about the things you do before you actually send your sales letter out to your marketplace, or place the ad, or whatever.** That includes attending seminars and similar events, learning to write copy, sharpening the ax with your education, and enhancing what you know about marketing. **It's knowing that effective marketing isn't just what you're going to sell to a customer the first time, but having your back-end marketing plan already in place.**

Before you make the first sale, what's your second sale? Do you know that? What's your third sale? What's your entire marketing strategy? <u>How are you going to take that person from an initial sale to a lifelong client who can be worth thousands and thousands of dollars to you</u>?

Napoleon Bonaparte was once asked why he always seemed to know what to say, what to do, how to act. And he said, "It's because prior to every battle and prior to every major event, I spend hours meditating on all possible outcomes and consequences." **He examined all the "what if's" he could imagine, so when something did happen, he already had a framework in mind that told him exactly what to do**. That comes from the process of preparation. Why do we practice basketball? Why do football players have so many drills? <u>Because it's necessary</u>. Yes, it's hard work, but it has to be done. You may be tired of sports and military analogies by now, but we use them, because, so often, they're directly applicable to business.

Preparation is especially important. **You need to have thought through every possible aspect of how you're going to approach your marketplace and your customers.** You need to know exactly what systems to have in place to automatically lead that new prospect — that new customer — where you want them to go, so that you can maximize your profits and ultimately better serve your customer.

Preparation is something a lot of people aren't willing to do, but it's where the money is made. That's good news for you, because <u>a lot of people who enter into business are really just</u>

<u>chasing cars</u>. They get an idea, they run off with no forethought of what happens, the project gets hard, they're out the door, and they never wind up making any money or doing anything sustaining. **The people who are really successful are those willing to devote the time, energy, and effort to preparation**. And not just preparation, but only realistic preparation. If you've read Napoleon Hill's *Think and Grow Rich*, you're aware there's something he calls "accurate thinking." **It's something a lot of people don't like, because it means you have to look at the world the way it is, not the way that you want it to be.** You have to avoid what Alan Greenspan used to call "irrational exuberance." If you're irrationally exuberant, you can't see all the things that are going to go wrong — and you need to, if only to plan for a just-in-case scenario and deal with things if they do go wrong. **If you do your due diligence and nothing goes wrong, great — you're fine. If you don't, then sure enough something bad is going to happen, and you'll be left holding the bag because you didn't prepare correctly.** This all comes back to that nasty four-letter word: work. **But that's what separates the successful people from the also-rans: the ability to sit down and focus on the nitty-gritty, the often onerous preparation, <u>because that's where the money is made</u>.** It's in the details. Chance favors the prepared mind.

At the time of this writing, there are a lot of reality shows on TV — basically, if you've seen one you've seen them all. They're kind of boring, really. But there's one new show on the market that's different: it's called "Kitchen Nightmares."

Basically, this celebrity chef named Gordon Ramsay comes into restaurants that are failing in the marketplace, and he explores all the reasons why they're failing — and then straightens them out. One week they went to a suburb of New York City and looked at a restaurant called The Mixing Bowl. **They'd been around for about 20 years, but they were just about ready to pull the plug and go out of business.** It wasn't a problem of quality; they served great food, and their kitchen was spic-and-span. One of the things Ramsay did was show them, a map of their own city as it was ten years before, with little green dots showing all the restaurants with which they competed back then. Then he showed them the same map today, with green dots for all the current competitors. <u>Little did they know that they had four times more competitors now than they had 10 years ago</u>.

It was the first time they realized this — you could tell that by their reactions on camera. In a way they were aware that there was more competition, but they were so locked into their little tiny restaurant that they forgot to realize that they needed to look outside the box sometimes. **Once they got over that shock, they decided to look at their competitors and find the gaps in the marketplace that weren't being filled.** Ramsay told them, "There's no competitor in this marketplace that's appealing to people who want to eat healthy." So they revamped the whole menu, and they found a wedge into the marketplace. It took some hard work and a lot of preparation, but they did it.

That's why I find the quote with which I started the chapter particularly relevant for business. **How are you going to prepare, to set things up, so that first of all, you can position yourself in a way that's totally different from all your competitors?** Well, first you have to look closely at all those other competitors in order to find a USP (Unique Selling Position). Think of your company as a product on a shelf in a busy grocery store. **You have to realize there has to be something about you that's uniquely different from all the products with which you're competing.**

Aristotle Onassis once said, **"The secret to business is to know something that your competitors don't."** John Alanis told me once that one of his competitive strategies over all the other Internet marketers offering products similar to his, is simply the fact that he knows all these offline strategies that he uses to compliment his online strategies. They let him go out there and kick the competitors' butts in the marketplace. **You have to ask yourself, "What can I do? What is my strength? What do I have over the other guys?"** Once you've identified this USP, you need to find ways to strengthen it as much as possible.

Here's a good example of that. McDonald's went out there and just wiped the floor with Burger Chef. But McDonald's still has competitors, doesn't it? Burger King didn't give up the way Burger Chef did; they fought. **In fact, some say they invented the concept of the swipe file, and started to use it effectively before anyone else**. They decided they were going to go head-to-head with McDonald's, that they'd locate their stores as close to a competing McDonald's as they could, and take up the choicest locations. **They weren't afraid to face competition, and they did it creatively and successfully.** You see, in a way what the McDonald's guy did to the neighboring Burger Chef guy — and hell, what McDonald's did that to Burger Chef in general — is what a really good poker player will sometimes do to another poker player who's less certain.

Even if the one poker player has worse cards than the other guy, he can still win if he bluffs that other guy into throwing his cards away. That said, he's got to have the resources to deal with the possibility of his bluff being called. McDonald's did have those resources, but they still won largely by bluffing. In the end, Burger Chef folded without even calling. **But look at Burger King — they called McDonald's bluff and are still around, and the competition is fierce.**

This has all turned out for the best not just for McDonald's and Burger King — both companies are doing very well — but also for the consumer. The products are more appealing to the consumer at both restaurant chains, and both have items that appeal to particular people or that are just plain better than the other guy's. Burger Chef could have stayed with it. **You don't have to be afraid of your competitors**. After all, McDonald's restaurants are franchised. **They're locked into doing certain things certain ways, and can't do the things that other outfits could have done.** Now, there's no doubt that McDonald's won over Burger Chef because they're the better company, from a business standpoint. They're probably the best in the business — but even so, there's room in the market for competition. That's my point here. <u>Don't be intimidated by the competition; look for ways that you can win in spite of it all</u>.

Don't give in to fear. **Too many people spend all their time focusing on the competition, looking for all the reasons why their competitors can win them over.** They're unable to see past the obstacles to the potential outcomes; they take little things and magnify them into big problems. While it's fine to be paranoid to some extent, too much paranoia can hurt you, by rendering you unable to compete effectively. **Realize this: no matter what your business is, you can compete with all those other guys, if you're careful and imaginative, and are willing to work hard.** If you walk away from this book having learned that and nothing else, then I'll be happy and you'll have learned an important lesson. **You've got to have a little swagger going into the game.** <u>You can't go in feeling like you don't stand a chance</u> — or you won't.

▼▼▼▼▼▼▼▼
MARKETING SECRET

Inspiration comes in the midnight hour. When the deadlines are creeping in — and your back is against the wall. When the gun is pointed at your head and you're forced to solve the problem.

- The key: You must consciously put yourself in these do or die situations!

Here's an example. Recently, a group of my friends were involved in a sporting event where our team was favored to lose. The point spread against us was eleven or twelve points, and the other team had won four out of their last five games. **But we went out there and beat them, despite the fact that our team came into the game as the underdog**. In business, you've got to have that attitude that you can win, in spite of the odds. You can't let your fears control you.

www.ingramcontent.com/pod-product-compliance
Lightning Source LLC
Chambersburg PA
CBHW022053210326
41519CB00054B/327